# Back on the Quality Track

## *How Organizations Derailed & Recovered*

**Kathryn Huddleston**

**American Management Association**

New York • Atlanta • Boston • Chicago • Kansas City • San Francisco • Washington, D. C.
Brussels • Mexico City • Tokyo • Toronto

Library of Congress Cataloging-in-Publication Data

Huddleston, Kathryn.
     Back on the quality track : how organizations have derailed &
recovered / Kathryn Huddleston.
        p.   cm.
     Includes bibliographical references and index.
     ISBN 0-8144-0282-8 (pbk.)
     1. Total quality management—United States—History.   2. Quality
control—United States—History.   3. Quality of products—United
States—History.   I. Title.
HD62.15.H855   1995
658.5'62'0973—dc20                                           95-18219
                                                                CIP

Printing number

10   9   8   7   6   5   4   3   2   1

# Contents

# Special Thanks and Acknowledgments

**DuPont**—Craig Binetti, Billy Joe Hinson, Kelli Kukura, Ronnie Pugh, Julie Rouse, Mickey Williams

**Eastman Chemical**—Buddy Bounds, Earnie Deavenport, Tom Dickens, Bob Kearns, Al Robbins, Mike Warner

**FedEx**—Bob Brown, Fred Smith, Jean Ward-Jones

**General Electric**—Al Palumbo, Jack Welch

**Jimmy Dean Foods (Sara Lee Corporation)**—Judy Baines, Bart Clayton, Jim Ellis, Bill Hardison, Jack Morton, Dick Perry, Ronnie Phillips, Bob Roberts

**Motorola**—Richard Buetow, Abbi Sedivec

**Promus Hotels**—Mark Wells

**Sara Lee Knit Production**—Barry Yeatts

**Saturn**—Bob Boruff, Robert Palmer

**Square D-Groupe Schneider**—Rick Agee, Catherine Bradford, Jim Clark, Bill Fightmaster, Jim Jackson, Eugene Martin

**U.S. Air Force**—Colonel Hank Firumara, Captain James Fritz, MSgt. Susan Homes, Colonel Scot Wangen

**U.S. Army Corps of Engineers**—Diana Brinhall, Robert Brown, Marvin Creel, Colonel Michael Diffley, Jerry Liebes, Brian Loggins, Colonel Robert Slockbower

And to my other clients over the past 18 years who have encouraged me and validated the material in this book

# Preface

Why did American competitiveness in world markets derail? How much did it have to do with veering from the quality road? The leadership road? What did Japan do that we didn't? Are we back on track? If so, what's it going to take to keep us there? These are questions both the public and private sectors are asking as they try to recapture the spirit of entrepreneurship, creativity, and quality consciousness that pervaded the U.S. organizations before smugness and inertia set in. This book provides some answers gleaned from those who lived through the derailment and have since been involved in business turnarounds.

As a trainer and speaker for the quality initiative, I have for some time reflected on the differences and similarities between today's quality imperative and the quality focus of the late 1970s and early 1980s. I had the opportunity to work for a major corporation when industrial America was just beginning to experience some international competition, primarily from Japan and Germany, and therefore felt the push to focus people on quality.

Previous to this time, we had the markets mostly to ourselves, and this monopoly made us a little smug and more than a little sloppy in products and service delivery. Add to this our incredibly layered organizations (which prevented most employees from feeling connected with the customer), entrenched habits, a love affair with the status quo, and management practices that were out of sync with the conditioning of the "baby boomer generation" and you come up with a recipe for lowered quality standards and productivity.

At this time American industry, for the most part, was in a state of denial regarding our competition. We wouldn't let ourselves believe this was anything but a minor setback. The hierarchical "modern corporation" structure still reigned supreme, despite occasional attempts to challenge it. It was a time when we placed a higher value on conformity and loyalty to that organizational structure and the accompanying culture than is done today, and a lower value on innovation and customer focus. After all, American industry had dominated the world, and the endorsement of these values by a homogenous workforce was considered by corporate management to have contributed to that status.

During the 1970s and early 1980s we had some of the greatest technology in the world and some of the greatest technical talent. Corporations like General Electric attempted to implement strategies, today considered novel, to address productivity and quality slippages.

But many of those innovative strategies did not work, because the political and cultural ingredients necessary for improved quality were lacking. Allocation of resources, which in many ways determines power centers, was out of sync with quality initiatives, and many of the innovations were just too far ahead of the prevailing beliefs and values to be sustained.

Then the U.S. approach to quality was driven by the chief executive officer or the design engineer. It was a time when U.S. companies "fixed" quality.

Things have changed remarkably since then. Leaders like Jack Welch have altered entire management systems, and the results are showing up in the bottom line. The delayering that is going on across the board is resulting in people executing, rather than administering. Business teams at DuPont and Eastman Chemical have built relationships with external and internal customers and with suppliers, leading to remarkable increases in customer satisfaction. FedEx continues to prove that high quality is not the special province of manufacturing companies, and Motorola continues to awe the world with its defect-free product goals and accomplishments. Square D-Groupe Schneider has proven what teamwork can do to decrease cycle time, and Saturn is the model of self-managed team success. Companies within Sara Lee are demonstrating that they can successfully meld into a third culture focused on the customer. Promus Hotels are offering their guests unconditional money-back guarantees and enabling their staff to enact them. And the government is proving that it, too, can reduce waste and improve processes that impact its customers. Yes, we're back on track.

The intent of this book is to review the history of the quality initiative and to examine how and where we got off track—from the perspectives of people who lived through the "derailment." It offers a brief look at our quality ingredients before the derailment, when the senior leadership of organizations was integrally connected to the front line and people cooperated with, rather than competed against, each other. It then examines cultures that tried to "launch the quality focus" during the early 1980s but lacked the cultural elements—organizational values, beliefs, and practices—needed to sustain it. Finally the book illustrates how organizations are recapturing the "quality basics" to get back and to stay on track. *Back on the Quality Track* shows ways in which the political and cultural elements are now being addressed in organizations that have been successful in retrieving market share and combating international competition—including some whose earlier attempts had failed.

The book focuses particularly on Square D-Groupe Schneider, Sara Lee, Federal Express, Motorola, Saturn, DuPont, General Electric, Eastman Chemical, Promus Hotels, the U.S. Air Force, the U.S. Army Corps of Engineers, and the U.S. Department of Agriculture, organizations that are successfully integrating quality throughout the organization. It is based on my personal involvement with these organizations as well as on the specific accounts and firsthand experiences of others who survived the 1980s and so far have survived the 1990s. Some of these people were yesterday's heroes, people not fully appreciated by the current leadership, but who nonetheless influenced others and whose imprint is still highly evident.

This book doesn't present a single formula for success. No one recipe works for everyone. In fact, the organizations cited here are quite varied in their approaches. But what is common to them is an all-out quality commitment that requires an uprooting of entrenched habits and, in some cases, virtually starting over. They connect quality with the bottom line and consider the cultural infrastructure as important as product development.

All of the individual contributors and managers cited in this book have verified one fact: There is and has always been a correlation between high-quality products and services and staying close to the customer. One of the overall dilemmas facing businesses in the 1990s is how to redesign, or at least reformat, the organization so that it can do this.

We have come a long way from when we viewed quality as a functional concern, unconnected with management practices. Today we recognize that quality must be integrated across the entire organization and aligned with the political and cultural infrastructure. Ironically, some of the organizations that have recognized this and focused the organization on quality have done so through a quality labyrinth that has ended up exalting the process over the goal—improved products and services. We still face the challenge of realizing that quality doesn't require a fixed formula but that it does require a *sustained* focus throughout.

That focus may take the form of corporate quality councils and quality directors who coordinate quality efforts. But it shows up more vividly in senior leaders who work alongside other personnel to make decisions and find new and better ways to serve customers; in multifunctional teams brought together to design and introduce new products; and in integrated customer teams that respond to customer needs on a twenty-four hours-a-day basis, resulting in faster response and improved trust.

Today, we recognize that we can't just impose quality on top of existing cultures, but that systems and processes have to be changed for any quality focus to really work over the long haul. Industries and government are still grappling with how to do this. I hope this book will help them.

K.H.

# Part I
# Before
# the
# Derailment

# I

# Before the Great Train Robbery

## The Basics of a Quality Culture

Two jobs early in my adult life furnished me all the basic ingredients I needed for my own quality journey. The first was a job I held when I was sixteen years old as a soda fountain clerk at Boyd Drugs, a small drugstore in Cookeville, Tennessee. I worked there after school and through the summer. The other was a job as a Mutual of Omaha insurance agent, a job I took to help me pay my tuition through graduate school. These jobs taught me the value of listening to the customer's preferences, responding to those preferences, working with others as a team, and the leadership required to do all three.

Actually, my job as a soda clerk involved more than serving ice cream. Most of the businessmen and women came to that drugstore at lunchtime for sandwiches, homemade soup, and homemade desserts. In fact, most of them wouldn't have considered going anywhere else. The store was run by its owner-pharmacist, Mr. Boyd, who taught me valuable lessons that serve me to this day.

One of the things I remember most vividly was that *everybody* did *everything* in the store. During the noon rush hour, Mr. Boyd would come from the pharmacy, don an apron, and scoop ice cream. In the late afternoon, when most people brought in their prescriptions, he had the soda clerks help him in the pharmacy. When customers came in to purchase cosmetics or gifts, we served as sales clerks. And then at night, we all cleaned up, Mr. Boyd himself often grabbing a broom and helping. It was such a natural thing that at the time I thought nothing of it. All I knew then was that we felt like we could rely on each other, we didn't have to guess at what the standard was, and, since everybody was involved, we didn't feel any of the jobs were demeaning. Furthermore, our opportunity to perform a variety of jobs—from cooking to washing dishes to waiting on pharmacy customers—reduced the fatigue and monotony that otherwise often characterizes these jobs.

There were no memos. No e-mail. No lengthy customer attitude surveys. No staff meetings. And yet there was very little ambiguity, and no fear of being left out of the loop. We knew what was going on. If we didn't, we asked Mr. Boyd. If we didn't understand his answer, we asked him again.

We knew the quality of the meals before they were served, because Mr. Boyd tasted just about everything before our luncheon customers arrived. If the quality wasn't right, we heard about it on the front end. His knowledge of the product and process, simple though they were, stemmed from his personal involvement.

At lunch, he chatted with the diners, asking them what they did and did not prefer. He certainly heard immediately if they weren't satisfied. Customers knew what our standard was, and if we slipped on any particular day, or if service became too slow, they told Mr. Boyd immediately, and he in turn told us immediately.

I can't remember a single time when Mr. Boyd chewed out anybody, but when someone wasn't pulling his weight, Mr. Boyd would pull that person from the soda fountain and hand him a broom, or ask him to come help in the pharmacy. I do remember specific times when he told us that a customer had particularly enjoyed his meal, or that another had commented on our quick service, or that another appreciated our smiles.

He also gave us opportunities to make decisions about our work, including work schedules, uniforms, and menus.

Mr. Boyd was actually a very quiet-mannered man who did not knock your socks off at first meeting, and I can't imagine him making stirring speeches. But he was connected with the operation of the business, and he motivated me to please the customers.

This way of running things was typical of businesses and industries during the 1960s before they became so layered and bureaucratic, when owners were vitally connected to the daily operations of the business. Since there was little layering, it was easy to spread the expectations for high quality. It was also easy to demonstrate commitment. And it was easy for people to "catch" the owners' passion for the business, because employees and owners worked alongside each other.

Ronnie Phillips, vice president of operations at Jimmy Dean Foods (a company in the Sara Lee Corporation), remembers this earlier time when the senior leaders "were personally involved with the business and very much connected with day-to-day operations. Their expectations were clear, and they truly cared." Jim Ellis, Vice President of Technical Services at Jimmy Dean Foods, agrees. Although rooted in a more autocratic culture than Phillips, he emphasizes the importance of "top" managers being integrally involved with the operation of the business. "Jimmy Dean [the owner and president of Jimmy Dean Sausage]," Ellis says, "majored in minor as well as major details, and everybody knew what his expectations were."

The other job that influenced my thinking about quality came along some fifteen years after my work in the drugstore. I was working on my doctorate at Vanderbilt and needed a job to help pay my tuition. Living on a graduate assistantship of less than $200 a month, paying rent out of that, and helping feed an "orphaned" elderly man, I realized I had to have another job. Scanning the newspapers, I discovered an ad for a Mutual of Omaha Insurance agent. Though I had no sales experience, I decided to telephone anyway and ended up with an interview.

This agency had a reputation for having some aggressive salesmen and a general agent who was a dynamic, builder type and the youngest general agent in the Mutual of Omaha company.

Mr. Pridy was the general manager, but I had never heard anything about him. Looking back, I realize that my less than enthusiastic first impression of him was probably colored by the aptitude test he handed me, which contained questions such as "What animal would you be if you were reincarnated?" and "Would you rather fight a bull in Spain or go home to your wife and children?" And the agency wasn't all that impressed with me, either, since I failed that aptitude test and had no prior sales experience. In fact, shortly after I turned in the test, the agency manager thanked me for coming by and dismissed me with the proverbial, "We'll get back to you." Before I left, however, I got the chance to meet Mr. Carell, the general agent; I momentarily forgot about those earlier questions and became excited about the possibility of working with him. I found him charismatic and articulate.

Somehow, I convinced Mr. Carell that I was hungry enough to sell "this stuff," and he in turn was eager to get a first woman into that agency. So I was given the chance and placed on straight commission. They and I figured that we had nothing to lose.

What began as a "filler" to get me through graduate school ended up giving me very valuable lessons about the need to listen to customers' preferences and to go that extra mile for them—the absolute first step in the quality journey. I also learned to value the balance that a visionary and charismatic type like Mr. Carell and a pragmatic "manager" type like Mr. Pridy can bring to an organization.

The so-called scrubby leads I bought from my manager (leads were sold to agents for three dollars each) sent me to people in the city who had no telephone numbers, poor health, and little money—people whom most agents probably would not have bothered trying to sell to. But these were the only "leads" I had, so I had to try.

That experience helped teach me how to match solutions with needs of customers. Many times I drove to those homes, afraid to get out of the car, honking my horn in the driveway, hoping someone would hear me over the barking dogs and come to the doorway. These customers' special needs and conditions required some "creative" selling—and a willingness to set up special conditions for payment. These experiences gave me a real good lesson in going the "extra mile" for the customer.

There were nights when I drove a couple of hundred miles to a prospective customer, only to be greeted with "I just wanted to get some literature in the mail." But by meeting their requests and giving them the information, I discovered they usually felt compelled to listen to what I had to say. And at a minimum, we established some trust—a major first step toward selling anything.

I was so naive in those days that I truly believed the manager and agents when they told me that selling disability income to attorneys was a great opportunity. Mutual of Omaha offered that policy at an association rate to the lawyers in the city, and I was convinced that I had been "chosen" to sell it to them. It's hard today to realize I could have been that stupid. Not knowing what "squirrely" (agents' term for any prospect in those days who was too weird to sell anything to) meant, I proceeded with enthusiasm to go "cold call" on my first prospective attorney.

Though those attorneys were generally more curious about me than the disability policies I had come there to sell, through listening and focusing on mission, I actually sold a few of them.

What success I had as an agent there I attributed in large part to Mr. Pridy. He was effective in his role and helped illustrate that an effective manager doesn't have to burn up the road. A quiet man who did not have a lot of formal education, Mr. Pridy had learned through the years the importance of listening to the customer—both the internal and the external customer—and he passed that on to those he managed. While sales schools fed us propaganda about the "smoke out" and other closes designed as overpowering, emotional, and intimidating tactics to get the prospect to *react* rather than think when buying a policy, Mr. Pridy exhibited exceptional listening skills when he went on calls with agents. He taught us to ask questions first to understand customers' preferences and to establish dialogue with them to build trust.

Mr. Pridy also knew the value of responding differently to different people, while at the same time treating them fairly. Recognizing my need for autonomy (aside from his initial efforts to conform me in my sales track), he let me sell pretty much in my own style and left me alone, unless I came to him for help, or my production started lagging, or I began to sell a new type of product or service he knew I was unfamiliar with. But even if my production was off, he didn't chew me out; instead, he expressed his disappointment that I wasn't meeting my potential.

While he himself had not been a high volume salesman, he was a good developer and manager of people because he was patient, could really listen, and ensured equity among those he supervised. He also valued learning, and constantly encouraged agents to work toward their CLUs (certified life underwriter) and enroll in other development courses. He was always helping us reach up. These strengths are required today to move companies into continuous improvement cultures.

Despite my considerable struggles, Mr. Pridy enabled me to reach my potential and earn President's Club the years I worked for the agency. Neither the other agents nor I ever quite understood at the time how this happened, since my volume was rarely higher than most of theirs was in any given week. Furthermore, I resisted various sales schools that promoted more aggressive tactics, I rarely used the smoke-out close, and I always called back. All of these were "should nots" in selling during those years.

Mr. Pridy taught me the value of listening to the customer. In those days, "talk" was considered power, and agents were given a lot of instruction on presenting the sales "track" to the potential client. Listening did not receive much emphasis as an organizational asset, and actually those in sales who were subtle and quiet were often considered passive and "too laid back" to sell anything. The most forceful agents usually sold the most insurance. However, their aggressiveness often prompted some prospects to give them a check for the first month's premium just to get rid of them. They then cancelled their policy after the first month.

I was able to make President's Club during those years primarily by retaining the clients I did sell, not by selling a vast volume of insurance. As best I can determine, they stayed with me, because they trusted me to be straight with them and to sell them the right policies for their unique needs. One woman I sold to told me once that she had never had an agent who had spent as much time with her *after* the sale, as before. So by retaining the business I did write, my bottom line production was as much as some who actually wrote much more than I did. I certainly made blunders—sometimes I couldn't even figure out how to fill out the forms of the business I had written; but my manager would just smile ruefully, sigh, and fill out the forms for me.

I developed personal relationships with these customers, sometimes over the protestations of my manager. "Kathryn, you are to sell—not to get involved with the claims," I heard over and over. Really, he was right. That was not my role, but I found it impossible just to sell and forget, since customers put a heavy value on help with claims.

During those years I came to realize the importance of listening to the customers' needs and interests and then trying to match those up with a product. Though I had not labeled it as such during that time, I received my first lessons in "value-added" properties and in using innovation to meet the customers' needs.

Besides helping me to "hang tough," selling helped me to understand the criticality of building a product around the customer's needs, rather than one's own. There's often a tendency to sell the product we want to sell, one that will make us the most profit, or one that we can understand comfortably. But this introspective view will eventually hurt the bottom line.

My work at Boyd Drugstore and at Mutual of Omaha together taught me lessons about quality and about serving the customer that have provided dividends for me in my business. Both jobs helped me see the importance of having managers be vitally connected with the job itself, the importance of listening to the voice of the customer, and the importance of building a solution around the customer's needs, rather than one's own. They also taught me a lot about the type of leadership that is required for the quality imperative—one that builds a team and treats internal customers, as well as external ones.

# Part II
# The
# Derailment

# 2

# Amnesia and Our Derailment

## The Lessons We Forgot

Japan is still teaching us important lessons about the central ingredients in the quality recipe, lessons that we seemed to forget in corporate America during the 1970s and early 1980s. As we watched a Japanese man following the Kobe earthquake in early 1995 poke through the rubble of the building that had housed his home and dry cleaning service, we were reminded of a major reason Japan was able to rise from the ashes in World War II to become the world leader in quality. Mr. Morimoto was not searching for his own personal valuables, but the clothes of his customers so he could clean them—a profound statement of the significance of the customer to Japanese business and of quality improvement particularly. Adults and children alike who took only small quantities of food for themselves so that others could also be fed likewise reminded Americans that there are requirements other than measurement tools required for continuous improvement—namely, patience, focus, discipline, and community spirit.

Ironically, though, the aftermath of the Kobe earthquake also points up a downside of this patience and discipline—the importance of speed in emergency decision-making. While consensus decision-making may be best on a long-term basis in certain quality matters, in a crisis people can actually starve and die waiting for a government (or an industry, as the case may be) to mobilize.

Before the earthquake, the recent Japanese recession had already prompted businesses to consider the importance of speed in product development and customer response time and the downside of consensus making. It also prompted Japanese industry to consider the importance of innovation, historically one of America's greatest strengths. Japan's acknowledgment of the importance of these two components of customer satisfaction—speed and innovation—has also prompted American business leaders to remember that these in fact had accounted for much of the higher quality of our product and services before our derailment.

## Lessons About the Role of Innovation and Speed in Quality

American managers are remembering our basic strengths of innovation, entrepreneurism, and speed and are recognizing their role in quality improvement.

For a while, U.S. industries undervalued America's strengths of originality and entrepreneurism, as they eliminated them from the quality formula. Today American industries recognize that while continuous improvement of existing products is necessary to compete, so is innovation. Clearly taking the "best in the class" practices and improving on them (*benchmarking*) in recent years has resulted in major turnarounds for various industries. But more than gradual improvement is required to remain competitive. In the late 1970s and early 1980s some in American industries were too quick to devalue their own creativity and self-reliance and too quick to grab gradual improvement techniques that had worked so well in Japanese industries imbued with a very different cultural infrastructure from their own.

While recently conducting some training for the Japan Engineering District of the U.S. Army Corps of Engineers, I picked up *The Daily Yomiuri*, one of the local papers, and was struck by the irony of an article that urged Japan to "shift its focus from catching up with others to creating something totally new." It stressed the need for originality and individuality—powerful forces in U.S. industry until the late 1960s—declaring that imitating others would not be enough to get Japan's economy back on track. Japan would have to make improvements in the way it organizes work life in both the factory and the office: restructuring, reengineering, and focusing on cost-saving benefits of new technologies. These are the same initiatives that U.S. industries have been emphasizing in recent years to help them recapture the speed and vitality that once characterized American companies. In particular, values of originality and individuality in product design—which we subsumed in the 1970s in deference to the latest corporate management mantras—are being hailed by the new class of Japanese business heroes. Here is Japan recognizing these strengths now and looking to the United States for examples. This is good news.

As customers' preferences continue to change more quickly and pressures therefore increase to reduce the cycle time of a product, American industries are again placing a greater value on speed. They have begun to reflect that too much patience—one of Japan's greatest strengths—can create an inertia that prohibits a fast enough response to changing customer demands. Many times it is as important to customers to get the product quickly as it is to get one free from defects.

## Lessons About Continuous Improvement

We indeed have learned valuable lessons from the Japanese about *kaizen*, their word for continuous improvement. They captured our attention during the 1970s and even more so in the 1980s with their willingness and ability to improve existing products and services through patience, focus, and discipline. They taught us that these attributes were just as important as great technical innovation in becoming international leaders in quality. This was a lesson we needed to hear. Those same attributes will, I believe, ultimately enable Japan to overcome its economic recession, just as they will enable the Kobe residents to rise from the tremendous devastation of the recent earthquake—and just as they enabled Japan to rise from the annihilation of its factories in World War II.

But the Japanese, in turn, have recently learned something that we also need to remember. If an industry's continuous improvement results in overdesign—that is, in embellishing a product with a lot of largely unnecessary functions at the expense of making new things (as in the case of some Japanese automobiles)—then that industry will fail to meet domestic and global demands. During the "bubble economy" of the 1980s, Japanese executives placed a high priority on satisfying every possible customer whim, regardless of how marginal the contribution was to the bottom line. This enthusiasm spread into what some see as needless variations in automobile parts. Confronted today with escalating costs and declining profits, Nissan has rationalized its marketing approach and is drastically restructuring product planning, design, and manufacturing. Its new priority is to reduce the number of unique parts and unnecessary product variations.

Today a new interpretation of customer tastes is guiding Nissan. Nissan's new motto is to keep it simple—through ease of operation, and plain execution of ideas and features.

Certainly, the pace of improvement in Japan was great after the war, for there was little choice. Japan had lost its major customer, the military, and companies were threatened with bankruptcy. The Japanese had to find out what to make, learn how to make it, and then try to sell it. They knew they had to have a better quality image if they were going to sell anything. In effect, they were starting with nothing. They had nothing to lose. So they listened, and listened well.

Today, however, things are different. Although the Japanese are still focused and listening, they are displaying a greater respect for entrepreneurship, innovation, and speed, qualities that have historically been American industries' strengths.

Despite the overwhelming dominance of engineers in management in Japanese companies, some of that country's technical functions have been weak because many engineers have spent the majority of their careers on cross-functional teams incrementally improving production processes. Though they have gotten better at what they already know, they have not always created new technical knowledge that leads to innovative products. And they now recognize the impact of that gap. Japanese leaders are also realizing that their corporate bureaucracies, the result in part of management policies of consensus decision-making and hierarchical organizations based on seniority, have become organizational barriers that inhibit greatly needed speed of design and production of new products.

## Lessons About the Customer's Role in Quality

For years many U.S. managers have been *verbally* hailing the willingness of the Japanese to imitate and continuously improve on others' innovations as well as their patience, consensus decision-making and teamwork, which are required for the process. But what many American managers left out of the equation during our "derailment" was the *reason* for the control charts, the Pareto diagrams, the cross-functional teams, and other quality improvement tools. Because the customer was not at the center of the efforts, many of those tools became ends in themselves, something quite separate from the actual work itself, and actually disconnected from the customer's needs.

Japan paid attention—even in the sixties and seventies—to what the customer wanted; we paid attention to fixing what the customer had not always indicated he wanted to begin with. Companies produced products and pushed them out the door to awaiting customers who had to buy them, for there was little choice. In the major industries, like the automobile business, we were making money without trying very hard. Many times, the customers' preferences played no role in quality considerations, because the United States was selling products without these considerations. The Japanese, on the other hand, had for years been putting effort into designing quality at the product development stage, factoring in the customers' preferences. Japanese workers were empowered to stop the line in the name of quality, while the U.S. emphasis was on measuring scrap at the end of the line—when it is too late to do anything about it. Within the Japanese team processes on the factory floor, those at the top were not very far removed from those at the bottom—at least on the factory floor; in the United States many layers separated workers from those at the top of the pyramid and from the customers themselves. This bureaucratic structure enabled many to hide mediocre performance within the system.

In Japan, customer satisfaction is perceived to be inherently related to employee satisfaction. Consequently, in the Japanese companies frontline employees receive respect and harmonious and cooperative interaction exists among all layers in the organization. While their historical predilection for autocratic control and a two-class society still sometimes surfaces (in teams waiting sometimes for the "head buffalo" to show for even the simplest decisions), the Japanese have adopted practices designed to eliminate the barriers between managers and workers that their two-class system had created.

## Learning From Japan's Willingness and Resolve to Change

If there is one thing that most agree on about the Japanese, it is that they have been more willing than the U.S. to change their way of operating, and they have the focus and discipline to do it. The magnitude of the recent Japanese recession has pressured Japanese industry as a whole to revolutionize the way its companies operate. Today Japanese business leaders are talking of dismantling the governmental bureaucracies and regulations that nurtured the economy in the past but now seem to get in the way. And the strong yen and increased foreign competition are forcing Japanese companies to become more efficient. The number of Japanese entrepreneurs is on the rise. Japan's setback could very possibly ultimately make the nation stronger than ever. The Japanese are employing resourcefulness and flexibility to put the temporary recession behind them. And they are looking to us for models. Toshiba is cutting more deals with competitors around the world. Toshiba already builds PCs, medical equipment, chips, and TV tubes in the United States, and it has enlisted a slew of powerful partners. For years it has been swapping valuable semiconductor know-how with Motorola, Inc., and it has formed strategic alliances with IBM, thereby cutting development costs.

Certainly the recent economic recession exposing some management vulnerabilities, along with the recent quake exposing some heretofore unknown structural infrastructure weaknesses, together are dispelling the image of an invincible Japan.

But we should be slow to think that Japan will not bounce back stronger than ever. We might remember just how quickly it bounced back from every economic crisis of the 1970s and 1980s—to say nothing of its rise from the ashes after the war. The energy crisis of the 1970s became a mere interruption in Japan's march forward. Between 1973 and 1989 Japan's economy doubled. Though there are some cutbacks in funding and a slowed pace of investment in manufacturing facilities, the updating of manufacturing prowess in the homelands is still proceeding faster than it is here among U.S. manufacturers. That same resolve, unselfishness, and community spirit displayed after the Kobe earthquake make for a formidable competitor. We should not assume that because Japanese industries have been the world leaders in quality that Japan has become complacent like U.S. industries became during the 1970s when they were lulled into a false sense of security, thinking they had no real competition to worry about. Nor should we assume that the Japanese economic engine is finally capitulating after its postwar miracle. Finally, we should not presume that the recent Kobe earthquake will reverse for very long Japan's economic regeneration, though it may cause some reversal in attempts to deregulate and slow for a while the recovery process.

## Remembering the Dangers of Loyalty to Past Cultures

As we watched governmental leaders in Kobe after the 1995 earthquake follow traditional consensus decision-making practices for the "long-term good," many Americans, like the Japanese people, were reminded that loyalty to past cultures has a price. The temporary individual needs were sacrificed for what government leaders felt was in the best interest of Japan as a country. But if short-term individual needs like hunger aren't addressed at all, the result can be a long-term loss, such as a decreased value on nationalism among the young and the old alike. Moreover, consensus is a time-consuming process, and in a crisis where people are starving from a sluggish response, clearly a quicker decision-making process is needed. So even a nation's great strength can become its albatross.

In our own country we have learned how costly loyalty to existing and past cultures can be. Loyalty to present and past cultural rituals during the 1970s came to be valued over creativity and innovation because that loyalty was perceived to have contributed largely to corporate America's success during the 1960s and 1970s. Today we often stress the need to have unifying cultural agents. But in the centralized culture of Fred Donner's GM or Reginald Jones's GE, those unifying elements actually resulted in the greatest barrier to keeping our companies vibrant and internationally competitive and to improving quality standards.

Bertrand Russell, in commenting on the consequences of autocracy, wrote in *The Taming of Power,* "Wherever there is autocracy, a set of beliefs is instilled into the minds of the young before they are capable of thinking, and these beliefs are taught so constantly and so persistently that it is hoped the pupils will never afterwards be able to escape from the hypnotic effect of their early lessons." He explained that these beliefs are instilled ". . . not by giving any reason for supporting them true, but by parrot-like repetition and mass suggestion."

The unanimity, conformity, and intense imitative capacity of the "corporation man" culture came to be perceived as the greatest stronghold of that culture. And thus, it was not about to be discarded. Those who did not conform were perceived as "boatrockers" who refused to be team players. The promotional system stressed loyalty to the boss more than performance, and if an employee didn't play by that rule, the price of that nonconformance was reflected in his compensation.

The presumed thinking was that employees were still primarily motivated by extrinsic rewards. After all, corporations had proved in the past that people will work harder and produce more for more "jelly beans": good salaries, good benefits, esprit de corps. Many of the older managers *had* lived through the depression of the 1930s and therefore felt the great need for economic security, which corporations like GE and GM had given to them. And though the younger employees were not so motivated, they learned not to challenge this assumption.

Corporations had also proved that social bonding of managers and their families contributed to this productivity. While working at GE during the early 1970s, I marveled at the extent to which GE managers and families lived in the same geographic location, socialized almost exclusively with one another, and held similar outside interests. For the most part, the lieutenants and generals didn't fraternize with the sergeants or the fighters. But they did spend a lot of time with each other, reinforcing how great things were going, and how great the company was.

There were no alarm signals to tell them otherwise. No outside voice. Even GE employees themselves who had come from other organizations outside of GE were often regarded with suspicion and were generally excluded from this community of "believers."

However, even before the United States began to lose a significant amount of its market share to foreign competition, some employees had begun to realize they had paid a high price for this unified culture. These employees, most of them in their thirties and forties, often felt they were under observation, to assure they displayed the "correct" habits and performed the correct rituals. While I was employed in that culture, I observed that fear of one's associates seemed to be the rule. Actually, management played a role in keeping suspicion alive by associating all diversity or opposition within the ranks with the "enemy," who might threaten the movement from the inside.

For example, when two people were found talking together in the halls, or in their offices, upper management often assumed that "the union was knocking," that people were "conspiring" to crack the existing culture. This fracture, then, might enable the "enemy" to get in. We might remember that the true believer's "sacred duty is to be suspicious," as Eric Hoffer said in *The True Believer*, and to be on the lookout for spies and traitors.

Interestingly, even though imitation or acceptance of outside cultures and rituals was sometimes branded as treason, this very trait, the imitiativeness of its members, could actually have made cultural change easier—if it were introduced from the top and lived internally. But since it was not, belief could not follow.

Such was the case in various other organizations where I was asked to implement quality circles. The theory behind quality circles—even in the late 1970s—was to give employees more input into resolving productivity and quality problems that affected their lives. But most employees just couldn't believe that management really desired their input, as there was too much pull from the old culture. Employees attended quality circle meetings, and then "went back to work," where they and their managers reverted to old habits. One employee at GE told me, "This is just one more fad that corporate has dreamed up. . . . I wish they would just let us alone. . . ." A staff member at a university medical center said to me, ". . . These quality circles make me feel dumber than I already feel. . . . I don't know about the long-term plans of this organization and my ignorance will now be obvious to everyone if I'm on that circle." An employee in a federal government agency remarked, "I really don't think most people *want* to be involved in the big decisions. . . ."

Some 40 years ago, Eric Hoffer wrote in *The True Believer* about his thoughts on change: "As long as the existing order functions in a more or less orderly fashion, the masses . . . can think of reform, but not innovation." This truth has been evident in the quality movement.

## The Human Element in Quality

In his autobiography Lee Iacocca declares that all business operations can be reduced to three words: people, product, and profits, with people coming first. For a while we forgot the value of the human element in producing and delivering quality products and services. And this memory lapse contributed to our derailment as much as anything. Oh, there was a great deal of lip service paid to such management ideas as consensus-building skills and team development, but the cultural infrastructure needed to sustain those quality components was often missing in corporate America. For example, distrust pervaded many organizations, members competed against each other for resources, and members' individual strengths were ignored. Consequently, no amount of team training or quality improvement techniques could result in anything more than a temporary or superficial quality improvement.

Messages about the human element had come from our own quality gurus, like Dr. W. Edwards Deming and Dr. Armand Feigenbaum, who much earlier had emphasized customer satisfaction and total quality as a process rather than a technical activity, and from our own visionaries, like Alfred Sloan and Peter Drucker, who emphasized the importance of employee involvement and upward communication.

During the 1950s Dr. Feigenbaum, then worldwide director of manufacturing operations and quality control at General Electric, was invited to visit Japan, where he emphasized the themes of customer satisfaction and results-driven quality. He was also instrumental in initiating the quality movements in Europe and Latin America. But his influence—like that of other quality experts including Deming and Juran—was less evident in the United States. Americans were too busy trying to make products more cheaply and quickly than their own domestic competitors to remember our own prophets' message that quality is more than a technical activity.

As industries became more layered and workers became more separated from customers, industrial managers were lured into using various management strategies to do a better job, and in so doing, began to be separated from the work itself. Even Dr. Feigenbaum admits getting caught up in some of these efforts. Management by objectives, zero defects, quality circles: All were tried by corporations, but all were done, for the most part, as a separate activity from the work itself—mostly from behind a desk.

I was working at the Small AC Motor Component (SAC) headquarters at General Electric in the early 1980s when Richard Pascal and Anthony Athos published *The Art of Japanese Management,* which all section and subsection managers were encouraged to read. I was attracted to the book's thesis that we should not try just to imitate the Japanese to recover our quality status but that we should take the best of Eastern tradition and apply it in such a way that American traditions remain whole. I was also impressed with the authors' encouragement of the "soft elements" over the "short-run, bottom-line, hard-ball" practices of "tough-minded" managers. I assumed that when senior managers directed us to read the book, they had endorsed its ideas.

As the communications and management training person, I figured it was my responsibility to adapt Pascal and Athos's ideas to SAC and deploy them in various ways. But none of my efforts were very successful. At one quality makers meeting, I remember the chairman rejecting an idea that came from one of the teams to improve telephone communication within SAC. Although we tried to persuade him of the connection with quality, we could not overcome his continuing resistance. "I don't see how this is related to scrap or rework, or defect rate," he continued to insist. Nor did he want to hear about how some team members had quickly responded to customer's concerns. He, like many others, simply could not be persuaded about the linkage of quality to responsiveness or timeliness—the human elements of quality which today's customers value. And when I reminded him of some of Pascal and Athos's ideas, he replied, "Kathryn, this is the real world . . . you're not in academia now." This incident was particularly ironic since much of the Japanese strength had come from the message of one of GE's own, Dr. Feigenbaum. As early as 1950, he had emphasized themes of customer satisfaction and some of those "softer" elements, as well as results-driven quality brought about in large part by process-oriented statistical tools.

Of course, companies in the 1950s were smaller, which naturally made the top closer to the bottom, and at the same time the front line employees producing the product closer to the customers. This leaner structure necessitated a belief in the values of innovation and customer satisfaction throughout the organization. As is always the case with smaller businesses, creativity cannot be the special province of the top; the full creative talents of everyone are required. Nor can anyone hide from accountability to customers. The cord from worker to customer is just too visible. Leaders like Alfred Sloan realized that all employees had the need to be connected to each other and to the product, and to continuously grow and learn.

Sloan, who became president of General Motors in 1923 and chairman in 1937, is credited with the vision and strategy that built GM into an automobile industry giant. But Sloan's understanding of people, his comprehension of the human element, as much as his technical knowledge, accounted for GM's status. Sloan was sensitive and believed in top management's staying in touch with employees' thinking. He stressed that the system worked best when management led by persuasion rather than command, and when decision making was forced to the lowest level at which it could be made intelligently. He believed that even huge corporations like GM must manage in a way that is highly people-conscious and that brings forth employees' creativity and commitment. His writings reflect these beliefs. In 1941 he wrote in *Adventures of a White Collar Man* that industrial management must expand its horizons of responsibility and "recognize that it can no longer confine its activities to the mere production of goods and services. . . . It must consider the impact of its operation on the economy as a whole in relation to the social and economic welfare of the entire community."

Thus, Sloan ran General Motors in a decentralized way. Even though he and his corporate staff set overall strategy and goals, company subsidiaries had full authority to make their own decisions in pursuit of these goals. Until the mid 1960s, subsidiaries such as Buick and Chevrolet were self-sufficient. They had the internal decision power and the resources to control their own engineering, assembly, and sales. A pride of craftsmanship and commitment to high quality were valued; functionality had not yet gained a stronghold.

Peter Drucker, considered the father of American management, believed in the importance of employees as a resource. Having more influence on the Japanese than he did on us during the 1960s and 1970s, he taught them that people are a resource rather than a cost and that employees therefore have to be managed to take responsibility for their own as well as for the team's objectives. He also emphasized to them that communication must travel upward, not just downward, and that top management is a function and a responsibility, rather than a privilege.

During the late 1960s and 1970s Americans derailed from this belief, as layered functionality and centralism widened the gap between the top and the bottom and between the front-line worker and the customer, while administration gained precedence over execution. Layering covered up accountability. Even when the decisions in the workplace concerned workers' own lives in an immediate sense—as in design of factory working space and offices, actual working conditions, and product and productivity problems within the employees' work areas—workers had at best participation only by an elite representative. The lower echelons of the pyramid structure were assumed to be incapable of making decisions.

In the short-run orientation of Wall Street, the human element had little place. Managers were driven above everything to make "this quarter's bottom line look good." In presentations to corporate management, local managers presented graph after graph and numbers upon numbers to try to convince themselves that they were still on track. The result, though, excluded new experience and learning.

## The Good and the Bad of Functionality

Only recently have we begun to remember the strength and the weakness of functionality. In the beginning of the twentieth century, American industries lacked strong functionality. And that was an advantage to American manufacturers in the whole process of mass production, as it facilitated collaboration between assemblers and suppliers. But as companies grew, so did the need to use and expand knowledge (in fact, the major benefit of functionality is technical depth). Consequently, companies organized their knowledge into functions—engineering, marketing, manufacturing, human resources, and the like.

It was after Fred Donner took over as Chairman of General Motors in the mid-1960s that centralism, vertical alignment, and functionality gained hold in that corporation—as they did in other U.S. companies. Engineering, assembly, and sales were fractured into separate functions, each consolidated internally. So much did functionality reign that functions were removed from each company and housed in large functional silos, such as the General Motors Assembly Division. Engineering and design functions were likewise consolidated into vertically aligned groups. There is no need to elaborate on the shortcomings of this functionalism within GM, since the consequences of that organizational structure have been widely acknowledged, the residue of which still hampers GM today. Suffice it to say that these functional silos became bureaucratic fiefdoms where technical talent and integration of talent became smothered. Responsibility became hard to pin down, since it was so diffused.

Functionality does have some merit. Strong functionality has been the backbone of German industry, where it has retained its original purpose—that of expanding and deepening technical knowledge. Because of its intense focus on deep technical knowledge organized into rigidly defined functions, German industry—at least up until the mid-1990s—has been able to compete globally by offering customized products with superior performance, however labor-intensive and sluggish the manufacturing process has been.

But as was the case with GM, in the United States this functionality came to be an organizational albatross, as functions became career identities for employees, rather than a means for gaining technical depth. As CEOs increasingly allocated funds to functions, functions began to compete with each other for self-preservation. Gaining technical knowledge became subordinate to building fiefdoms, as success came to be measured not so much by wealth of technical knowledge, or the success of the company relative to its competition, but by the accumulation of political power and departments. When the reject rate increased, there was a lot of finger pointing between functions, and it was usually the "manufacturing ghetto" that was blamed for scrap and rework.

Not only did functionality result in internal competition, which hurt our ability to compete outwardly, but the centralized bureaucracies ended up smothering the human spirit and creativity and the ability to execute on the front line. There was a lot of discourse about overcoming shortcomings of vertical, functionalized structures with matrix management, but the assumption in many organizations was still that those who had authority had functional responsibility—unlike today where vibrant, customer-focused organizations recognize that authority should be vested in those with multidisciplinary *product* responsibility.

Craig Binetti, general manager at DuPont Films, Old Hickory, Tennessee, who lived through the derailment, explains that functionality often prompted managers to spend time on functional excellence items that may have had a lot of value for individual functions, but held little value for customers. "As opposed to supporting an overall business need/priority for the customers, functionality tended to support what was good for the function," he says. He illustrates this weakness of functionality with an example of an R&D function whose existence may depend on creative and innovative products responding to new trends, where in actuality, the primary business need may be a cost-reducing focus in R&D. But in trying to ensure functional excellence, that priority is lost.

To help counter the effects of extreme functionality, in the 1970s managers began to hire generalists with professional credentials such as MBAs and generic expertise independent of a particular function (e.g., finance, design engineering, or planning). They gave individuals opportunities for rotational assignments, in part to develop an allegiance to the entire company—a remarkably current prescription for crafting lean organizations. While this practice had the benefit of encouraging employees to develop an overall view of a company, it decreased the depth of technical knowledge that comes primarily from functionality. We seemed to forget that employees need both an overall view of an organization *and* the depth of technical knowledge that comes primarily from functionality.

## Remembering the Damaging Effects of a Limited Vision

One important lesson American organizations are remembering today is the price paid for a limited vision. Until the 1970s the United States enjoyed an absence of strong outside competition, which forces introspection and inhibits change. Unlike the 1990s when discriminating consumers look for the best value wherever they find it—inside or outside the United States—during the derailment, U.S. industries were insulated from any overseas competition.

American companies did, of course, compete vigorously with each other. This intense company focus caused companies to act as individual, autonomous entities ("this is the *GE* way"). General Electric employees, for example, were rotated from component to component, to get an overall view of the company and to build allegiance to it, so that they would be able to resist temptation from competing companies that might try to lure them away. Much of the internal communication to employees had to do with beating U.S. competitors. Newsletters were filled with data about how one company's benefits outweighed benefits in other companies. We became less concerned about raising our own individual standards and more concerned about beating our U.S. competition. As a matter of fact, as a GE employee, I tried on more than one occasion to move beyond previous standards on training and communication assignments, only to be met with, "Kathryn, that is not the way it is done here." So intense was this inward focus that we simply were not watching the competition in the rest of the world. Believing that our corporate labs were all-knowing, we lost the ability to spot innovations outside our United States.

This company focus seemed to work until the baby boomers appeared on the scene, and demanded attention for their individual needs. Then the individuals *within* companies began to compete with each other. "Every company for itself" seemed to give way to "every person for him/herself." From inside GE, I watched "the American way" translate into "career advancement" and limited promotions and accompanying perks to determine a person's self-respect. These came to be the predominate yardstick for determining if the individual were going anywhere. In many cases, ambition and ego grew over ingenuity, and our creative energies came to be employed for playing the system to move up the corporate ladder (meeting individual needs), instead of using it for product innovation (meeting company needs). But in both cases, it was an inward focus, which had little to do with customers or contributions to the overall value stream.

## The Price Tag for Our Forgetfulness

By the beginning of the 1970s, the United States enjoyed the number one industrial status in the world. By the mid 1980s we had lost 40 percent of our market share to foreign competition—most of it to Japan and the Pacific Rim countries. U.S. industry had possessed more than its share of technical talent. It had experienced the leadership and vision of people like Alfred Sloan and Dr. Armand Feigenbaum. It had proved that its products were durable and long-lasting. How, then, did it manage to get so off track? How could we have forgotten what really had given U.S. industries their strength?

The answer is that the proponents of centralism and functionality managed to convince most of corporate America of the efficiency of this management structure, and their evangelism resulted in too strong a driving force for the individual spirit. As centralism gained hold, individual talent and vision were smothered, and a lack of accountability and commitment was fostered. Managers came to be further and further removed from the front-line worker *and* from the customer, and came to see their role as administering the status quo, failing to take into account the needs of the individual employee or the customer. Companies came to disregard the impact of the human elements of quality—trust, ethics, and respect for each other—on the bottom line. This internal focus on functionality and centralism not only kept the focus off the needs of employees, but also off the needs of customers. While there may have been functional excellence, that did not necessarily factor in internal or external customers' needs or priorities.

In the 1970s when corporate America began to lose its market share and quality sank to an all-time low, we just couldn't figure out exactly how this could have happened or seem to remember what we had done differently before this derailment. The baby boomers, who had entered the world of work, thought they knew why and made stabs at questioning established practices and policies and offered tentative attempts at solutions. These employees had been conditioned not during a depression, but during the "Happy Days" of the 1950s and 1960s when the overwhelming need was neither money nor benefits. As they offered up their notions about how the company wasn't responding to individual employees' needs, or letting them use their creativity, the veterans smiled patronizingly and said, "Children, when you've been at GE as long as we have, you will realize that's not the way it's done here."

So industrial leaders for the most part continued to operate with the same philosophy that had worked so well during the 1960s and 1970s. Those who had been "reared by the company," who had signed on right after high school, pretty much accepted the organizational culture—for they had known nothing else. Others had a tougher time, but they were told if they didn't like it, they could leave.

This scenario was complicated by the fact that much of American industry during the late 1970s and early 1980s was still in a state of denial that we had lost that much ground, and that it would take a major cultural shakeup to get us back on track. Middle management tried to imitate words from the corporate office and to follow directives for this and that quality initiative. But most employees thought that this "quality fad" would pass, and they could get back to business as usual. Most workers I found wanted to be left alone to follow their normal work routines. Habit and inertia were too strong; corporate managers had mastered a set of bureaucratic traditions. We simply couldn't remember, or refused to remember, what had gotten us off track.

The United States paid a high price for its memory lapse. In the years since our derailment, we have remembered why our products were as good as they were before the derailment, and why today our mothers hang on for dear life to their forty-year-old GE refrigerators. The price has been so great, that we surely will not dare forget again.

# 3

# Fast Train to Nowhere

## *Our Frantic Effort to Scramble Back*

The price of American hubris was high. The loss of market share to foreign competition sent American managers into a frantic effort in the early 1980s to regain lost ground. American managers were compelled to try to achieve quality by copying overseas competitors' strategies, some of which were out of sync with the American culture—or at least with what had been the strengths in our culture. For example, *kaizen* (the Japanese term for gradual continuous improvement) frustrated many of those American managers working in the trenches who had been used to quicker fixes and who were working in industries whose systems did not support the continuous improvement principles of Joseph Juran and W. Edwards Deming. Collaboration and consensus techniques proved difficult for those groomed for quick and unilateral decision making and who were working in organizations still headed up by managements with top-down, command-and-control styles.

When our status began eroding in the early 1980s and our trade deficit increased, U.S. corporations began scurrying around to retrieve declining market share and trying various strategies to turn back foreign competition. As the pressure to survive intensified, departments frantically tried various approaches to ameliorate the situation and to improve quality and productivity. The bottom line governed what was "really OK" to do, and short-term profit took precedence over ethical behavior.

Many companies took initiatives in the early 1980s to do something about quality—to "fix" it. Edicts from corporate offices everywhere ordered employees to get out there and "get into this quality thing." Companies and components within companies went in different directions, sampling various quality theories and programs. Some did Crosby; others did Deming. Some did quality circles; others did zero defects. Some stressed skill specialization; others stressed cross-functional movement. But all interpreted quality from an internal perspective, rather than from the customer's perspective, which resulted in doing what was best for the organization rather than for the customer.

The American automobile industry, for example, earnestly believed that the automobile engineer knew more about what the customer wanted than that customer did. Even though that may have been the case from a technical point of view, in terms of buyer preference, it was not the case. And American industries still measured quality at the end of the line, rather than design it into the product from the beginning. "Sell cars quickly and cheaply" was the motto; if there were problems, the buyer could always use the safety net of the repair shop. Implicit in that idea was the suggestion that the customer ought to be grateful for that opportunity!

Moreover, according to John De Lorean, a vice-president of GM during the early 1970s, since top managers usually were furnished with company cars that were serviced daily in the company garage, they often had not purchased a car themselves or dealt with a service garage for twenty years. They were out of touch with the real world. Contrary to Alfred Sloan's teaching, GM did not have the best information from customers with which to make decisions, often prompting a reactive, rather than a proactive approach. Bill Gossett, Chevrolet's finance manager during the 1970s, spoke of the " 'cloistered executive' who has no basis to judge public taste."

Overall, the notion continued even into the early 1980s that the inspection department alone was responsible for quality. As a result, U.S. industries tended to emphasize inspection rather than prevention.

During this time, many American managers denied reality and blamed what they called "unfair trading practices" by foreign competitors for those competitors' low costs, and consequently, increasing market share. Ironically, the main competitors were the two countries that had been defeated by the United States in World War II—Japan and Germany. U.S. industrial managers, particularly those whose great technological accomplishments had earned them their market shares, had to begin scrambling to recapture those shares.

## The GE Way

In the early 1980s, General Electric began increasing its emphasis on productivity and quality in response to the increasing competition from foreign competitors, such as Toshiba. Jack Welch had just arrived on the scene, and he vowed to cut off any component from the company that could not carry its weight. He proclaimed: "There will be no room for the mediocre supplier of products and services . . . the winners in this slow-growth environment will be those who search out and participate in the real growth industries and insist upon being number one or number two in every business they are in." The company's leaders were threatened, and as they saw their power begin to crumble, they began circulating horror stories about Welch. *Ruthless* and *cold* were adjectives I heard used to describe him.

Near the end of 1981, ironically, Welch identified three "soft" elements wrapped around the idea of being number one or number two: reality, quality and excellence, and human factors—those same elements that our own prophets had identified twenty years earlier and that Japan had taken up. Welch urged "creating an atmosphere where every single individual across the whole company is striving to be proud of every product and service we provide . . . and an atmosphere where people dare to try new things—where people feel assured in knowing that only the limits of their creativity and drive, their own standards of personal excellence, will be the ceiling." At the Small AC Motor Component, where I worked, individual contributors were excited; managers were terrified.

Today, Welch is hailed as a master in radical change. Since his arrival at General Electric in 1981, he has been touted as leading a corporate revolution that is transforming the entire GE culture and getting it back on track. But it did not happen quickly. For some GE components and for some employees, it would never happen.

When Welch arrived, GE managers had mastered a set of traditions, from cloned newsletters to a "tried and true" compensation system based on loyalty to the boss, which had produced an inertia and a nonglobal business. I was hired into that culture where changing anything about the past was virtually impossible . . . unless the change came from the inside.

And there were so many layers that even if corporate leaders endorsed changes initiated by individual contributors that were contrary to the old "GE way," that endorsement had too far to travel for it to do any good. The person trying to change things had already, in many cases, moved on.

My division, the Small AC Motor Component, or SAC, was convinced that Welch and other senior leadership were overreacting and that the Japanese inroads into our market share were only temporary. The department, in particular technology, attributed Japan's success in part to quick delivery of products and a limited number of offerings. Mostly, it tried to convince itself that the success would be short-lived.

Still, it was enough to capture SAC management's attention. Managers decided that they had better take a look at why the Japanese had made these strides and what they needed to do to turn back the competition. They discovered that the Japanese had grabbed Deming's statistical tools for improvement and involved the entire workforce in improving levels of productivity and quality. Because Japanese companies had been plagued by startup problems when new products or models were introduced, they had been motivated to improve design so that when a new product was introduced to production, it was right from the beginning. As early as the late 1970s the Japanese had developed matrix processes to improve communication between design and manufacturing departments to better consider the function of the product, potential failure modes, and possible new modes and to facilitate systematic analyses of engineering bottlenecks.

By the early 1980s the Japanese had recognized that all employees could contribute to the design effort. They implemented organizational changes to enable employees to try their own improvements. These changes contributed to the gain in market share in electronics and automobiles. American companies—including GE—started paying attention.

Some American industries tried adopting these "Japanese" practices and made some progress in their quality journey. But most of the quality effort in the late 1970s and early 1980s did not work out very well, for several reasons.

First, the efforts were fragmented, lacking a unifying element. A unifying mission guides workers in decision making on a daily basis; the only unified mission during this time was to turn back the competition. The focus on the customer needed to sustain a quality initiative was missing. Second, as is the way with fads, quality was, more often than not, layered on top of existing organizational systems. The quality effort was not integrated and aligned with job design, performance measurement, and selection systems. Third, and perhaps most significant, the cultural elements, such as the belief in the skills and talents of individual contributors and the basic trust generated by mutual respect, were often missing. For any quality effort to work, a corporate culture has to be created that establishes high expectations and supports everyone involved in the quality process. The human contribution has to be recognized. Every man and woman must have the tools to do quality improvement. This component was missing, and quality efforts deteriorated into Band-Aids, not addressing the infrastructure needed to support any quality initiative.

## The Band-Aids

GE's Small AC Motor Component seemed to be inundated with "quick fixes." Corporate teams were brought in to diagnose production problems. Committees within SAC were formed to address what technology and manufacturing considered to be the root of our profitability and product quality problems. And corporate literature carried continuous slogans on quality and articles on how to improve it. The result was many conflicting and frankly overwhelming explanations for our problems. Management's thought was that we could reduce quality to a program, a formula—if we could just find the right one. And although each of the various strategies had merit, they were piecemeal and implemented more or less in a vacuum, lacking a unified focus. They were also superimposed on a structure that lacked basic elements of trust and respect, further inhibiting their effectiveness.

One debate within the SAC headquarters centered around how much model diversity was necessary to keep existing customers satisfied and capture new markets. Design definitions had always been based on an endless file of customer requests, and thus the model count was actually infinite. SAC had always recognized that the real needs of the industrial motor market would require a large variety of models. But in the beginning, the intent was to structure the motors to make them adaptable without redesigning basic components. What SAC ended up doing, however, was redesigning basic components in virtually all lines of motors.

Technology's assumption was that excessive model count was increasing indirect costs and decreasing profitability. It urged a reduction in the model count and an analysis of which models brought in the most money and most influenced customers. The new process was to look first at where the motors were going—at the market, for example, for the polyphase motor; then to look at outside data, breaking down key markets; to interview marketing personnel to determine motor characteristics needed; and, finally, to look at SAC's relative share of each market. The ultimate objective was to provide a product-model mix that optimized profitability and also served the customer by reducing the production cycle. This initiative made sense, but, as one engineer explained, "it eventually fizzled, because it was too little too late."

Another Band-Aid solution to SAC's declining status and one of the most frequently heard answers within SAC for meeting increasing competition was the ongoing development of the department's energy-saver products. In the early 1980s the first Extra-Severe-Duty Energy-Saver Motor had entered production. This product attempted to capture in cast iron all the good features of the aluminum motor, including stack length capability and high structure. In addition, it had a longer bearing life and extra protective features to serve customers who use motors in extra harsh environments, such as the chemical, petroleum, and cement businesses.

A lot was riding on this product. The whole development process had been expensive both in time and in money, and the motor's virtues were hailed by managers and employees alike. The hope was that it would allow SAC to maintain a leading edge in the marketplace.

This was a natural hope, since the predecessor of this product, SAC's energy saver motor, had helped the Industrial Motor Group, of which SAC was a part, to win the lead share of the motor market. This new product was to help secure SAC's future in that group.

The technical theory was sound from an internal perspective, but SAC appeared to be out of touch with the needs of the market. One manufacturing contributor explained:

> GE had ridden for a long time on its reputation; it had begun to believe that as long as the product had the "GE" label on it, customers would buy it. While that might have been the case at one point in time, it ceased to be the case by the early 1980s. That arrogance got SAC into troubled waters that an energy-saver motor could not overcome, regardless of how technically strong it was. . . . And there were too many problems for one invention to overcome.

By the time the product was launched, plans were already being made to absorb SAC into GE's Ft. Wayne operation.

Product innovation proved inadequate to turn around this ailing component. It was ailing not because of a dearth of technical talent or new and innovative products but because it lacked the cultural infrastructure needed to capitalize on the existing technical talent and innovation.

During the early 1980s most discussions within the company focused on what products were good for SAC, rather than on customer preferences—a situation typical of other maintenance-oriented organizations in the late 1970s and early 1980s. Although engineers were concerned about whether SAC products were meeting customer needs, that concern was overshadowed by continued speculation over what would keep the department afloat.

The next attempt at a quick fix for SAC's market share slippage and quality gap involved the synchronous flow system, in which the work in each unit depended on materials coming in from another unit. Because of the interdependence of the work units, if the work was disrupted in one area, work was necessarily halted in another.

Delays and disruptions became so great in one of the plants that an outside control team was brought in to diagnose the production problems. As is often the case in functionally structured companies, accountability had become diffused, and fingerpointing had resulted. The team proposed a procedure that would alert Requisition Control as soon as possible when a production problem occurred, in an effort to isolate the source of the problem early enough to reduce the domino effect of slowdowns on other work areas. There was still some fingerpointing, but the new procedure required documentation. Also, the process implied a response from the source of the delay.

The proposal was hailed by manufacturing as the answer to time scheduling problems. The commitment was made to implement it.

When the procedure was presented to the front-line shop unit managers as one of our plants, they pointed out that a similar process was already in place. All the new procedure would do would be to add a redundant activity, with unnecessary and tedious paper work, to an already strained process.

This exercise in futility highlighted how far removed section managers had become from the factory floor. They had attempted to solve the department's problems without "interference" from the people, staying in the office and going through countless analyses and mental exercises. Ironically, in the process they had damaged their chances of keeping abreast of what was really happening on the firing line. In their quest to make management more "professional," they had made it overly analytical, overcomplicated, and at times totally ineffective.

Finally, there was the "zero defects" program, a pioneering effort in U.S. manufacturing based on Philip Crosby's book, *Quality Is Free.* The basic principles of this initiative called for conformance to interdepartmental requirements: Manufacturing must conform to requirements of engineering, engineering to marketing requirements, and marketing to customer requirements.

SAC established a committee to define the concept for the entire SAC department and to establish a measurement system for quality. While product specifications at SAC were usually defined in terms of customer needs, that was not always the case. As products matured and became refined, they sometimes became subject to all sorts of compromises and modifications. Engineering changes, for example, were often done to reduce costs. It was not unusual for these compromises to be made, as long as customers would still buy the product.

I and other members of the cross-functional quality committee spent considerable time explaining to each other what zero defects really meant. In essence, the term itself meant that a product had to meet certain prescribed standards or it would not leave the factory. But different committee members interpreted this definition differently. The technology representative, for example, felt that if we could not meet the standards we had set, we should change the standard so that we did not fail. Crosby himself had advocated that the requirement be changed if it was not what the customer really needed. But the customer was the key player in Crosby's plan for changing the standard, and in our meetings the customer was rarely mentioned.

Clearly, if we lowered the quality requirements, variance would be lessened and the number of rejects decreased, while the acceptable ratio would be increased. There was a certain corporate appeal in this proposal, but some of us saw a contradiction between accepting this interpretation and achieving high quality. While "zero defects" might be achieved with the lowered standard, it would not result in higher quality. It might even result in lower value. While this standard might be appropriate if it met the customer's expectation and he were satisfied with it, the inherent quality would be lower.

Ultimately, we considered it our first task to explain this definition so that all the employees could understand it, an action consistent with the Crosby plan. Ironically, though, this was step seven in Crosby's plan; the first step dealt with management commitment. We seemed to have bypassed this step, along with several others.

Our second step was to articulate the tasks necessary to achieve the quality goals and quality levels established by the company. No longer was quality relegated to manufacturing or engineering and then promptly forgotten by upper management. The program made a lot of sense to me then; today I recognize how forward-thinking it was as a cross-functional approach to quality.

Unfortunately, like the other strategies, this zero-defects program did not achieve the success it might have due to gaps in the human elements of quality, including trust and open communication. To its credit, however, SAC had made a stab at advancing Crosby's theory that quality was not the special province of a functional department but everyone's job. The failure came in trying to practice this theory in daily operations.

During the late 1970s and early 1980s SAC's workers were not primarily focused on what customers value. Discussions usually centered around what was important for SAC or around functional imperatives rather than around ways the relationships between functional areas contributed to or detracted from specific aspects of customer value. And we were primarily concerned about fixing the things that we thought we were doing wrong, not improving the things that would most affect the customer.

Today it is common to define high quality as that which satisfies the customer, although in practice this definition is still challenging for many. Some people feel that we have the responsibility to raise the customer's quality consciousness and provide a product that goes beyond what the customer has prescribed. Customers will almost always accept the higher standard if we give them more of what they already value. But, if we are just giving them bells and whistles they don't care about, embellishing with nonvalue properties, that is a different story.

### Movement Across the Lines: The Pros and Cons of Functional Mobility

During the 1970s a popular practice was rotating people around. Like other corporations, GE practiced this cross-functional movement, a practice now commonly upheld as a way to give employees a greater sense of security. GE experimented with moving people temporarily into other work areas to give them an understanding of the interdependence of work within the company and to foster development of skills across functions. As part of that practice, I shifted from employee relations to engineering, where I worked for a while as a keypuncher. Although I was not very effective in that job, I gained appreciation for what keypunchers did and for how that function related to other functions at SAC.

Cross-functional movement was most popular among the more senior employees who had been conditioned by GE to "wander around." This was GE's term for rotational assignments intended to give them an overall understanding of the company's products and systems. (GE had its own special vocabulary for programs and practices to increase the perception of uniqueness, such as "wander around" and "synchronous work flow," even though many phrases referred to practices that were common at other corporations as well.) An employee might move from quality control to advanced engineering or from manufacturing to engineering. Sometimes these work assignments lasted only a few weeks; at other times, they lasted a year or longer.

Not everyone appreciated this attempt to help people understand their interdependence. Had this initiative been implemented in a culture characterized by trust, it would probably have been perceived as adding to employee security. As it was, many saw it as another strategy to keep them off guard and perpetually insecure.

Employees saw various drawbacks to this mobility. When the production process required that each specialist modify goals or develop a new set of skills, specialized employees sometimes became confused and even hostile. A systems man argued, "Bring a scheduler in here, and in one day our whole system will be down." And a marketing guy screamed, "That's the problem now—engineering trying to stick its finger into our business. They need to stay away from 'our' customers." Even Lee Iacocca has expressed skepticism about this strategy, which was used also at General Motors. In his autobiography Iacocca says that it's like taking a heart surgeon and saying, "Now let's let him deliver a baby," as if all skills were interchangeable.

Cross-functional movement was particularly resisted by the younger employees who had just recently been trained in colleges to be marketing analysts, mechanical engineers, or employee relations specialists, and who sometimes resented being moved around.

A design engineer related some other problems created by this mobility.

> You know, our section manager was a production man—a manufacturing man—who had been placed over design engineering to relieve some of the animosity between Production at the plant and Engineering at the Rivergate operation . . . the philosophy of manufacturing types is to get the job done, at any means . . . there were different difficulties with this move. First, manufacturing typically doesn't have a lot of sympathy with engineers, as they're concerned with production, not design. Second, the two groups—design engineers and advanced technology—who support each other are separated from each other by being in different functions, and in different physical locations, as well. Third, engineers are used to planning; manufacturing tends to be firefighters, to whom planning more than two weeks away is out of the question.

This statement demonstrates how tough it is for people to move out of a functionality mind-set, however theoretically sound cross-functional movement is.

I experienced some of the drawbacks of functional mobility in my work area of employee relations. The manager of this function had come from manufacturing, and his closest aide had been an accounting clerk.

Their talents and skills clearly lay elsewhere than in employee relations. I spent an inordinate amount of energy and time trying to get them to understand the relationship between management practices and communications and the bottom line, usually with little success. While there is value in having personnel people acquainted with operations matters, it is also important that operations employees be trained in human resources issues. Here we had a situation where no one had trained these men in employee development, management practices, or handling grievances. That failure was costly. It produced an insecurity that manifested itself in various damaging ways (see Chapter 5), including positioning people throughout to report on "traitors" to the system. These tactics kept employees threatened and off-guard and contributed to the deterioration of the entire operation of SAC.

In the end, SAC was not able to capitalize on its cross-functional practice. Employees who were shifted across function lines and placed in critical areas for which they were totally unprepared often felt insecure in their new roles and viewed the practice as manipulation by management to keep them tentative and unsure of their jobs.

Employees crossed over not only to new functions but also to new components (e.g., from Electrical Devices to the Small AC Motor Department). Because employees mistrusted management, they often viewed these rotational assignments as corporate attempts to keep employees tied to the company, not as efforts to give them an overall view of the scope of GE products and systems.

### The Impact of Ignoring the Cultural Infrastructure

GE was a leader in management approaches designed to improve product quality and promote an understanding of the scope of GE systems and products. Unquestionably, cross-functional movement and rotational assignments gave employees an overall view of the GE operation—not just of the interdependence of different functions (marketing, manufacturing, technology), but of the diversity in GE products.

Unfortunately, the distrust embedded in the cultural infrastructure of some GE components prevented innovations like these from having the positive impact that they might otherwise have had. Employees were suspicious that cross-functional and cross-component movement would tie them to one employer and increase their risk of becoming largely nonmarketable to other companies. One of the goals of cross-functional movement today is to enable employees to gain skills that will make them *more* marketable, not just to other business units inside the company but to other companies. During the 1970s and 1980s at GE, however, the perceived primary intent was to develop an understanding of and a loyalty to the company itself. Each business function was peculiarly "GE." For example, employee relations involved GE benefits, GE communications, and GE newsletters. Every unit trained personnel on the "GE way." Employees remarked that while they had received much training, they didn't know if they would be considered employable by other companies. Would their GE accounting course, for example, be valued outside GE?

Further, there was always the problem of conflicting goals of the functions as well as conflict between the short-term orientation of Wall Street (numbers) and the costs of high quality. Manufacturing was concerned about the number of models sold and shipped, since that was what manufacturing was measured on. Indeed, the entire SAC operation was governed by these numbers, and managers received their incentive bonuses on the basis of these numbers. Design engineering, on the other hand, was concerned with keeping the defect rate low to reduce customer complaints. In both cases, their priority goals were based on what was good for the function and for SAC, rather than what was good for the customer. The customer was brought into the equation, but often at the end of the process, as in "Will he buy what we've built?," rather than at the beginning, as in "Can we build what he wants?" (This was true of most industries during the 1970s.)

If the SAC culture had had the needed cultural elements of trust and respect for each employee's contribution, and if it had in turn connected these elements with customer satisfaction, SAC would probably have been able to capitalize on its innovations and remain in business.

### A Lack of Customer Emphasis on Front End Production

The quality initiatives tried at SAC failed to make the difference because the "quality people" typically did not get involved with the customers unless there was a problem. Today, we stress the need for engineering and manufacturing to interact with customers and for contractors to define product expectations up front. In the late 1970s and early 1980s, engineering and manufacturing had little or no part in obtaining product specifications and often interacted with customers only after a problem developed. As a result, specifications occasionally tended to drift away from specific customer needs if the designs needed to be modified to accommodate the manufacturing process or if cost reduction was essential. For example, a cheaper material might be substituted, but it might result in a shorter product life and only then would the quality people intervene.

The original request from a customer was sometimes modified by production because it didn't happen to have the products requested. Sometimes these substitutions proved to be unsatisfactory to the customer. In one case, when the customer was displeased with a product he had received, marketing blamed engineering and technology blamed manufacturing, when in fact the field salesperson either had not understood what the customer required or, if he did understand, had not accurately documented the specifications. That marketing person had altered the customer's request to fit a mold the component happened to have but that did not meet the customer's needs.

Some people believe that such modifications are justified, as this is what standardization is all about. Justified or not, the error in this case occurred in the initial contact with the customer, not in the "manufacturing ghetto" which was often blamed for "white-collar crimes." In this case, if engineering had interacted with the customer, the error might not have occurred.

Like most organizations at that time, quality was considered primarily a manufacturing issue, despite fragmented attempts to move it out of a single function. We had not identified managerial and administrative functions as places where there could be substantial losses as a result of redundant tasks or rework.

## Summary: Barriers to Inventiveness

Perhaps General Electric's greatest strength historically has been its inventiveness. Yet in the 1970s and 1980s GE was not able fully to capitalize on its tradition of inventiveness for three reasons. First, the overgrown size and layering of the company impeded the innovation process. As early as the 1900s, the company had had difficulty coordinating research and development in factories spread all over the country. Second, the strength of traditional rituals overpowered new process ideas, especially if those new ideas came from people who had not been reared in the GE culture. Third, the cultural elements needed to sustain these inventions were missing: Specifically, younger employees did not believe that corporate practices were driven by what was good for customers, both internal and external, rather than by what was good for GE.

In steering SAC through this rocky period, GE managers forgot the advice of their own prophets, such as Dr. Feigenbaum, who had in the early 1950s emphasized broad management themes of customer satisfaction and results-driven quality. Total quality was not about defects but about increasing the number of good values that customers receive.

If the GE "fixes"—cross-functional movement, zero defects, rotational assignments, and all the other strategies to survive—had been driven by customer preference, rather than by company preference, I believe that GE components like SAC would have stayed on track and in business. As it was, those employees who had not been "reared" by GE came to view these practices as strategies and manipulations that might help the company but wouldn't necessarily help either internal or external customers. Consequently, those businesses were swallowed up. Plans to phase out SAC and absorb it into GE's Ft. Wayne operation began late in 1982, and by the end of 1983, many SAC employees had been terminated.

# 4

# No Way to Run a Railroad

## Quality Is More Than Slogans and Surveys

By the early 1980s, then, the Small AC Motor Component of GE had initiated various plans to improve quality. These were aimed at reducing motor failure rates, most of which were caused by product defects and mechanical failings. Engineers began emphasizing the high costs of doing things wrong. Advanced Technology began stressing measurements to determine conformance to requirements. SAC seemed to be doing the "right stuff" to turn itself around.

Corporate management decided that one way to improve quality and productivity throughout the company was to offer incentive programs, such as contests and dinners on the town, for employees. General Electric spent hundreds of thousands of dollars on employee incentives to improve quality, much of it on the Quality Makers program. For employees in shop operations, quality meant reducing scrap; for office workers, it implied speeding up the flow of work, saving costs to the department.

Initially, motivation seemed high. Posters were hung; conference rooms were decorated with pictures of employee quality makers. Early on, suggestions about quality improvement proliferated. Soon, however, as employees continued to see their daily business being conducted as usual, enthusiasm gave way to skepticism, and then to cynicism. Employees bemoaned the emphasis on what they began seeing as gimmicks. Grumbled one employee, "If the company would spend the same money they're spending on all these gimmicks and send us some qualified managers, we wouldn't have a quality problem." Another one wrote in a management attitude survey I conducted, "Management doesn't want a quality product; this whole quality makers program is a joke . . . it's only being done because the company says to do it." Even employees who continued to offer written suggestions within their quality teams complained that their suggestions were falling on deaf ears.

## SAC's Attempt to Use Quality Makers Teams

Quality teams were established at SAC to study production and service problems that were affecting quality and to make suggestions on ways to improve quality. Like the quality circle program in Japan, they were intended to give employees power and authority to influence the organization; but unlike in the Japanese system, the emphasis was on technique and not on the human aspect of production.

At SAC I was a member of the quality steering committee on which my boss, the employee relations manager, served as chairman. Our goal was to coordinate the efforts of the various quality teams and to reduce the potential for replication. Employees were at first excited about the possibility of having some input into improving things, and they introduced some great ideas for reducing scrap, rework, and replication. As the program developed and we began considering these suggestions, however, problems developed.

The chairman began rejecting all suggestions related to what he called "the soft elements," such as engaging in more direct communication with customers, taking the pulse of customers, and having clearer internal communication. For example, when one member suggested a method to improve telephone communication with customers, the chairman could not see the relationship between cutting response time to customers and achieving higher quality—and, ultimately, improving the bottom line. Therefore, after only a few meetings, team members' interest turned to cynicism as they concluded that their suggestions were being stonewalled. Eventually, they gave the process only lip service and ceased being serious about it.

The rewards system was another problem. The plan was that the quality team that generated and implemented the most valuable and creative quality improvements over a particular time period would win and be rewarded with belt buckles, dinners on the town, coffee mugs, and other tangibles. This emphasis on winning prizes rather than on the intrinsic rewards of quality backfired. As the same teams kept receiving the rewards, the program became a negative motivator for the rest of the employees.

I had been initially excited about the Quality Makers program because I thought it would draw attention to quality problems behind the accumulation of scrap at the end of the production line and provide focus for the quality initiative. I was disheartened when the program fizzled.

## Why the Program Failed

There were two underlying reasons for the failure of the Quality Makers program—employees' basic distrust of senior management's sincerity and their feeling that the program, like other quality improvement efforts, would end.

Employee distrust was in large measure a result of management practices, particularly in Employee Relations. This unit, which directed and coordinated the Quality Makers initiative, had low credibility stemming from its reputation for unfair practices. Nonexempt and exempt employees alike felt that the unit used its power to punish those who were disloyal to the existing culture, who resisted the tried and true ways. I frequently heard the ER manager, who had come from manufacturing, talk about his people whom he had positioned throughout SAC to report on these "traitors." When employees questioned practices or tried to change things, they often ended up being put on lack of work, or they failed to win promotions. Employees especially resented the unit's abuse of its power over their compensation and classification.

By analyzing employee attitude surveys, interviewing employees for newsletter articles, and observing workers in meetings with the ER manager, I had come to understand that there was a particular hostility to the ER manager. (Later I came to realize from personnel in other GE components that other ER managers within GE had similar problems.) He and his assistant projected the insecurity that often exists when power has been granted on the basis of position, rather than merit. They suffered, along with everybody else, as a result of this action.

The manager's insecurity, based on his inability to understand the underlying causes of quality problems or the relationship between human resources practices and quality, caused him either to reject ideas he could not understand or to react with suspicion to ideas that came from within "the ranks." This lack of understanding derailed many of the teams' suggestions before they could be implemented.

This scenario served to reinforce the already existing skepticism about whether management was really interested in hearing employees' suggestions about quality improvement. Employees simply could not really believe that an historically autocratic culture all of a sudden wanted employees' ideas on quality problems and solutions, especially when they saw contradictions between employee involvement slogans and managers' behaviors in quality meetings. The perception that their ideas were being stonewalled was reinforced by some operations managers who, like the ER manager, had difficulties connecting quality improvement with anything but the manufacturing process.

The other reason the Quality Makers effort couldn't be sustained was employees' belief that quality was a "program" that would inevitably end. People asked, "What happens to quality when our Quality Makers program is over?" Some employees really did see quality as a journey, but they did not dictate the culture; change was directed from the top and driven from the top, and workers had seen management impose one campaign after another on them.

## The Employee Attitudes Survey: Perplexing Results

Despite the plethora of articles and books written to the contrary during the 1970s and 1980s, in practice industry leaders had a tough time relating job satisfaction or dissatisfaction about management's intent and practices to producing a quality product. And so when skepticism and suspicion about management practices did surface in attitude surveys, senior managers became concerned primarily because they feared losing people and trade secrets to the competition.

In the survey introduction, which had been communicated through the local newsletters, GE officials explained that the 1981 survey could do one of two things: "It can give employees an opportunity to candidly express their feelings about their job and work-related matters, or it can test their willingness, when confronted with leading questions, to supply the answers management wants to see."

Even though employees were encouraged to answer openly and candidly, some employees still indicated skepticism to me about the survey. They suspected their answers might somehow be traced, and they therefore supplied what they believed to be the "right answers" in preference to candid responses. Jack Welch was new to GE, and his philosophy, radically different from some predecessors, had not had time to translate into belief at the local levels. Also, the bureaucratic hierarchy of companies then contributed to employees' skepticism about whether corporate management really cared about them. The voice of the corporate office was too far removed.

Questions related to management's communication practices, and those related to trust between employees and managers—performance appraisal issues, complaints, involvement in decision making, enough information obtained to do their jobs—were given largely negative responses. These responses reflected attitudes they personally expressed to me. Few of the employees felt they were given candid answers to their questions, and most indicated that the major source of information was the grapevine or rumor mill.

There was an overall paranoia about sharing information. Financial data were guarded. The playing field was, at best, dimly lit. People worked overtime, many times because of down time, waiting around for the "information giver" to show up and give them another task. As a result of power/information being held by a single person, people were forced into operating independently rather than interdependently and had to go to that single source for information on how to proceed. This approach had worked in organizations that were productivity driven, rather than quality driven, and as long as workers had assembly-line mentalities. But as employees became more knowledgeable and creative, they were frustrated about being forced into a reactive mode.

Surveys during those times also revealed that employees did not feel their opinions and ideas mattered to management. Few people felt that sufficient effort was made to tap their brains. Nor did they feel that management was concerned about their problems. I believe that some senior leaders were actually concerned, but employees were too removed from senior leadership for that concern to reach them. Even if they read about it in newsletters, local practices were often so out of sync with it that they saw it as just some "pretty theory."

Interestingly, on questions related to "communication," more employees indicated that management was "frank and honest." This apparent discrepancy can be attributed to the fact that employees were conditioned to view "communications" as information about benefits and salary, something quite separate from interpersonal communication between themselves and their managers. Newsletters had been a big part of the company's history, but they had primarily contained information related to GE benefits or company regulations. "Communications" and "communicators" were considered concrete "things," apart from everything else. This was ironic since the information communication network has proved over the years to be more significant to employee morale than formal newsletters and bulletin boards.

GE managers, many of whom were themselves primarily motivated by pay and benefits, often expressed bewilderment over the fact that responses related to benefits and pay received relatively high ratings, and yet the questions that asked about overall "job satisfaction" received considerably lower ratings. Questions about overall "job satisfaction" were positioned separately from management practices or communications, demonstrating that even the corporate office did not see the connection.

Though the questions about overall "job satisfaction" received lower ratings than the ones about pay and benefits, their ratings were higher than any of the questions related to management practices, such as conducting performance appraisals, communicating clearly, or sharing information with employees. This response demonstrated that even employees themselves had not crystallized the connection between job satisfaction and communication, involvement and recognition, but still reflected the corporate connection of job satisfaction primarily with pay and benefits. They had come to the general awareness, though, that overall they weren't happy.

Significantly, categories on employee attitude surveys in the 1970s generally omitted customer satisfaction, as that focus was perceived as the special province of the marketing function.

Corporate "blueprints"—models that "communicators" were often sent to follow in analyzing survey results—grouped pay, benefits, and other perks under the category "job satisfaction," attempting to perpetuate the view of employee satisfaction as only satisfaction with extrinsics. Senior level management during those days did not pay much heed to the theory that money and benefits were beginning to lose their force as sources of job satisfaction compared to such things as recognition. They should have.

## Slogans and Programs—No Match for Dissatisfaction

Slogans and programs proved not to be enough to get SAC back on track. Real job satisfaction needed to attain and sustain high quality and productivity was missing in the quality formula. These areas of discontent which had showed up in attitude surveys had a devastating effect on the bottom line, but managers were too concerned about the costs of "quality" to listen to the causes of poor quality. Dissatisfied employees ultimately create a lower quality product and provide less-than-satisfactory customer service.

At SAC, individual employees showed more concern about the customer than did some of the managers, although neither really gave the customer the proper weight. SAC did stress conformance to requirements. The general manager himself stressed that quality in manufacturing was conformance to engineering and that quality in engineering was conformance to marketing. It was only in marketing, though, where quality meant comformance to customer requirements. To the degree that initiatives were not undertaken as a response to customer expectations, no quality program or effort could have made a real difference—at SAC or at any other GE component.

## Employee Awareness

When I began writing articles for the SAC newsletter on topics such as how to handle conflict, how to negotiate, and how to communicate clearly and on the "soft issues" of quality, such as communicating with the customer, I was challenged by my manager. He warned me that the newsletter was not supposed to be a vehicle for these matters and that employees did not want to read about these superfluous topics. So I decided to survey employees anonymously about how they rated various newsletter articles. They were asked to divide 100 points, according to the value that articles in several categories had for them. Articles about the employee concerns just listed received twenty-eight points; those related to customer reactions received seventeen points; service award features, sixteen points; locally written features about product quality, fifteen points; news releases from corporate, fifteen points; and quality makers features, eight points. One employee wrote, "I am sick of hearing about productivity and quality . . . I think we all know they are important to the business . . . show more human interest and that will solve those two problems." Another wrote, "Individuality is being lost in the work atmosphere . . . so no one fully knows the contribution effort by some to achieve quality."

Individual employees showed a concern for doing a quality job and appreciated efforts to help them, but they associated quality more with the way they were treated than with programs and slogans. I found it also interesting, judging from the difference in points awarded the customer reaction articles and the quality articles, that the employees still considered the customer separate from quality, except in the marketing function.

## Missing Cultural Infrastructure: The Other Bottom Line

While organizations like GE successfully focused people on quality initiatives, they did not have the cultural elements in place needed to sustain quality. The first problem was trying to change an entrenched paradigm.

Management's sudden interest in getting all employees involved in improving quality was introduced into cultures that historically had been autocratic and unconcerned about winning every employee's involvement. Employees simply could not believe that management suddenly wanted their input. Managers' behaviors in quality makers meetings and managers' responses to employee attitude surveys intensified this disbelief. I believe that Jack Welch really did want to change the culture, even in 1981, but proving this to employees in the local offices was another matter, especially when they saw contradictions between the slogans and daily actions. Not unlike employees in many organizations today, employees were highly skeptical of slogans that seemed out of sync with the "way things really are."

The perception of change—that is, people's belief that it has really occurred—always lags behind the facts of change. Even if senior leaders are sincere and even if their daily actions do match their words, they will require patience and persistence to overcome this lag. Welch's statements and actions in 1981 implied that he was serious about the need for radical change in the way GE components did business, but his words were not always reinforced by management actions at the local levels, where a culture is really changed.

Second, GE and other corporations attempted to superimpose quality initiatives on top of existing cultures. The programs came to be viewed as just new slogans, campaigns from the corporate office. An overall systematic management strategy needed to unify the initiatives was missing, as was the willingness to recraft the cultural infrastructure. Because the organizations' past cultures, including corporate initiatives such as quality makers programs, employee attitude surveys, and benefits newsletters, had brought them so much success in the past, management lacked a plan for liberating the culture from its past. Habit and inertia were too strong. For the most part, the rules and rituals of changes were dictated by the old culture; because of those embedded beliefs, values, and behavior patterns, the changes that were introduced focused, for the most part, on technology, rather than on ways of operating or managing. The result was that while innovations such as zero defects and quality circles were introduced, the systems changes needed to support technological changes and to alter day-to-day behavior were ignored. The bottom line therefore continued to deteriorate.

This scenario was common throughout corporate America during the 1970s and early 1980s. Even those few organizations that attempted to redesign themselves on the basis of internal and external employee responses dictated that the redesign come from those who had long been a part of the corporate culture. "Insiders" were the only ones who were allowed to drive the effort—a radical difference from many of today's reengineering efforts, which are driven primarily by either "out-of-the-box thinkers" who often have not been accepted in the organization or outsiders.

Slogans, surveys, and quality articles were not enough. It was too little too late. With the continuing decline of both "bottom lines," SAC began to be merged with GE's Ft. Wayne operation within two years of these dramatic "quality" initiatives.

# 5

# Getting Railroaded

## *The Threat of Continuous Improvement*

When empires are built from position and gamesmanship, their foundations are shaky. When people within those empires don't have the substance to back up their positions, an insecurity results that makes it virtually impossible to introduce any improvement of process, since that improvement magnifies existing or past weaknesses. Today we view continuous improvement as our savior; in the 1970s and 1980s, it was mostly seen as a threat.

## Corporate America

During the 1970s and early 1980s, entrenched rituals and practices in corporations like General Electric took precedence over continuous improvement. In GE's case, these cultural elements had helped secure the company's leading position in its industry, and they were not about to be discarded or changed. Written company communications, especially newsletters, sounded and looked largely alike. Puzzles, games, quality makers winners, benefit statements, and salary increases—all had their place in GE newsletters. These communication vehicles reinforced conformity within the ranks. Even though many employees ignored these "cloned articles," no one could alter the format or the subject matter without an uphill battle. The style and content of other business communications also remained the same year after year. They were part of the "GE culture."

One aspect of my job at a General Electric component headquarters was synthesizing data from employee attitude surveys and, from these data, preparing a report with recommendations about communication and other management practices. This report in turn was sent to the corporate office. My boss directed me to follow the historical corporate blueprint for my report, even though employee and organizational needs were changing, given the current state of quality and productivity. Clearly, the slippage that SAC was experiencing was in part the result of the company's failure to meet some of these changing needs. When I suggested that I update and revise the report on the basis of the new conditions and values, the response was always, "You must do it that way because that's the way we do it here."

Each time employee attitude surveys were administered, local Employee Relations units prepared a report of "significant questions and responses" based on the corporate report and then distributed that report to employees. This report compared the particular department's responses with those of the larger group and with those in the overall company and compared the percentage of "positive" responses with the figure for the previous year.

Historically, the process had largely been a matter of cutting and pasting information on certain areas—mainly pay, benefits, and perks—drawn from the corporate report. But these highlighted summaries never told the full story. Before I had actually gotten the assignment of preparing the report, I had studied previous years' reports and was bothered about how questions were categorized. From employees' generally positive responses about pay and benefits, the senior management at SAC as well as the corporate office had always drawn conclusions that most employees were satisfied with their jobs—an incorrect conclusion.

I grabbed the opportunity to do something meaningful; after months of fetching donuts and lining up the cream and sugar for birthday meetings, synthesizing and analyzing data seemed stimulating. Though I had been hired as SAC's "communicator" and trainer, most of my time up to that point had been spent on tasks almost any seven-year-old could have handled. I later realized, however, that I had been naive not to realize one very important rule of the game: No subordinate manager in those days preguessed key executives about anything, particularly about changing business needs or gaps in the information possessed by management.

When the corporate report was sent to SAC, some of the questions and responses that had appeared on the actual survey had been omitted. Realizing I had insufficient information from this study to compile a useful analysis, I asked my manager whether I might secure additional data from the corporate or group sector. He seemed almost pleased. Whether it was because he thought I was serious about the job at hand, or if he was merely glad to have me out of his hair, I do not know to this day. Whatever, he gave me a couple of names to contact for more information.

Phoning these individuals, I explained, "I am trying to bring some meaningful analysis to the exempt attitude survey and find I do not have the responses to some key questions. Can you help me?" Both individuals were supportive and gave me additional data.

After obtaining the information, I worked on the report for some time and saw a pattern emerge. I decided to organize the report around various employee needs, such as the need to be kept informed (involvement), the need to perform creative and challenging work, the need to have open communication, and the need to have competitive benefits. When I showed my manager my plan and a rough draft of the report, he looked somewhat puzzled but responded, "That's fine, Kathryn." Even though I wondered at the time if he really meant what he said, I decided to let well enough alone.

When I presented him with the final report, however, he became livid and told me that I "would not go to print with *that*." I asked him what the problem was, and he responded that I was presenting a negative picture of the department. He said, "You were supposed to use the corporate report, and just add the department's responses to it."

As my mouth dried out and my adrenaline started pumping, I said in as even a tone as I could muster, "Why didn't you tell me in the first place when I showed you a rough draft?" Raising his voice, he responded, "You never showed me any draft; this is the first time I've seen it." I realized there was no point in arguing, so I asked him to explain how this was being negative and why we had to copy previous years' reports. The answer was simple: "You will do it this way because I say so."

To this day I remember my frustration. My time and effort had been completely wasted. I knew I had done a responsible job, presenting as accurately as possible a complete picture of employee attitudes at SAC and suggesting solutions to problems. I was more concerned, however, that he was asking me to omit important information, the result of which would give a distorted picture. "I don't know if I can do what you want me to, and still do what is right and accurate," I responded. He quickly seized the chance to say, "If you can't, then you should resign." I had unwittingly given him the perfect opportunity to try to move me out. I realized belatedly that my attempts at improving the report were just too threatening to an entrenched GE tradition.

I returned to my office to try to think logically about what was happening. Was he firing me? I knew he wanted to, but had it happened? I really didn't know. Later I also realized that I had violated the number one rule in the game: Show absolute deference to the boss. The situation had escalated beyond the simple matter of improving a report, although I did not have the good sense to see it at the time.

The next day I heard my manager tell his secretary to call me in to his office. Although we were within earshot of each other, he always told her to have me come in, rather than asking me directly. Going through the secretary increased the distance between supervisor and employee, which in turn increased positional power.

"Here, I've done your work for you; do you think you can fill in the blanks?" he asked sarcastically while handing me some scribbled sheets. I was confused by these notes and asked him if he could be a little more explicit about what he wanted. His voice rising, he responded, "This is what I want," and with that he handed me the corporate blueprint. Here we were—back to where I began.

I wanted to make a formal protest but realized that I had no one to go to. At GE, as with any corporation at that time, the immediate boss had supreme power over a stipulated area. Even though his superior could technically remove or reprimand him if he proved to be inept, the power inherent in the rank remained with that supervisor, until he was physically removed. Besides, in the department, my manager's superior appeared to be his protector. So I managed to turn in a superficial report by the deadline, which was the next day. I copied the corporate blueprint, included only the data that would be the least damaging to SAC, and made no analysis. I left it on his desk and waited for him to read it.

After a short while, I heard him tell the secretary to have me come to his office. He told me to close the door, a bad sign.

He began, "The report you turned in shows an indifference; you just halfway did it."

Within a few weeks, SAC began to be restructured, my job was eliminated, and I was laid off in the name of "restructuring."

The exempt attitudes survey was only one small example of the degree to which the status quo reigned supreme and managers had come to identify themselves by the rituals. On one occasion, a manager instructed me, "Kathryn, don't you know by now that employees are paid high wages to put their minds on the shelf and do as they are told? And above all, they're not to go beyond their scope of work."

Letting us go was a correct action in one sense, since our values were clearly out of sync with the "GE way," and it was too great a struggle to maintain the status quo with our constant questioning and attempts to improve things. The "GE way" had been dictated by those who had been reared in the culture, and a few of us "baby boomers" who had come from the outside had not paid our dues and were viewed with skepticism.

We probably should have been more patient, but we simply found it too difficult to go along with practices that were dishonest or had limited value for employees or customers.

After the various GE components began to feel the influence of Jack Welch, many of these ritual practices were eliminated, and the managers who could not operate without them were terminated. But that was a couple of years down the road, and many other workers were sacrificed before the changes could happen at the local.

## The Fear of Continuous Improvement in Service Organizations

The fear of continuous improvement was not confined to corporate America. During the early 1980s I had the opportunity to design and deliver management training for a major university medical center. I found a situation similar to that at GE.

This medical center faced dilemmas common to university medical centers, which have to set priorities among goals for teaching, health care, and research. Not only were there differences among the three divisions as what the primary goal should be; there were differences about how goals should be carried out. This particular university medical center had historically been autocratic and top down, but employees like researchers resisted tight controls and young medical staffers had begun pushing for more autonomy. Responding to a politically charged situation like this one is always challenging for any human resources function; to have any hope of credibility and success, HR personnel must be strong and capable.

The provost of that university, whom I knew, encouraged me to take the job as management trainer, since the training being provided by the personnel department had some serious weaknesses. These were beginning to manifest themselves in university and hospital employees' work, and the provost thought I could restore credibility. At the same time, however, he warned me that it would be tough getting any changes implemented because of the department manager. The provost explained that this person's training approach was considered too elementary to be very helpful for hospital and university administrators, many of whom had advanced degrees. He also explained that she had gotten her position through political alliances and close personal involvement with one of the medical administrators. (This situation seemed to show up frequently in personnel departments that have potentially great power over employees' work lives). Looking back, I probably was foolish to think I could help things given that scenario. But having come originally from academia, I knew what professor and research types expected, and believed I could close the credibility gap. So I decided to respond to this challenge.

On my first day, I approached the manager's office, passing the department's secretary who was rearranging books in the next office. I said, "Good morning." No response. I asked where I might find my manager. No response. Finally, the secretary, without looking up, muttered, "You may as well sit in this office, until we can find you another one." I never saw the manager that day, and no one spoke to me that entire day. The other trainer in the department did not speak to me for one month. I later learned she had wanted my position, but the higher-ups felt she wasn't qualified. The secretary remained cool to me for six months.

Perplexed about this less-than-warm introduction to the job, I determined to concentrate on what I had come there to do and began reviewing results of needs assessments and previous training evaluations. Between analyzing these reports and interviewing some of the internal customers, including researchers, hospital administrators, and operations managers, I realized that the training that was being created and delivered reflected more the language and knowledge level of the training manager than that of the intended audience. The curriculum hadn't been changed in years. Things were further complicated because participation in training programs was voluntary, and funding for the department was in large part dependent on the number of employees who participated in training sessions. So I needed to figure out how to raise the standards.

After presenting to the manager an outline and a rough draft for one suggested program that the medical center staff had requested, I quickly learned she was not really interested in changing anything. She told me that not only must I retain the topics already taught, which many customers had indicated were insultingly childlike, but I must use the same method of delivery, which included many games and activities and which I knew would turn off professional audiences. This posed a challenge, since I had the job of designing and delivering credible training, and besides the funding dilemma, my own performance evaluation would reflect the success of this initiative. How could I develop programs and get them accepted by the immediate manager and still satisfy the needs of the ultimate customer and recreate value for that branch of personnel?

I ended up cloning her design, keeping much the same topics, writing "lesson plans" much like hers, and asking her advice on simple items, such as choosing visual aids, seating arrangements, and training room information. This way I deferred to her judgment on things she was comfortable with and followed her existing process. I wrote a second set of programs for the audience, keeping the same general topics but tailoring them for the customers' needs by targeting their knowledge and language level and delivery preference. I was determined to accomplish this mission without incurring the manager's wrath.

That strategy worked for a while, until she began to receive positive comments and written evaluations from trainees. The more satisfied the customers were with the training, the more it highlighted the difference between past and current training, and the more critical she became. She eventually learned that the training was being delivered at a higher technical level than before. I had earned enough credibility with the ultimate customers by this time to give me a little bargaining power, but it was not enough to prevent her from exacting her revenge. I was the only person in the entire personnel department of forty-four people who did not get a pay increase that year, although the evaluations of our programs were better than those for the previous six years. Eventually, the administrators removed me from her jurisdiction, ending her management status. With the loss of positional power, she left the organization. I continued with my mission, and the programs continued to receive high ratings.

There is a certain psychological strength and energy that can come from focusing on the customer, knowing you are contributing to a better product. Unfortunately, the constant change and reassessment that are part and parcel of continuous improvement can be threatening to fragile departments. For you too, it can produce some short-term pain, including financial setbacks. But if you can stay committed to higher quality for the customer and keep your focus on that end rather than on *who* it is that's making you uncomfortable, usually you will ultimately succeed.

In the case of the training situation, improved quality was helping the internal customers by giving them skills needed to serve patients and other staff members. *Customer impact*—not just a different product, or one that was broader—saved higher quality. Creating value for customers is different from just changing things because they are not good. A new product may not be any better, unless it is driven by customer value. Fortunately, today, successful organizations consider higher quality as the savior, not a threat.

Of course, realistically you must consider whether you can manage financially and psychologically until the higher standards eventually pay off and gain so much force that things have to turn around.

## The Keepers of the Systems

Every supervisor and team leader in an organization leads by example, even when it's a bad example. Every one of them has influence on the organization, even if it is a bad influence. We just naturally imitate those in charge. What senior leaders do, what they believe and value, what and whom they reward, are watched, seen, interpreted, and imitated throughout the whole organization. That becomes a major barrier to the quality initiative if their philosophies are out of sync with it. If they find continuous improvement threatening, the culture simply cannot change, however many programs they initiate.

Not only was American industry off track during the 1970s in its thinking that quality could be reduced to "programs," but it was also off track in its thinking about what managers and leaders are supposed to do and be. Loyalty to the status quo had as much to do with our derailment as anything. Leaders often looked at what was compatible with the company's past practices rather than what was good for the customer.

Corporations had grown so much that by the late 1970s they pretty much ran themselves, as long as those at the helm were loyal to the system and the tried and true ways. Self-gain and ambition were often more important than mission and were manifested in various strategies to climb up the corporate ladder.

Leadership played a major role in America's high quality consciousness and productivity before the derailment. As organizations became more layered and bureaucratic in the 1970s, they increased strategies and tools to recapture efficiency that had become lost as senior leaders became further and further removed from both the internal and external customers. Sophisticated decision-making tools, performance measurement strategies, and controlling techniques surfaced to address daily and weekly operations.

During my experience with GE I learned how much that value for the status quo restrained the culture for continuous improvement. Many of the philosophies and practices that managers were expected to uphold had a lot to do with the ultimate decline in quality and productivity. These philosophies and management practices were a far cry from Jack Welch's dream today of a horizontal corporation. Since then, Welch has worked hard to change the GE style from management to leadership.

## The Refusal to Improve and the Consequent Loss of Competitive Edge

During the 1970s and 1980s American industry's refusal to move past entrenched rituals hurt its ability to raise its quality in both the manufacturing and service organizations, and thus adversely affected its ability to compete. Though corporate America was in trouble, and industries like GE and GM were floundering, it alternated between panic and complacency. Even when corporations tried quality "fixes," they were generally not motivated to improve things as much as they were to accommodate an edict from the corporate office. And it was only when someone *inside* the business considered a problem important that it was attacked. Outsiders had not *earned* the right to make suggestions.

The reluctance to raise quality standards also hurt service organizations, and like manufacturing companies, political alliances and entrenched rituals carried more weight than raising the standards for the customer. As in corporate America, positional power in service organizations had often been granted to those who administered the status quo and catered to past practices.

# Part III

# Back
# on
# Track

# 6

# Reversing the Engines

## *The Status of Our Quality Effort Today*

By the late 1970s U.S. industry had received its wake-up call. The loss of market share had taught it valuable lessons, and by the beginning of the 1980s it had begun to recognize what it had to do to get back on track.

These businesses began to realize that there's more to quality improvement than measuring scrap at the end of the line. They acknowledged that the absence of the human component can keep us from capitalizing on our inventions. They recognized that quality cannot be delegated to a quality control department. They realized that we had allowed ourselves to become complacent about the dominance of American manufacturing and its value to society. They acknowledged the price of not listening to the customer and the criticality of having the right kind of leadership. And they recognized Philip Crosby's message that companies pay for poor quality in several ways—low employee morale, decreased market share, increased lawsuits from dissatisfied customers, and with 25 percent of the product price!

Having moved from denial to awareness, we spent our energy talking and writing about the importance of quality and the importance of the customer in defining quality. Corporate newsletter articles admonished employees to be more quality-conscious and to think more about the customer's preferences. Feature articles in trade journals everywhere resounded with the message that the customer is king!

However, awareness that the customer was important didn't necessarily translate into changing operations. In actual business operations during most of the 1980s, customers were still treated primarily as sales targets to be manipulated. Companies still preferred to sell what they made, rather than make what customers wanted. Although Total Quality Management (TQM) was often the subject of great celebration, its application was clumsy, inarticulate, and in employees' faces all the time. In the beginning years, it was a model for reality, not reality itself. Quality was something of a spectacle; when the quality training was over, it was time to get back to work.

Things have changed. In the 1990s organizations are moving from mere awareness to action. Total Quality Management has matured. Successful organizations have learned that when the primary focus of improved quality becomes the number of hours of training, the number of team meetings, or the number of suggestions, rather than the impact of those activities on business results, the organization's time and money are wasted. As a result, organizations are focusing their quality efforts on visible outcomes, recognizing that quality cannot be an activity separate from the real work of the organization and that value inheres not just in price but in intrinsic product features and service.

Businesses are making significant gains in retrieving market share and staying competitive by integrating quality throughout their organizations and leveraging it throughout the world. Many organizations have been successful in focusing all their employees on the benefits of high quality and the high costs of poor quality. They have persuaded employees that all of them are responsible for high quality. And they have paid homage to the quality principles of prophets like Joseph Juran and W. Edwards Deming. In short, total quality is helping American industry bounce back.

Manufacturing is redefining itself. Leaving behind old management techniques in favor of market-driven lean manufacturing, it is beginning to recapture the power it lost to the service sector, particularly to the financial wizards of Wall Street. The changes call for cooperation rather than for the rigid hierarchies of the past. Once strictly compartmentalized, manufacturing, design, engineering, and marketing are now working jointly on product development and delivery. The question of who's in charge is less important than the question of who is to lead the effort at each stage of development.

Manufacturing is not a discrete function consigned to a factory building. It is a time- and quality-sensitive activity linked to several areas within a company—and to customers, suppliers, and distributors outside the company. Industries have put into place reliable technology and information systems that can play the role of safety net.

Because of these changes, we are finally drawing close to equaling the quality achieved by our Asian rivals in products such as automobiles and office equipment. In some electronic products, we are outdistancing them.

Not only is manufacturing retrieving lost market share; it is reclaiming some lost status as well. Americans are dismissing the idea that the service sector can support the American economy. American manufacturing seems to be gearing itself up for the fast track once again, as it regains lost respect.

I remember the old days when the guy who was running the manufacturing plant in my home town was proud of what he did, and others were proud of him. He created jobs for the neighborhood, and he was highly respected. Over the past fifteen or so years, that plant owner has been blamed by academics and consultants alike for ruining the environment and for needlessly laying off workers. The word *industrialist* long ago ceased to conjure up visions in American minds of the entrepreneur who illustrated the can-do age of American industrialization. We must remember, though, that today some of the most exciting things going on in the country are happening in manufacturing. Manufacturing is starting to hold its head up high again.

Some people remain skeptical about these improvements; they cynically respond that companies have been using quality tools and techniques since at least 1980. "We've been through all of this before, and we still lost 40 percent of our market share to foreign competition. So what's the difference?" they ask.

It has become trendy to talk about why some quality initiatives still fail. Various business periodicals reported early in 1994 that, while more than 70 percent of companies had a TQM effort under way by 1993, two-thirds of those efforts had fallen short of their goals. Baldrige applications rise and fall; even some of those organizations that have received the Baldrige award have started to lose market share. Quality seminars are decreasing in popularity and there is a plethora of articles about TQM failures. Even ISO 9000 has been criticized for placing more emphasis on process and documentation than it does on what the process is intended to produce. Even though it was 1985 when in his book *A Passion for Excellence* Tom Peters first declared that quality has to be more than a technique, we still are challenged to accept that quality is not a program or an initiative that can ever end.

## Why It's Still Tough

Unfortunately, there are more ways to fail at continuous improvement than to succeed. Some mix of these five obstacles is usually behind such failures: (1) Business leaders can't agree on what quality is; (2) Management fails to match its intent and words with its daily actions and structures because it still thinks quality can be reduced to a "program" that is somehow separate from performance appraisals or strategic planning; (3) Management thinks the quality initiative is the result, rather than the means; (4) Leaders are not willing to invest the time and resources needed for measurement and cultural changes; or (5) Management fears that endorsing continuous improvement will imply to both customers and employees that interest in quality is something new.

1. **"What Really *Is* Quality?"** One of the biggest problems initially is simply coming to an agreement about what quality is. For most senior managers the words "quality" and "customer satisfaction" have become synonymous. Where people line up in an organization on the "hard" or "soft" elements of quality depends largely on their functional conditioning. As a rule, successful organizations consider that customer value is the goal and assume that customer value requires both the hard and the soft elements.

Historically, the engineering profession has defined quality as conformance to requirements, measured by how closely the product or service meets the "specifications" set for it by the industry. Any deviation from the standard is a defect. Motorola's tough goal of six sigma (3.4 defects per million processes) demonstrates that "zero defects" can be worth it, as the company's cellular phones and pagers gain the lion's share of their markets.

A second definition of quality may be termed "value-based." This definition expresses quality in terms of conformance to requirements, including the cost of meeting these requirements. What is best for certain customers' conditions, including the actual use and the selling price, is taken into account in determining customer value.

The most common corporate definition is that quality is what the customer deems it to be. This definition is founded on the premise that only the customer can be the true judge of how well the product or service is matching his or her needs. Contrary to its philosophy in the 1970s, General Electric today sees its mission as providing a level of "overall performance and attitude that makes General Electric the natural choice of customers." This concept pledges a company to do whatever it must to improve those quality characteristics of a product that are most important to its customers. This concept is about how people and their jobs are linked to facilitate the easiest, most efficient, and most logical flow of material, ideas, or information to result in customer value.

2. **"How Do You Make Quality Ongoing?"** The second challenge, bringing daily operation into sync with a quality vision, takes commitment and time. Thinking of quality as a "program" separate from everything else sometimes excuses managers from investing the time, energy, and resources needed to redesign systems and structures required for employees to change their behavior. It is easier to plan a program than to change the way a company operates. For one thing, programs end; even if those who are called upon to implement the program cannot always endorse it, they can put up with it because it will soon be over.

A lack of commitment from senior management is a major reason that some organizations continue to conduct business as usual, regardless of new vision and mission statements. In such organizations the frontline and middle managers and leaders struggle with how to drive the quality quest from the bottom up and how to do what they can in their circle of influence to change systems and structures that are out of sync with the company's vision statements. This effort to drive change from the bottom up is remarkable in the federal government, where federal employees have a much bigger rock to climb anyway, and where the head of the agency is often a political appointment who may be gone in three or four years. It's one thing to post a vision statement on the CEO's wall. It's quite another to get top management to allocate resources—time and effort—to translate this vision into doable strategies throughout the organization, especially if that management may be around for only four years.

Even in cultures where senior management has committed to total quality and where operations managers and individual contributors alike concede that a quality turnaround will require a major overhaul of the organization, some managers have not figured out how to move beyond councils and committees and pareto diagrams. They still stress "quality initiatives"; quality circles, zero defects, and statistical process control have given way to problem solving teams, pareto diagrams, scattergrams, and the Deming chain reaction. Fishboning has given way to process action teams. But in many cases, these are all simply repackaged quality circles.

Managers still prefer to make investments in information technology rather than in organizational structures and systems because it's a lot easier to change a computer system than to change an entire classification or compensation system. As a result, companies still struggle with classification systems that are totally moribund or at best are out of sync with the direction in which they're trying to move.

3. **"Process Improvement Is Our *Goal*."** The third cause of quality failures to achieve continuous improvement is that leaders often view process improvement as the goal, rather than as the means for keeping customers satisfied and therefore improving market share. Some quality devotees have become so obsessed with cost cutting, defect reduction, and improved cycle times that they have lost sight of customer concerns. While standards have risen, sales have dropped.

Some quality initiatives have gotten stuck in a labyrinth of internally focused process measures that have no reference to the customers who are supposed to benefit from them. Leaders have become so immersed in the process, with compilation of documentation and analysis, that they've created another bureaucracy and a heavier workload for employees, the very opposite of their original intention. This seems particularly true in service industries and in the public sector, which may be the result of their grabbing onto the quality initiative in an effort to recreate value for themselves in the eyes of the customer. Here the quality process has become its own reward and a means of justifying labor intensity. Whatever the reason, when the strategy or the process overtakes the result, then it's really hard to justify the investment.

In some organizations, a "program" helps create value for certain departments, such as personnel or human resources, whose value has often been questioned by operations managers and by those on the front line. "Quality" is often tackled as a way to create a mission to justify their staffing and budgets.

It is particularly difficult to focus on the result rather than the process for projects that take years to complete, such as civil works projects undertaken by the federal government. Members of the Army Corps of Engineers, for example, find it almost impossible to focus on the ultimate result when that result, such as a dam or bridge, may not be evident for nearly two decades. A part of the answer in these situations has to lie in focusing on benchmarking components of the project—the planning process, the design, and so on.

4. **"We Don't Have Enough Time and We Don't Have Enough Money."** The fourth barrier to continuous improvement is the amount of time and resources required to change an entire culture. Many managers want to think that quality is an orderly, sequential process and believe that there should be smooth, consistent progress. But the fact is that change is often a sporadic, nonlinear journey. Market changes, including changes in customer preferences, require continuous design adjustment. This nonlinear movement produces great disruption, which is unsettling for employees who remember that the old culture was at least orderly.

Managers' modes of operation have developed over long periods of time, and they are not going to change overnight. We learned in the 1970s the significance of management styles and practices for creating a quality culture, as centralist practices hurt both individual and team efforts. But we can't expect managers to relish the thought of sharing knowledge and power with those they just yesterday considered to be inadequate to handle the information. Besides, just trying to keep people informed about the "big picture" so that they will have a feel for the whole game takes a lot of energy, and this is energy that many managers feel they don't have to give.

Nor can managers change automatically from boss to coach when they were reared on principles of "tough-minded management" and are not yet convinced that that was all so bad. They realize that working alongside people and trying to get them to make the right decisions in alignment with the broad strategy and direction is always more time-consuming than either simply telling them how to do it or doing it themselves. A lot of mission statements contain the right words about empowerment and respect, but crafting vision statements requires relatively little time compared to changing cultural practices. Some of the same people crafting those statements still keep people "out of the loop" to maintain their own power.

Time and energy are also required to establish ongoing methods and goals for quality improvement and to measure and hold people accountable for quality results. Process action teams and quality councils can take up a lot of time. As the amount of time and effort involved becomes evident and executive attention often begins to wander, there is a temptation to delegate quality so that everybody else can get to "work." In some organizations, paradoxically, the initiative ends up creating an internal bureaucracy even though it started out as an attempt to streamline and improve operations.

Documentation and benchmarking are especially time-consuming components of any continuous improvement culture. This is especially true of ISO 9000, the set of international standards on quality management and quality assurance. Even if a company has the required quality indicators and does daily tracking, incomplete or out-of-date process controls, obsolete supplier lists, or any other absolute information technology may sabotage the effort. And managers may have to explain and defend its documentation of its efforts to auditors or suppliers who have little knowledge about their product or process. Some companies feel that they can't afford the time and effort to prepare for these auditors' visits. It also takes some time for some organizations to adjust to the "new" concept of quality as determined by the customer.

5. **"We're Already a Quality Organization."** The final reason organizations delay complete commitment to continuous improvement is their fear of what their customers might think they've been doing in the past. If they suddenly endorse total quality or customer service, they think their customers will conclude that they have been passing along defective goods or performing slipshod repairs or other service. Some federal agencies have been slow to board the total quality train because many of their leaders believe that they have always placed a high premium on quality and that to "jump on the TQM train" might imply that the idea of quality is something new for them. Many people in private industry also feel that to endorse a quality initiative is to concede that quality was unimportant in the past.

## What Successful Organizations Are Doing to Overcome the Obstacles

With all these challenges to continuous improvement, it's tough to maintain commitment to quality initiatives. While no organization has made it to its destination, everyone that hopes to make the trip has at least boarded the train. Some have taken the express train; others have taken the local. Some have taken time for their passengers to stop and catch their breath; others have taken detours. One thing is certain: All have taken the important first step of moving from treating quality as a separate component of the organization to realizing that it has to be integrated into the culture. Those organizations that have successfully retained market share or retrieved lost market share are those that have a strategic quality vision and are living by it day by day. They have invested resources in designing systems and structures that foster continuous improvement of their products and services.

Both private industry and the public sector are bringing needed cultural components into alignment with the quality vision. Organizations that are back on track have put into action Deming's message that quality is not the special province of the manufacturing floor. They have emphasized that everyone is responsible for quality and can be taught how to apply quality control techniques, and they have empowered their employees to effect quality improvements. Whether it's reducing defect rate, decreasing cycle time, or increasing overall quality consciousness, these organizations have succeeded at continuous improvement only when systems, structures, and values have been altered to integrate continuous improvement into ongoing operations and processes.

While some companies still exhibit bureaucratic tendencies and some still shun risk takers and miss opportunities, many others have earnestly tried to reinvent themselves so that they act more like small companies. They're chopped layers; they've decentralized; they've restructured to move employees out of functionality; they've endorsed the latest nostrums, from just-in-time inventory to TQM. Successful organizations today recognize that networks connect people to people and people to data. They allow information that once flowed through hierarchies—from the front line up through the middle to the top, and then back down from the top through the middle to the front line—to move directly between employees. These networks have inspired an informal style in which people interact as peers, rather than as bosses and subordinates.

## Shifting the Focus From Company to Customer

Competitive automakers and sausagemakers alike have shifted their focus from the company to the customer. They see the customer's needs and expectations as the starting point and then develop products or services around them. They restructure their organizations to reduce functionality in favor of horizontal movement to replace inward focus with a customer focus. They design the entire operation—from conception of the product to delivery of the product—around the customer. Their selection criteria factor in consumer service, and their evaluation systems measure it.

The seriousness of the effort to effect a total quality culture is evident in the American automobile industry. Both the Chrysler Corporation and the Ford Motor Company, after missteps in the 1980s, have found the strength and the resourcefulness to turn themselves around. They have done so well that they have been gaining market share from Japanese car makers.

Chrysler is benchmarking everything from accounting to manufacturing. A team that included senior executives from all areas of the company and representatives of the United Auto Workers visited sixty-five companies in the United States, Asia, and Europe, looking for ways to improve operations. It overhauled its top-down autocratic management structure. After an in-depth study of the Honda Motor Company by fourteen young employees who hadn't been steeped in traditional Chrysler-think, the corporation dismantled rigid departmental lines and replaced them with nimble, Honda-like product development teams. The teams brought together in one location experts in areas as diverse as design, manufacturing, marketing, and purchasing. Each team had the power to make decisions on everything from styling to suppliers.

One team of eighty-five people designed the $50,000 Dodge Viper sports car in just thirty-six months (the company traditionally has taken at least four and a half years to design new products). Even former Chrysler president Lee Iacocca was affected, acquiescing in team decisions. "I used to go in and tell them everything," conceded Iacocca, "but you can't do [design] by the seat of your pants."

### Integrating Quality With Customer Service

However much their internal managers may occasionally disagree about what constitutes quality, most successful industries today endorse the integration of quality and customer service. They recognize that service is more than just "being nice to customers" and that quality is more than "measuring scrap at the end of the manufacturing line." They still view conformance to requirements and zero defects as important, but they recognize that this is only one element of quality. They have a new concept of delivering customer value—a value that comes from tangibles, such as decreasing variation, as well as from intangibles, such as the customer's overall perception. This new focus on value has forced companies to rethink service. Analyzing the work helps them deliver solutions, instead of just products.

This is particularly true in industries that produce essentially interchangeable products, such as steel. The definition of an outstanding product in steel is that a company produces an exact copy of what the customer already gets from another source. The only way for a company in a mature industry such as steel to differentiate itself is by the quality of its customer service.

Quality improvement is incorporated into many overall strategic plans and translated into specific objectives for work units. Although some companies have occasionally allowed their improvement efforts to center on internal processes that may not make much difference to customers, in general the quality focus has produced a mind-set that treats the customer's satisfaction level as the centerpiece of the business effort.

There is more to the quality equation, however, than zero defects. Organizations that are committed to wholesale quality efforts know that world-class quality and competitive pricing are merely the requisites for beginning the journey. They realize they have to provide compelling reasons for customers to buy their products and services, rather than someone else's, and that at a time when rising quality expectations are forcing them and their competitors toward the same standard, perhaps the only way to differentiate themselves is in service and price. Only a few years ago, corporate leaders were arguing that price shouldn't be factored into the quality equation. Today corporate and government buyers are getting used to high standards of quality and are being squeezed by budgetary constraints. So organizations have had to become cost competitive merely to be allowed to bid for contracts.

## A Shift in Emphasis to the Front Lines

Whereas during the derailment most of the responsibility for transforming corporate cultures came from top management, today the front line is considered the force that can enable an organization to compete worldwide. Whereas at one time they were given their directions and told to respond, today's front-line workers are encouraged to solve quality problems themselves and to make whatever decisions are necessary to contribute to higher quality and customer value.

Take the role of technicians, for example. Since the 1950s the number of technical workers has increased nearly 300 percent—triple the growth rate for the workforce as a whole. Because increasingly powerful, versatile, and user-friendly new technologies are eliminating the need for workers to perform many time-consuming routine tasks, they are free to tackle more challenging activities that require judgment and skills. As more companies rely on technology to help eliminate quality defects, speed up product development, and improve customer service, technicians become the critical front-line workers.

As corporate hierarchies collapse and the boundaries between organizations dissolve, employers are beginning to gain a new appreciation for the work technicians do and for their insights into how it should be done. Who better for the smart employer to enlist in the effort to gain a competitive edge than those who actually operate the equipment that will carry industry into the future? Engineering technicians test the integrity of materials used in the construction of bridges, buildings, and dams. They are the developers and caretakers of the computer and telecommunications networks that keep businesses running.

## Adding New Strengths While Leveraging the Old Ones

U.S. organizations shouldn't try to catch up to foreign competition merely by grabbing programs and initiatives that worked for industries in other countries. What we need is more Yankee ingenuity. America must leap ahead not just by improving existing products, as the Japanese have been excellent at doing, but by focusing on what have historically been its greatest strengths—innovation and speed. The Japanese recession of the mid-1990s is demonstrating that creativity and speed may indeed be just as important to a sustained competitive edge as perfecting existing products.

Until the 1990s, research in the United States overshadowed the importance of shop-floor innovation. Japanese managers, in contrast, used their best engineers in production, not just in design. Today, many American managers are likewise breaking down the walls between research, development, and manufacturing and recognizing that industry needs not just incremental improvement but innovation on the factory floor.

Instead of looking inward for a solution as to why they lost their market share to foreign competition, U.S. executives in the past tended to blame "cultural differences," usually implying the Japanese penchant for teamwork. But few cultures have been more autocratic and class conscious than Japan's. The truth is that the Japanese listened to America's quality prophets long before Americans did, and applied their theories. By carefully analyzing customer requirements, being willing to make gradual but continuous improvement, and collaborating with one another, Japan's industries became the world leaders in quality. If Japanese businesses used teams more than American companies did, it was not due to a team culture that already existed. If we did not use teams enough, it was because we never had to. We were self-reliant, and we had the market. And our managers crafted their corporate cultures from those strengths. That culture worked well and produced good quality until we became too big and too bureaucratic.

While consensus decision making in Japan is presently proving too slow to respond to increasing competition, it has been successful in building commitment to a shared mission. American organizations today recognize the importance of consensus decision making to a sense of shared mission. And while the Japanese are trying to become more entrepreneurial, U.S. companies are recognizing the strength of consensus and collaboration in addressing product and process dilemmas.

Americans have gained respect for incremental improvement. Today successful organizations are employing *kaizen*, the Japanese term for continuous improvement. But they also much realize that improvement must be allowed to happen within America's innovation and entrepreneurial spirit.

## A Glance at Some Successes

Organizations that have successfully regained market share and that are competing successfully in the worldwide market look at quality from the customer's viewpoint at the product development stage, rather than at the end of the line. They have successfully deployed teams which not only cut across vertical functions but increasingly go beyond the bounds of the corporation to include partners, such as suppliers of critical parts. In the 1980s some of these were focused on inspection and problem solving and were structured functionally.

Consider just a few examples:

- Companies like Ford, General Motors, and AT&T now use Quality Function Deployment to help ensure that customer needs drive product design and production, rather than what is best for a particular function. This system provides a means of translating customer requirements into the appropriate technical requirements for each stage of product development and production (marketing, product design, and prototype evaluation).

- The Grumman Corporation, an aerospace company, saved $30 million in rework and scrap costs during the first two years of its quality-improvement effort by redesigning processes.

- DuPont, long a proponent of continuous improvement, has reported benefits such as on-time delivery increasing from 70 to 90 percent, and a reduction of cycle time from fifteen to one and a half days; one product line went from 72 percent to 80 percent first-pass yield.

- Square D-Groupe Schneider has cut cycle times and reject rate in half and has increased market share by examining key processes that impact the customer.

- ABB is delivering value by improving quality and slashing costs. Since 1990 product cycle time has been reduced 60 percent, inventory is down 40 percent, and quality has improved 75 percent.

- Some AT&T units are now basing annual budgets not on functions or departments but on processes such as the maintenance of a worldwide telecommunications network. And the company is basing employee bonuses on customer evaluations of each team's performance.

- Eastman Chemical Company's ongoing comprehensive worldwide customer satisfaction process, which measures its progress in satisfying customers and identifies improvement and reinforcement opportunities, helped earn it the 1993 National Quality Award.

- General Electric in Fairfield, Connecticut, uses work-out sessions in which groups of employees and managers discuss how to eliminate unnecessary work and improve business practices to make the organization less complex. This company, which fifteen years ago could not capitalize upon its innovations because of its allegiance to its past culture, is moving toward a horizontal, "boundaryless" organization in which senior leaders from various functions come together to allocate resources and ensure coordination of processes and programs.

- Motorola, with its commitment to zero-defects management, has won recognition for its "six sigma quality," or a near-perfect defect rate of 3.4 per million operations. This intense focus on quality has made Motorola's MicroTAC portable phone the best-selling cellular phone in Japan and Asia.

- Sara Lee's Chairman, John Bryan, is reorganizing plant floors in his casual-wear apparel division so that stitchers work in teams to turn out finished products, instead of using the old assembly-line approach in which each worker does the same job on garment after garment. This change has reduced defects as much as 75 percent while increasing productivity by up to 30 percent.

- A massive effort is under way in the federal government to make government work better and cost less. The National Performance Review, made up largely of federal government employees, is examining ways to streamline procedures such as procurement to liberate federal workers from strangling regulations. Most government managers want to do their jobs more efficiently, but they have been prevented from doing so by bureaucratic red tape. The review has produced some good results:

> —As early as 1988, the Navy saved $1.8 billion by eliminating paperwork and purchasing spare parts directly from subcontractors.
> —Senior leaders in the Army Corps of Engineers have identified and eliminated work processes that complicate jobs, to the tune of tangible savings of millions. The Corps now emphasizes partnering as a teamwork approach to construction project management, resulting in improved efficiency and cost effectiveness, as well as better quality of products and services.
> —The Internal Revenue Service began its quality improvement drive in 1986. Its Ogden Service Center in Utah received the fed-

eral government's Quality Improvement Award in 1989 for a program that helped save more than $11 million and reduced by 14 percent the amount of mail that never gets to taxpayers. From 1988 to 1992 the agency increased the proportion of accurate information provided to taxpayers from 33 percent to 88 percent.

—The Commerce Department's Patent and Trademark Office reduced the average time needed to mail receipts for patent filings from thirty-seven to eighteen days.

—In 1993 the Atlanta office of the Social Security Administration reduced the cycle time for disability claim payment by sixty-six days by merely having claimants bring their medical records with them.

The rest of this book provides greater detail on how these and other organizations have gotten back on track and are staying on track by a relentless pursuit of all the quality ingredients: customer service, continuous improvement, and total involvement of the workforce.

## Getting Back on Track

Organizations that have had the greatest success are those which have successfully dealt simultaneously with what may seem like two conflicting objectives: obsessively improving performance, quality, and the value of existing products while forging ahead in pursuit of new technologies and products. Teamwork, empowerment, and improved communication are being employed by these organizations to increase customer value.

The organizations are taking advantage of one of their most precious opportunities—the ability to give millions of individuals with diverse interests, backgrounds, intellects, and talents unique opportunities to create products that create wealth for the company and in turn create a need for services.

Tremendous energy and focus are being poured into continuous improvement. Much of the criticism being hurled at quality initiatives is coming from those who are living in a vacuum, believing somehow that things will automatically get better without considering the customer's perspective on quality, without raising their bar, without measuring, and without changing personal and organizational paradigms. I suspect it is coming from those who are reluctant to even buy the train ticket, much less have any chance of staying on track.

# 7

# What Was That the Passenger Said?

## Listening to the Customer

One of the most important lessons I learned during my insurance days was that in order to sell someone, you have to find out what he wants or needs. People don't buy products. They buy benefits and solutions to their problems.

People also buy service. As differences in quality and reliability diminish, automakers are realizing that car buyers are basing their decisions more and more on how they're treated by dealers—including the service they'll receive *after* the car is purchased.

It's not just a matter of having the right technical components or good service. Quality no longer means only conformance to a set of specifications. Nor does it mean only fair treatment. A combination of tangibles, intangibles, and experiences that delight the customer make up customer value. Quality is the measure of the customer's satisfaction with the total package, which may include reliability, durability, communication clarity, empathy, or timeliness, as well as freedom from defects. The customer's quality *perception* also depends on the degree to which quality expectations are confirmed by experience. If experiences exceed expectations, the customer thinks the quality is high (even if the intrinsic quality is low); if the experiences do not reach the level of expectation (even though the intrinsic quality may be high), the customer thinks the quality is low.

Many insurance agents during the 1970s and 1980s were inwardly focused, not unlike most employees in other industries during that time. They tried to sell their preferred "products"—usually the policies that carried the highest commission—whether or not those policies really fit the needs of the prospective buyer. Manufacturing companies also concentrated on production and sold what they made. They were obsessed with planning, logistics, and technical achievement, which resulted not in a defect-free product but in one produced with mechanical efficiency.

Today, however, companies are beginning to concentrate upon consumption—to make what they sell. They realize that "one size doesn't fit all" and that customer needs cannot be driven into standard patterns. Before the Lexus automobile went into production, Japanese engineers—not marketers—visited Americans in their homes to understand the lifestyles of potential buyers so that the car would fit those lifestyles.

Although tailoring products to meet customer needs is more common in manufacturing than in service industries (e.g., banks, hospitals, and hotels), service industries today realize that customers have increased options. They are therefore beginning to go the extra mile and abandon the standard operating procedure mind-set.

## Service Makes the Difference

Customer service is the centerpiece of quality. Customers have expectations about two aspects of service: process and outcome. Process is the way you treat the customer. Outcome is the result—what you actually deliver to the customer. Process can be even more important than outcome for some types of services, particularly for those whose outcome cannot be judged until significant time has passed (e.g., medical treatment in a hospital or help with claims in an insurance company).

### Service Organizations

Nonmanufacturing organizations seeking to exceed their customer's expectations in order to enhance their quality image should take advantage of the best time for doing so—during service delivery. It is during delivery that customers directly experience the service skills of the organization's employees. This is particularly true of the insurance business.

Although the service rendered by an insurance agent who is handling a customer's claim has always been one of the most important factors in customer retention, during the 1970s and 1980s agents were often told to avoid getting involved with claims. Today, however, insurance agencies tuned in to what customers value most from insurance companies and agencies are responding by considering attributes beyond "prior sales experience" when recruiting agents. They look for empathy, interpersonal skills, and the willingness to serve the customer after the purchase. Today agent training moves beyond "smile training," dramatic closing strategies, and product knowledge to include listening skills and techniques to use in targeting customers' needs.

I learned during my selling days that customers choose one insurance company over another not so much because of price differences between one company's policy and another company's policy, but because they feel that some agents are willing to treat them as individuals and communicate honestly, while others aren't. There's actually very little difference in price or features between one company's whole life policy and the next one's, but there is a world of difference in the way agents treat clients and prospective clients. The degree to which agents treat "prospects" as individuals and take into account their preferences and level of understanding when explaining policy features often makes the difference. The agent as conduit becomes particularly critical in selling insurance because the policies are usually intimidating, with their jargony language, and they are about the most uninspiring documents one could read. Consequently, people often rely on agents to interpret the terms and to explain features to them with clarity and friendliness.

The same can be said for the banking business. Because there is little difference between the return on one bank's one-year certificate of deposit and the next bank's, what customers buy is accurate information and personalized treatment. Banks find that most customers don't understand all the language in an annuity contract, but they are willing to trust the bank if they feel that they are treated with respect and concern. Consequently, banks are beginning to think of their business as more than accounts and products. They are recognizing that intangibles, such as having tellers know customers' names, may significantly add to the customer value equation.

Similarly, hospitals have discovered that patients' hospital choices and rate of compliance with outpatient treatment plans depend more on clear one-on-one communication and understanding from both physicians and staff than on the most up-to-date technology.

### Nonservice Organizations

Customer responsiveness is certainly not confined to what we think of as "service organizations" (today hopefully all businesses are service organizations). A couple of years ago I was in the market for a laptop computer. My major interests were word-processing capability, weight, compatibility with my desktop, and available technical support. Over and over computer salesmen tried to sell me this or that capability and software. Their own preferences spoke so loudly, though, that they couldn't hear mine. Consequently, I ended up responding to an ad in *The Wall Street Journal* and buying the computer directly from the manufacturer. So much for the need for salespeople, if they can't hear your preferences. Many salespeople still have not learned that it doesn't matter how many features they can offer the customer if he isn't interested in them in the first place.

## The Importance of Exceeding Customer Requirements

Today those organizations that are regaining their competitive advantage recognize the importance of the customer's voice in defining quality. Although organizations differ in what other factors must be considered (e.g., consistency, price for value), they realize that the customer must be a major determinant of what constitutes high quality. Instead of internally focusing on their idea of great quality, American industry today places great emphasis on the value added to the end user—as determined by that end user. That's more than just meeting customer expectations. If customers can't say, "I wouldn't consider doing business with anybody else," then you are at risk of losing them. If they aren't rating you ten out of ten, then you are not delighting those customers in a way that ensures their loyalty.

### The Best Listen

World-class organizations are dedicated to and driven by superior customer service. Their vision statements, value statements, and leadership center around it.

The most important group of criteria for the Malcolm Baldrige National Quality Award are customer satisfaction measures; these account for up to 30 percent of the total points that can be earned. It therefore stands to reason that Baldrige winners like Motorola and Eastman Chemical are constantly surveying, testing, and adjusting their products and services in their pursuit of one goal: giving the customer what he wants. These companies realize that unless you know what your customers actually think about your efforts to please them, you will not be able to focus those efforts for the best results. It is not just a high-quality product that wins the customer. Most customers switch their business to a competitor, not because the competitor's product is significantly better but because the service is of a higher quality.

World-class organizations use various strategies to ensure the customer is the focus of the business. Among these strategies are the following:

- *Including everyone in customer service.* It used to be that listening to the customer was reserved for the customer service department, just as quality control was relegated to the QC department. Today the best companies recognize that working for customers is everybody's job. Engineers, for example, realize that they have to become marketing engineers. Their day-to-day decisions are relevant to the customer and are therefore actually marketing decisions. Infiniti dealerships include their receptionists in customer training to help them answer any question about the cars and to understand buyer demographics. The training emphasizes the view of customers as "honored guests."

- *Communicating in high-tech and high-touch ways.* The best in every class communicate with customers in both high- and low-tech ways. Some companies have installed state-of-the-art customer service information systems linking sales and operations. Many companies and government agencies provide tollfree telephone lines for customers with complaints and suggestions. Detailed customer information from surveys and profiles helps business units link operational goals and recognition systems to these customer priorities.

- *Organizing to hear the customer.* Successful customer-focused organizations centralize functions when doing so enhances quality; they decentralize operations when being close to the front line is more important. Decentralized execution of centralized policy usually enables marketing and sales staffs to respond more quickly to changes and opportunities within the local market. Companies such as General Electric have found that when management, operations, policy execution, and authority are decentralized, employees tend to execute, rather than administer; having fewer levels between top management and those on the front line moves everyone closer to the customer.

- *Interacting with customers.* Robert Galvin, Motorola's former CEO and the man responsible for that organization's highly regarded achievements in manufacturing quality, began visiting at least one Motorola customer each month after he realized the need to eliminate process mistakes, such as sending products to the wrong address. He didn't just go to the company's top managers either. He went to the people who used the products—and then wrote up his findings for the rest of the company. Now all the Motorola officers make these visits.

This customer focus pervades Motorola. The second step in the company's six sigma process for becoming "Best in the Class" is answering the question "For whom do you do your work?" This step of identifying customers and what they consider important is more complex than it sounds. If there are multiple customers for a product or service, they may have different definitions of what constitutes a defect. Only by seeking and listening to each customer's voice can the company truly know how to identify defects. In addition, listening to customers helps pinpoint the specific aspects or characteristics of a product or service that matter most to those customers. If a customer's critical requirement is accuracy, for example, then an essential element might be that all part numbers be correctly recorded. Without this identification of essential elements, any further activities become relatively meaningless.

Jimmy Dean Foods realizes that there are more customers of its products than just the grocery chains or the consumers. Jim Ellis, vice president of technical services, explains how important everyone is in the chain of production, even those who handle the product on the receiving docks. Consequently, when Jimmy Dean surveys its customers, it includes the receiving dock personnel, who are asked questions such as "When the product was delivered, was the paperwork legible?," "Was the truck trailer clean?," "Was the shipment on time?," and "Was the carrier helpful to you?"

- *Focusing outward.* When we look at improvements from an internal rather than an external view, that is, when we set standards without considering their impact on the customer, we may look better to ourselves, but we haven't necessarily improved customer satisfaction.

Bob Brown, Manager of Global Personnel Programs at FedEx, discusses the difference between what customers expected when FedEx began and what they expect now:

> Back when we started, people were willing to pay a premium for good service. I'm not sure they're willing to do that any longer. People today want value, which means that people are still demanding the same service but at better prices. It's no longer good enough to have good service and charge a lot of money for it.

In an effort to achieve its goal of 100 percent customer satisfaction, FedEx has moved from an introspective measure of customer satisfaction (e.g., number of on-time deliveries) to an external measure using the customer's standards (e.g., ability to track packages). The Memphis-based shipper is trying to isolate quality improvements that don't add value to the service that the customer receives. This has meant rethinking its original quality goals. In its sorting operation, for example, FedEx formerly stressed speed over accuracy. Workers met schedules, but the number of misdirected packages soared as they scrambled to meet deadlines. FedEx eventually fixed most errors, but redirecting each wayward package cost it about $50. To ease the sorting crunch, FedEx has invested $100 million in new equipment that accurately routes packages to their destinations.

Jean Ward-Jones, Director of Corporate Quality at FedEx, explains:

> We came to realize that even though deliveries may be on time, there can still be disgruntled customers over other matters. Or if they aren't on time, most customers don't report it. We evolved a system whereby each category of service failure (e.g., misdirected packages) is weighted to reflect its relative impact on customer satisfaction.

Jean adds that the company has tied its customer satisfaction/service quality gauge to the service component of the people-service-profit corporate objectives.

FedEx understands that its customers are probably not that concerned about what they don't see. They are more impressed by the employee's uniform, the hand-held computers carried by FedEx employees, the service center hours, and the timely arrival of their package than with behind-the-scenes activities. But as FedEx officials are keenly aware, the "invisible" process has a major impact on the visible components of the process that do create customer value.

A primary advantage for FedEx is the commitment shown by its CEO, Frederick Smith, for the quality initiative. Because of this commitment, the customer service vision has been transmitted throughout the organization to all involved with both the visible and the invisible processes—those who deliver the packages, fly the planes, sort the packages, take the phone orders, and staff the pickup stations.

### Dividends at DuPont

Craig Binetti, DuPont Chemical Film Enterprise's business director and site manager at Old Hickory, Tennessee, affirms the importance of having DuPont move closer to the customer: "It used to be that products were produced and handed on to the customer; all that's changed. Customers today design their own specifications." Mickey Williams, process control systems and ISO team member at DuPont's Sontara plant (Polyester Blend Fabrics), adds: "If marketing gets a call for a certain product, we can have it on the line and make it. Through programs such as the customer satisfaction survey, DuPont has kept the lines of communication open to their customers in categories such as product quality, marketing, and technical support." He continues, "In the old days, whatever DuPont put a label on, the customer bought. We didn't worry too much about the product being perfect. Now it has to be right. We don't want anybody to come back with a problem."

DuPont's customer complaint teams deal with engineers as well as operators to search out problems; a lot of time the correction is done on line. Says Williams:

> Sometimes we are performing a run for somebody; they may have part of the product and they need something changed. If R&D, for example, needs some alteration, we make the change on the production line while it's running. We can correct it right there. That's a lot different from earlier days when the customer was the one to analyze and inspect it at the end of the process.

Sam Bogle, a thirty-year veteran of DuPont, including twenty-two years as manager of customer service, adds that DuPont has become so customer-focused that customers no longer feel they need to analyze products shipped. Bogle explains: "DuPont customer teams share all their quality data with customers on a monthly and quarterly basis . . . for example, if there is an upset in the process that might result in a defect, we share that with the customers." DuPont guarantees all its products that leave the site by bulk transportation.

Bogle says that building partnerships with all its customers (which were started in the mid-1980s) fostered a level of trust "so high that the customers don't even sample the truck. You might remember also that the integrity of the equipment has to be good for the product to be good when it gets on the other end."

DuPont team members explain that these partnerships have resulted in a lot of mileage with their customers. Bogle explains how the customer teams work:

> For example, there are ten of us on our GE team—including central transport and two drivers. We have a great deal of inter-

action between us and our GE customer, and that extends to various roles throughout the GE plant. . . . For example, GE will probably have twenty-five of their operators that handle our product—including those who unload our truck, their managers, and their engineers. All of these people—not just the managers—have the opportunity to communicate with our customer team members any time day or night. That's the type of rapport we have with our customers.

Bogle explains that when DuPont began to form these partnerships, it found there was a missing link in the chain—the carrier who was moving the product to the customer. "So our carrier is now involved in the partnership with our customers and that includes involvement in the team meetings with our customers." Bogle adds:

If our customer has a quality problem and we think it might have a relationship with our production process, we send our engineers to the customer's plant to help troubleshoot and fix that problem there in his plant. The customer knows he can get in touch with anybody here at our DuPont plant twenty-four hours a day. All of our operators and managers on the customer end know our teams face to face, and when they call their respective team, they personally know who they're talking to. This makes a big difference.

DuPont also schedules regular team meetings with customers to share any problems with the carrier and to discover anything—including productivity items—it can do to improve performance. Bogle explains that DuPont team members don't wait for the customer to call; they have weekly contact and stay on a first-name basis with these customers: "We call our customers regularly just to see everything is going all right. We don't really have many problems to work out, but in this interaction we look at productivity items and ways to become more efficient in the future."

This approach has paid off for DuPont's Dimethylterathalate (DMT) Plant. According to Bogle, out of more than 10,000 loads of product shipped to its customers, in addition to transfer of product to its on-site customer, DuPont has had only one customer concern.

The DuPont team listens just as intently to its internal customers as to its external customers, and it shares similar types of partnerships with them. That philosophy has also paid dividends. Sam Bogle speaks with pride about a supplier recognition award given to the DMT plant by another DuPont plant for quality and on-time delivery: "This resulted when that plant didn't have the equipment to get some DMT, which had gone bad, out of the tank. They didn't have the proper piping and equipment to get it. So we sent our equipment and helped set up piping to get the DMT out of the tank."

Unlike other companies, whose functions or plants often compete against each other, DuPont operations partner with other DuPont operations for the sake of customers. DuPont has learned the meaning of shared mission and teamwork and goes the extra mile to respond to internal customers (fellow plants), even when those plants are serving different customers.

### Earning the Gold

Customer satisfaction at Eastman Chemical has been achieved through the company's strong focus on understanding, meeting, and anticipating customers' needs. While Eastman has had a long history of dedication to customers, it was in 1982 that it began a process called "Customers and Us." Through that program, Eastman opened its plants to customers for the first time. Says Al Robbins, Eastman's quality management coordinator, "Our people actually met customers. We also took our people to their plants and had an exchange, basically. We were made aware that customers were real people with real needs." Today, customers regularly visit Eastman's plants and provide input on process improvement.

This strong focus on customers is reflected in Eastman's vision, "To be the world's preferred chemical company" by exceeding customers' expectations, and in its quality goal, "To be the leader in quality and value of products and services."

Eastman's customer emphasis has paid off. Since 1990 more than 70 percent of its worldwide customers have ranked Eastman as their number one supplier. On the five factors customers believe are most important—product quality, product uniformity, supplier integrity, correct delivery, and reliability—Eastman has been rated outstanding since 1988. In 1993 Eastman's dedication to continuous improvement and to listening to the customer earned the company the coveted Malcolm Baldrige National Quality Award.

Like DuPont, Eastman Chemical works closely with the customer on the front end of the process. Eastman's "right from the start" philosophy has been put into practice with a multifunctional team approach to development and production, which involves the supplier, processor, manufacturer, and customer in the innovation process. Eastman recognizes that working closely with its customers from the start of the project can eliminate costly surprises and reduce cycle time, leading to excellent value and satisfied customers.

Eastman's ongoing quest for unexcelled customer satisfaction actively targets its seven thousand worldwide customers who use more than four hundred types of chemicals, fibers, and plastics. The company possesses deeply embedded strengths or core competence in several fields, including cellulose technology, organic chemistry technology, polymer technology, and innovation of new products and processes. In its extensive program called "planner-to-planner," all employees, from production workers to senior executives, are in regular contact with their counterparts at customer operations. Thus, production-floor workers, after first coordinating through sales, are encouraged to phone the customer people who use their product and inquire if everything is satisfactory.

The company monitors customer responses in a variety of ways, including all reports and nonsales contacts with customers. These efforts provide input on customer needs and customer satisfaction, according to Richard Byrd, director of customer satisfaction. A customer satisfaction process and a customer interface core competence team were established to conduct companywide analyses of customer satisfaction from all sources. This team monitors and detects changes in customer satisfaction measures, determines the causes of problems, and develops ways to improve operations. And it communicates its findings to business units and functions within Eastman.

The two most valuable tools for determining customer satisfaction are the company's complaint process and its customer satisfaction survey. These have also become the Eastman sales force's most powerful tools for building customer relationships.

Eastman's customer satisfaction survey, which is managed by the sales team, includes about twenty-five "performance factors," including order entry and processing, proportion of on-time and correct delivery, product quality, pricing practice, and introduction of new products. Customers are asked on about an eighteen-month cycle to rate Eastman on a one-to-ten scale on each performance factor. They're also asked to provide one-to-ten ratings for their best "other supplier." Eastman uses this information to track how it's doing over time on each performance factor, as well as how its performance compares to that of other suppliers. More than two thousand surveys are sent out each year, with a return rate of more than 70 percent.

After the survey is completed, sales reps go back to their customers and discuss the survey results, focusing on where each customer's rating differs significantly from the composite or where the customer has rated Eastman significantly higher or lower than a competitor.

The company's no-fault return policy on its plastics is a direct result of Eastman's extensive customer surveys. Believed to be unique in the plastics industry, the policy states that a customer may return any plastics product shipment for any reason for a full refund. Byrd recalls that it wasn't always this way: "We used to have to call about three committee meetings to get agreement to enter a complaint . . . the manufacturing people particularly didn't want complaints entered because they thought it was a black mark on our abilities."

Now Eastman makes it easy for virtually anyone to register a complaint, asking about problems and complaints on the satisfaction survey, encouraging salespeople to ask about problems, and operating a seven-day, twenty-four-hour, toll-free number through which problems and complaints are recorded on an electronic complaint handling system. Trained operators route the caller to the desired contact, and each function has designated people on call. On-line, telephone-accessible technical databases also are available twenty-four hours a day. Other companywide databases help Eastman track customers' preferences, future requirements, concerns, and expectations, as well as complaints. Customer advocates follow up and resolve the complaints.

Sales plays a prominent role in Eastman's high customer satisfaction record. In effect, the sales organization contracts with the company's ten separate and diverse business organizations, which range from packaging plastics to coatings to fine chemicals and each of which has its own specific set of business strategies. George Trabue's sales organization of five hundred people is responsible for $4 billion in sales. It often finds itself in the position of coordinating many of Eastman's eighteen thousand employees in team efforts focused on improving customer relations.

For Eastman, a key phrase in connecting quality management to the sales effort is "linking in." That's the phrase used when an Eastman quality improvement team officially announces that it's taking aim at a specific customer problem. Al Robbins clarifies the focus of the company's "MEPS" ("Make Eastman the Preferred Supplier") program: "The objective is to identify ways to improve the processes that link us with our customers. . . . We want to make those processes as simply to use as possible, so that when a customer wants something, he thinks of us first."

MEPS projects range from improving response time to providing answers to customers' technical questions to identifying issues that need to be addressed when a new European office location is being considered. A project often arises out of a specific problem with a customer or group of customers. One sales rep, for example, initiated a MEPS project when a customer was having a persistent problem with black specks in a chemical product Eastman was delivering. A cross-functional team that included representatives from supply and distribution, manufacturing, and product support services, as well as the customer, studied the problem and resolved it by recommending that new equipment be installed at the customer's facility.

Another project arose out of customer complaints that Eastman's standard "conditions of sale" printed on the back of order sheets were somewhat offensive to customers. Buddy Bounds, District Sales Manager for plastics, explains:

> The conditions made it sound like we were saying to customers, 'We know you're out to get us and we're going to make sure you don't.' As a result, the legal people put together a MEPS team that refined and shortened the conditions of sale. Actually, it reduced the number of conditions and made them a little more friendly.

Based on the voice of the customer, process improvement projects are implemented in virtually all areas—manufacturing and nonmanufacturing.

### To Whole Hog or Not to Whole Hog

According to Bill Hardison, former corporate Vice President of the Sara Lee Meat Group, Sara Lee's philosophy of determining quality from the customer's point of view and not from what management thinks the customer wants evolved only after much deliberation within the Sara Lee Meat Group. Hardison explains the differences between yesterday and today in responding to the customer and preserving the quality vision:

> You get to a situation where some things are questionable in terms of operating costs. It is much more difficult to operate today. We're trying to satisfy the customer with value received and doing much more research to try to find out what really makes a difference to customers. In the earlier days, it was much easier, because someone had a vision of what that standard for the product should be . . . that vision was clear to

everyone because that person talked and walked it that way all the time; there was no compromise. Also that person was in touch with customers himself . . . he didn't have to depend on other research. Well, that guy's gone. The person that replaced him either doesn't have the same concept of quality, or the concept was wrong to start with.

As an example, Hardison cites one of the biggest product dilemmas in the sausage business—whether to use the whole hog or only trimmings or pieces to make sausage. As the name implies, using the whole hog produces a product with less fat. This use of the whole hog was the standard at Rudy's Farm Company (a company within the Sara Lee Meat Group), which emphasized it in their marketing.

Even though Hardison admits he was a hard sell on the compromise to use trimmings and pieces, he acknowledges that Sara Lee's research showed that customers could not "care less about whether this sausage was whole hog or not." In fact, many consumers didn't even know what whole hog meant. Hardison explains the dilemma that faced the business:

What it boils down to is what does that use or nonuse of the whole hog actually do that's obvious to the customer? One of the most obvious in using whole hog is that it [the sausage patty] shrinks less in the frying pan. Of course, you can't be all things to all people. And somewhere you have to make educated choices. At some point, you have to stick and say, "This is it; we're not going to compromise any more." If you have a process that costs seven cents a pound more, and you can't back it up with the customer, you have to reevaluate your reasons for it. Of course, in the old days, where we killed the hogs, we had total control of product from the live animal through the end product; if we have to go out and buy parts, then we lose part of that control. We then have to consider bacterial counts, the age of [the parts], the condition of the shipping, the trucks; that's a lot more chance you have to take. The customer, of course, doesn't see much of this sausage raw, and so they don't know always if it doesn't look right, or if it shrank a lot before it was cooked.

Hardison explains that for him, it was a tough decision to lower the intrinsic quality, but operating costs demanded that he do so. The lower standard, he explains, has been acceptable to some customers of their competitors, which have never used whole hog.

Says Hardison, "You still have to make that product—however many compromises you must make in that product—the best you can."

Jim Ellis, Vice-President of Technical Services at Jimmy Dean Foods (another company within the Sara Lee Meat Group), notes that emphasizing the customer's notion of quality is not the same as endorsing the perception of quality. Ellis does not subscribe to the idea that the perception is the important thing. "That philosophy can only carry you so long; then you have to have real quality to back it up," he says.

He also contends that companies have the obligation to set a standard, which will then guide customers in setting their own standards. Ellis, perhaps internalizing Jimmy Dean's attention to detail, remarks that some details that can make a difference in customer's overall reaction to the product may be totally unknown to the customer. For example, Jimmy Dean Sausage demands a particular standard for the plastic film used on some of its packaged products (related to permeability of film to oxygen), and Jimmy Dean is the only meat manufacturer that does so. The supplier of this particular plastic film reserves a selected portion—the highest-performing film—for Jimmy Dean, as competing companies have not expressed interest in meeting that standard. One may argue that this is a frivolous detail, but Jimmy Dean believes that it combines with other details to produce an overall perception of quality in the customer.

Bob Roberts, Marketing Director at Jimmy Dean, believes that it is important to use outside research firms to take the customer's pulse. Otherwise, Roberts says, companies tend to ask questions that confirm "what you already want to do." He says that Jimmy Dean has institutionalized benchmarking; the company is continuously examining the "best in the class" in terms of product and speed of development. Roberts himself participates in a cross-functional team, called a "speed team," that works to reduce cycle time for product development. Roberts adds that at Jimmy Dean, the freedom to interact with colleagues is conducive to moving across functions.

### Beating the Industry Average

It is no accident that Hampton Inn hotels, a member of the Promus Hotel chain, has enjoyed a 15 to 20 percent growth over the past several years. Much of that growth stems from the chain's high guest satisfaction, which outranks the industry average by about twenty percentage points. A *Busi-*

*ness Travel News* survey rated Hampton number one in appearance, quality, courteous service, and overall value.

Their formula is simple. Promus Hotel employees want their guests to feel like they're in their own homes, and employees are committed to doing whatever it takes to make that happen. All employees—from the front desk staff to the housekeeping staff—sign a commitment to guest satisfaction when they begin work, and they are empowered to make decisions that affect the customer's satisfaction level. Promus has enacted a 100 percent unconditional guarantee to customers, which covers everything and guarantees 100 percent satisfaction or guests stay free. And all Promus employees are encouraged to enact it.

Mark Wells, Senior Vice-President for Marketing, explains that Hampton Inn has found that important moments of contact determine customers' perception of service. These insights were not gleaned from sophisticated marketing strategies or from complicated decision analyses. They came instead from listening to customers through interviews, written questionnaires, and letters received. Significant "moments of contact" include having the reservationist call customers by name and answer the phone within three rings; having an efficient check-out staff that asks about customers' perception of quality and service. (For more on quality measures in the "moment of truth process flow," see Chapter 8.)

Hampton goes beyond the basics of what hotel customers expect. It offers special features for those with special needs, including nonsmoking rooms (75 percent of all guest rooms), facilities for guests in wheelchairs, and low-sugar selections at its continental breakfasts.

Wells explains, "Our guarantee, we feel, is the minimum we owe customers . . . our business is rather unique in that it is one of the few businesses where customers must prepay before they've received the service, and we, on the other hand, have the opportunity to inspect [the product] immediately before the customer gets it." Wells adds, "Therefore, we have the obligation to pledge value. Upon their leaving is really too late. We have an obligation to make certain beforehand that the carpet isn't stained, or that there is little noise in the room next to the one the guest is scheduled for."

What Hampton doesn't do is worry too much about trendy features that the competition offers, which many customers don't take advantage of anyway and only mean a higher cost for the customer.

## The Challenge of Excellence Still Exists

Companies are still being challenged to focus on those aspects of product or service that are most meaningful to customers, potential and current.

They don't need to be exceed customers' expectations about things that don't matter to the customers in the first place. While fax machines in hotel rooms may at first blush seem to give a hotel an edge, how many people really value having one enough to pay the difference in price for the room?

Once an organization determines what the customer really wants, it must determine what it needs to do internally before it can meet this need. Then it has to prioritize those processes that need to be addressed, estimate the cost and time involved, and begin to reengineer accordingly. And it must make these processes part of every employee's job.

Organizations face the challenge of meeting the needs of existing customers while trying to secure new ones. Although research reveals that it takes less investment to keep existing customers happy than to bring new ones in, businesses often forget this point and neglect their traditional customers.

One major grocery chain in Tennessee has historically attracted older shoppers because it offered short lines, help with grocery bags, and individualized attention from the staff. Since the owner of the chain died in 1994, the chain has made noticeable changes in order to compete with another leading grocery chain in the area by staying open later, broadening its offerings, and in general jazzing up the place. The effort appears to be working, since the grocery is attracting more young people and is even taking some customers away from other competition. The irony is, though, that because of the increased business at the chain, the lines are longer, the service is less personalized, and its traditional customers are starting to grumble and to go elsewhere to shop. A company takes a risk when it moves "too far away from its knitting," as Peters Tom put it. Sears found this to be true when it tried to upscale. Every successful business has a niche in the market and "core competencies" that are responsible for that niche. The challenge is to develop those core competencies and to broaden their application, rather than abandon them in favor of imitating those of the competition.

Another major challenge is trying to anticipate customers' future needs so that you can offer needed services and products before the competition does. This effort is limited by customers' ability to tell you what their future needs will be. Rosabeth Kanter said in *The Change Masters* that you can lead the pack, but you can't get too far removed from people's frame of reference. No matter how proactive you think you are, if you are perceived as too "blue-sky" or theoretical for your audience to see the applicability of your offerings, they will probably reject your products entirely. You may earnestly believe in your product, but selling a future need is harder than selling a current customer-defined need, however much the product may reflect the direction in which the customer needs to move. Even if you're right about their direction, the arrogance of setting that direction without the client's involvement will cost you business. It really doesn't matter if your thought is right; what matters is the extent to which the customer is convinced that it is. And that means beginning with where the client is at the time.

A third challenge is to remember that all the listening in the world is inadequate without appropriate technology and systems to back it up. If, for example, your information technology is inadequate and information cannot be retrieved quickly enough for the external customer or moved quickly enough in the internal customer chain, then all the beliefs about the importance of the customer's voice won't help much. Although a business may be willing to take the customer's telephone call, if it doesn't have someone on the front line who can properly direct the caller to the appropriate office or if the telephone system is inadequate to handle all incoming calls, attitude won't matter.

While many people get on soap boxes about "reinventing" government, some leaders in corporate America still lag behind in the actual practices of redesigning their own businesses to enable the voice of the customer to lead in improving business performance. At least those businesses that are back on track realize that sticking with the old way today hurts too much—and that the arrogance of not factoring in the voice of the customer is not an option. They are beginning to go through the difficult and sometimes agonizing work of talking to the user. And they are making rewards and sanctions consistent with their new focus.

### And Mostly It Requires Heart

In a trip to Japan I was impressed by the lengths to which a young college girl went to help me get to my destination. Japan's train system is the most efficient way to get from place to place, but the traveler must understand the different lines and be able to read the platforms—most of which are written only in Japanese—to capitalize on that efficiency. Even though I knew some Japanese, I became confused by the platforms and boarded the train going to the town of Zama rather than to Camp Zama. It was getting late by the time I discovered my error, and I deboarded. Finding myself alone except for one young girl in a rather desolate small depot, I communicated my plight to her and asked if she could help me. Not in my wildest imagination did I expect her to personally take me to my destination, but that's exactly what she did, even though she was not intending to go there herself. I have often reflected on the extent she was willing to go for a stranger, and thought how great it would be if we felt that way about visitors to the United States. It also caused me to reflect on the care and concern that Japanese workers have shown for their customers since the 1950s.

Many American quality initiatives failed in the 1970s because they were not focused on the customer. During the 1980s when a lot of books and articles emphasized the importance of the customer, many quality initiatives still failed because they were sterile and mechanical and omitted the human element in actual practice. Therefore they couldn't become part of the culture. Just as philosophy and belief without systems and processes are not enough to sustain high quality, neither are process and structure adequate without passion. Customers must feel they are getting more than they expect and more than the company is required to give, either technically or legally. They must feel that they're cared about. This calls for more than SOPs and legalistic guarantees.

Caring takes many forms. It may show up in the housekeeper in the hotel who leaves handwritten notes asking you if everything was OK today; it may be the waitress who tactfully directs you away from an item on the menu; it may be a trainer who gives up his lunch hour to deal with a special need of a trainee who was too embarrassed to surface it during the formal session.

## Basics to Becoming a Customer-Focused Company

There are a few basics that are required to become a customer-focused company. Most of these were first articulated by American consultants like W. E. Deming, Philip Crosby, and Peter Drucker. These basics keep organizations on track in their quality journey.

• *Create a customer vision throughout the culture.* At FedEx everyone from the receptionist to the courier not only feels the criticality of the mission—"it must be there on time"—but the importance of other sources of customer complaints. They use customer survey results to change their internal systems and policies. Discover how much every employee in your company feels a personal commitment to exceeding customer expectations. If that commitment is absent, determine why; does it have to do with the way workers are treated? The Marriott Corporation puts all its hotel workers through empowerment training, which gives them wide latitude to step outside their normal jobs and solve guests' problems.

- *Integrate the voice of the customer throughout all your processes.* Prerequisites for this include hiring, training, and keeping the right employees. Disneyland interviews prospective employees in groups of three so that it can watch how they interact. Interviewers look at whether the prospects show respect for one another by paying attention when the others speak. Ensure that your staff and state-of-the-business meetings are infused with references to customer value. Involve customers and suppliers in your product innovation teams. Work customer satisfaction into operational objectives in all employees' performance plans.

- *Regularly measure quality of your products and services and benchmark against the best.* Benchmark your quality measures against those of your competition. Study those organizations that have enjoyed the highest customer satisfaction in products and services similar to yours—or dissimilar. Robbins Air Force Base has used FedEx to benchmark its customer service. Companies like DuPont, Xerox, and Eastman Chemical contact customers at least once every ninety days to seek ongoing feedback about their standing with customers.

- *As leaders, do what you're asking others to do.* Successful leaders who are staying on track in their quality journey constantly seek new ways to learn about customers' preferences. They build customer-focused teams and celebrate successes, and they personally stay in touch with customers.

# 8

# Riding the Rails

## Living the Vision

The first step in creating a customer-driven culture is to develop a clear vision statement, a singleness of purpose that everyone can embrace and that energizes and challenges people to make a difference. For an organization trying to retrieve or improve market share, that statement should incorporate a clear quality vision with a focus on customers.

Words alone, however, rally people only temporarily. For any vision statement to have a real impact, it must be lived. People can stay inspired to serve the customer only if that vision is translated throughout the organization and used to guide decision making. That means it has to show up in all systems and structures, from empowering employees to make decisions in behalf of the customer to conducting performance evaluations that factor in customer service objectives. It is when every department and every individual adapts and uses a quality vision on a daily basis in their sphere of influence to determine how they will serve both internal and external customers that the vision statement really comes to life.

I always remember the time one of the housekeeping staff at a medical center reminded me, as she proudly displayed a new way to clean the floor, that she was taking care of customers. That's what localizing a vision means—employees creating their own visions of how they will serve the customer.

When every person sees himself as a mini-CEO and embraces the organization's core values, the organization gets reenergized.

## Modeling the Way: Senior Leadership's Role

I have heard hundreds of people over the years in both the public and the private sectors express cynicism over a vision statement that they felt was

written just to sound good for a brochure. Many times the cynicism resulted from seeing senior leadership act in ways that contradicted the
principles embodied in the vision statement. In order for quality vision
statements to be believed by people across the entire organization, and in
order for them to be used to make decisions on a daily basis, leaders
themselves must walk their talk by putting the customer first, empowering the front line, and illustrating continuous improvement in their systems and policies. Customer-driven leaders live their vision, and they
have personal power as a result. You find them doing whatever needs to
be done for the customer—often things that they hate to do. They are
never far removed from the customer or the product.

They demonstrate the courage to tackle anything—structures, systems, even beliefs and values—that prevents increased value for users.
And then they celebrate progress toward removing those barriers.

One of the reasons for McDonald's success is that Ray Kroc, the
founder of the hamburger chain, lived his business vision of "quality,
service, cleanliness, value" by staying in touch with the franchises and
keeping his finger on the pulse of the operations. He would often show
up, unannounced, at a franchise, where customers might see him picking
up hamburger wrappers in the parking lot.

Good leaders constantly communicate and find opportunities to
focus employees on quality. They make their rounds and know what's
going on. They take the guesswork out of what constitutes "exceptional
performance" by giving employees clear examples in their frame of reference. Realizing that "the best" comes from focusing people on details as
well as on the overall picture, they model continuous improvement in
their own work. They share their optimism and get those they're leading
to respond with belief in what can be accomplished. And they create the
systems and structures to get other people there.

People watch and emulate them, not out of fear and paranoia, but
because they respect and trust them. This respect and trust result from
seeing leaders model their words about quality and continuous improvement in their actions. One cannot simply order peak performance; people
have to be motivated to give it, and that motivation often is the result of
observing exceptional performance. Those with personal power are those
who are not threatened by losing position or status, for they know that
real influence comes from sharing information and power and that status
and position are inconstant, anyway. They major in quality *all the time.*
They lead others in the quality journey, not because they are clever but
because they are consistent.

Continuous improvement leaders know what is currently of value to customers and what will be of increased value in the future. They then reinforce these ideas throughout the organization. They promote discussions about products and services that emphasize customers, rather than functions. And they promote discussions about performance that center on process improvement, rather than people.

Quality leaders understand that for all employees to really feel ownership in the organization's vision, that vision must be translated down and across the organization—from lock operator to sausage maker to project manager to marketer.

The vision has to be localized. Leaders who live the quality message help employees translate vision statements to specific actions and understand what the service strategy means for their own work unit. At a hotel, for example, does better service mean personal involvement with the guests to give them a final personal touch, or does it mean speedy electronic checkout? At a bank, does it mean more frequent bank statements, or does it mean more personal approaches from the tellers? At an automobile dealership, does it mean having all employees able to answer customers' questions, or does it mean emphasizing written communications comparing automobiles' features with the competition?

Sometimes translating the vision means defining for the employees the impact on the customer of repairing locks in a timely fashion; sometimes it means defining the impact of retrieving information quickly for physicians; sometimes it means explaining the impact on contractors of clearly writing requests for proposals for bidders. It means empowering employees to make decisions about quality.

This is the way leaders energize talents of the organization. People, at first nervous about the new vision, can get excited when they are given the opportunity to rethink how they can do things differently. When they begin to see the results of their own involvement, their contribution, and how they fit into the overall vision, the vision becomes clearer.

### Promus Hotels

Mark Wells, Senior Vice-President of Promus Hotels, explains that one of the chain's biggest challenges is to ensure that every employee of the hotel—from housecleaner to groundskeeper—catches the quality-service vision: "If our president were there, he could create that excitement and demonstrate to the customer himself what our mission is, but since he can't be everywhere, the only option he has is to find ways to actualize his notion of customer satisfaction."

Wells explains that since the hotel business asks for acceptance and payment before the product is purchased, hotels must get their "feed-back" in advance. The way Promus does that is by translating into specific behaviors what "customer service" means. "We have to make sure that Emily the maid is motivated herself to remove the carpet stains, or replace the remote control that doesn't work properly," says Wells.

Promus Hotels places great emphasis on transmitting its vision of customer satisfaction to all employees. Quality measures have been speci-fied for nine components of customer satisfaction. Each of these compo-nents then has quality measures, enabling employees to understand the actions required. These components and their quality measures in Hamp-ton Inn, one of the hotels in the Promus chain, are shown in Figure 8-1.

Many organizations talk and write about the importance of values as guiding principles for policies and practices. Many, however, fall short in defining for employees how these translate into action.

Promus Hotels enables its employees to deliver on their values pledge. For every component in the pledge, there is a delivery statement explaining how that value translates into action. Table 8-1 gives some examples of the way Promus translates its values pledge.

### FedEx

Fred Smith, CEO of FedEx, had a clear, customer-focused vision and built a great organization around it. He said, "We will produce outstanding financial returns by providing totally reliable, competitively superior global air-ground transportation of high-priority goods and documents that require rapid, time-sensitive delivery." Visitors to the massive 280-acre FedEx SuperHub sorting facility in Memphis, Tennessee, can see the incredible interplay of people and technology and the attention to detail that keep the company on top of its game. Meteorologists track weather patterns from Bangkok to Bangor to anticipate the weather's influence on flight patterns and delivery schedules; package handlers need only four-teen minutes to remove thirty-three thousand pounds of freight from a Boeing 727. Inside the facility, more than eighty thousand packages pass through a SuperTracker scan, a part of the tracking data that connects shippers to receivers inside FedEx's mainframe computers.

FedEx has done what the vision promised. It has worked with com-puter companies to invent the technology needed to make its involved communications network and delivery service function efficiently.

But Smith understood that it took more than technology to live the customer service vision. He realized customer satisfaction begins with employee satisfaction. FedEx knows that only if the company responds

**Figure 8-1.** Hampton Inn and Hampton Inn and Suites "Moments of Truth" process flow

Important moments of contact that form customers' perception of service

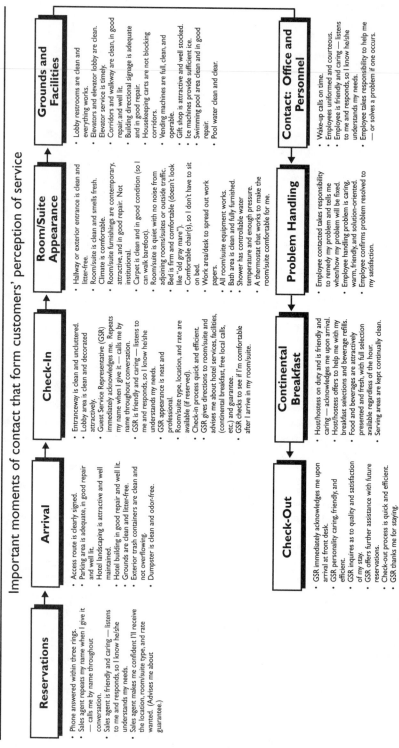

Source: Reprinted with permission of Promus Hotels.

**Table 8-1.** Values and actions of Promus Hotels.

| *Where We Stand* | *How We Deliver* |
| --- | --- |
| We will consider every opportunity for adding greater value. | By providing extras like free continental breakfast, free in-room movie channel, free stay for kids, no charge for third and fourth adult, and free local phone calls, we will give guests more for their money. |
| We guarantee guest satisfaction. | By offering an unconditional "100% Satisfaction Guarantee," we promise that our guests must be completely satisfied, or we give them their night's stay free. |
| We will be sensitive to the special needs of our guests. | By offering features like 75% non-smoking rooms, facilities for guests in wheelchairs, and low-sugar selections at the continental breakfast, we will express concern for guests' preferences and requirements. |
| We will make doing business with us simple. | By providing 1-800-HAMPTON reservation service and inventory shelving in the travel agent global distribution system; by establishing simple pricing guidelines—guests and travel intermediaries will prefer to do business with us. |
| We will treat every guest as we would hope to be treated ourselves. | By maintaining the highest guest satisfaction ratings of any hotel in the upper-economy and mid-priced segments, so our guests will be happy. More than nine out of ten guests tell us they will come back. We won't be content until it is ten out of ten. |

*Source:* Reprinted with permission of Promus Hotels.

to employees' needs and interests will employees in turn align with corporate goals. In Smith's words: "When people [employees] are placed
first, they will provide the highest possible service, and profits will follow." Every quality initiative, every management guideline, and every
recognition program at FedEx embodies this philosophy.

FedEx officials insist that it is this "people" commitment and the
willingness to act on that commitment that won FedEx the Malcolm Baldrige National Quality Award. It's a level of commitment that drove the
corporation to assemble one of the world's most extensive private television networks, not for its return on investment, but because the network
would allow prompt, open, two-way dialogue with employees on critical
company decisions, goals, and performance issues. That same commitment lies behind the practice of converting the annual Survey-Feedback-
Action into a comprehensive "report card" of employees' assessment of
management's leadership capability, along with employee recommendations for fixing any perceived problems.

### Jimmy Dean Foods

Judy Baines, Director of Customer Service for Jimmy Dean Foods, believes that each person has to feel the criticality of his job to the overall
mission. In the sausage business, explains Baines, "sanitation workers can
shut a whole plant down . . . they can make a huge difference to the
outcome. It is vital that they know that."

And Baines knows that firsthand. Beginning at the Rudy's Sausage
Company in 1960 when she was seventeen years old, she has learned the
business from the ground up, literally. She was first hired as an office
clerk and later moved into coordinating sales production and scheduling
production. She has lived through the purchase of Rudy's Farm Company, a small, family-owned business, by the Sara Lee Corporation, as
large and diverse as corporations get. She has survived the merger of
Rudy's Farm Company with Jimmy Dean Sausage, two completely different cultures within Sara Lee. She has been led by five different company
presidents, each with different preferences and styles. She has been able
to survive all this, relatively unscathed, because she has the courage to
tell the truth to her superiors, even when it may sting, and the willingness
to do what she's asking others to do. She is willing to challenge, but she
does so with a great sense of loyalty to organization and to current leadership.

Baines reflects on the difference—and similarity—between years ago
when she began her career and now. "Then it was easy to have a sense of

urgency about our mission . . . we were all connected because we were smaller . . . we had a passion for a quality product, and for the customer . . . now with the shift in the mode of operation to brokers, it is more challenging to maintain that sense of urgency." But what doesn't change, says Baines, is "the importance of doing the right thing—all the time—for the customer. I advise the people I supervise not to try to identify the level of authority of the person on the other end of the telephone line . . . you must do the right thing regardless of rank or status." When asked which lesson has been the most valuable over the years, in terms of the customer, she responds, "You cannot relegate customer service to a department or a person; everybody must be a quality assurance representative and a customer service representative. . . . Everybody must be connected to serving the customer." She insists on the importance of developing personal relationships with customers and then following up.

### DuPont

DuPont believes that every person should feel empowered to make decisions that affect quality and customer service. Sam Bogle, customer service and distribution manager at DuPont Chemical Film Enterprise, remembers a time when clerks were not allowed to "color outside the lines." He himself supervised two clerical nonexempt employees who had been told to stick to their paperwork. "I gave them the majority of work that exempt employees had previously been doing. I gave them authority, for example, to work directly with our suppliers, to take orders from those suppliers. It used to be that managers set up meetings with our suppliers that furnish us our raw materials; today nonexempt people set up those meetings."

The U.S. Coast Guard regularly checks DuPont's barges and wharfs before shipments are unloaded. Bogle explains that, in the past, managers interacted with these officials. "Today, nonexempt employees interact with the Coast Guard. . . . They even interface with the Department of Transportation to assure our facilities are in proper working order. They work with the railroad inspectors, specifically. They are even helping to rewrite the Coast Guard manual."

Another example of "powering down" occurs in districts within the Army Corps of Engineers. Those employees, including plant mechanics, who are closest to problems are allowed to solve them. In the Portland District, for example, two power plant mechanics suggested ideas to reduce handling of migratory fish during annual maintenance work on the dam's fishway, resulting in an estimated $10,000 savings in the first year of implementation. Another employee suggested revising the method of removing and reinstalling the main unit thrust-bearing temperature gauge at The Dalles Dam, resulting in a tangible savings of $307,200.

## Integrating the Vision Throughout All Operations

A company's vision and mission statements, advertising and customer communication, internal communications, displays on the factory floor, plant design, and selection, training, and evaluation practices—all must reflect the quality components of defect-free products, superior customer service, front-line orientation, and continuous improvement. As much as any industry today, Motorola has demonstrated that quality cannot be confined to the manufacturing floor, but that it must be integrated throughout the culture. For years Motorola has focused on customer service and quality within all its operations. This focus, which won the Malcolm Baldrige Award for the corporation in 1988, has increased sales throughout its divisions, including its communications, semiconductor products, and general systems sectors. Hailed as the best-managed company in the world, Motorola's annual costs savings based on the improvements made from 1987 to 1992 resulted in cutting $950 million in 1992 manufacturing costs. Over the six-year period, manufacturing costs savings exceeded $3.1 billion. The company's sales jumped to a record $17 billion in 1993, propelling the company to the number 23 spot on the Fortune 500. Its transformation from a slowly declining American electronics company to a world-beating, Baldrige-award-winning company— attributed in large part to its fanatical pursuit of six sigma quality—is widely chronicled. It continues to be a model for companies on how to use total quality management to re-energize the organization. It demonstrates that U.S. companies can use a quality management system at least as strong as those used by the Japanese.

### *Quality Goals and Strategic Plans Throughout*

Motorola has clearly demonstrated its belief that the message from the top, which involves changing values and expectations, must be institutionalized in procedures and policies that guide all actions and decisions, so that quality becomes an integral part of the day-to-day operations. Here businesses within Motorola incorporate strategic thinking and plans into the company's long-range plan. At least once a year, the company examines its strategic direction in all facets of the business, such as new-product programs, finance, technology, and quality, for the next five years. The specific quality goal in the annual plan is then driven down through the entire organization.

At the organizational unit level, the mechanism for setting these targets is the participative management program (PMP). All Motorola's employees are involved in the PMP process, and the bonuses they receive are tied to accomplishment of the specific improvements targeted by their own PMP teams.

Managers at Motorola are as accountable for achieving quality improvement goals as they are for any other business goal. It is a part of the job's requirements.

The corporate operation and policy committee, a group composed of the highest level of senior management of the corporation, conducts frequent reviews. At these meetings the group ensures that Motorola's day-to-day operations are actually reflecting its long-term strategic goals. To demonstrate the priority quality deserves, it is the first topic on the agenda, followed by finance and operations.

### Reducing Defects Beyond Manufacturing

Motorola began stepping up its quality effort in 1979 when, at the close of a company meeting that April, a senior executive told Robert Galvin, the CEO, that customers were telling him that Motorola's quality in his division "stunk." It was quite a shocking statement, given Motorola's reputation for superior quality, even then, and its record profits and excellent growth. But the problem was that not only were too large a proportion of products failing after they were taken from their boxes, but other annoying process mistakes were being made *outside of the manufacturing floor*, such as shipping products to the wrong address, or sending erroneous invoices.

Motorola understands that reducing process variability in manufacturing is only one part of building a world-class company. Every sector/group/staff organization and business unit develops its own supportive policies, and the details are oriented toward every phase of the business. Each one establishes and maintains regular improvement programs in product quality, reliability and services, and customer-driven satisfaction and responsiveness.

Achievements are targeted for a ten-times reduction in defects every two years. Specifically, each sector/group/staff organization has documented and installed a quality system detailing responsibility for executing its quality goal, and each has a formal process for planning and achieving continuing improvements in quality and reliability of its products and services. By the beginning of 1993, Motorola could point to the 170× improvement that it had made in error reduction and improvement of quality services.

As a last example, in one of Motorola's order entry operations, improvement of the process for doing work entailed designing and implementing a new computer system. The system was successful, and the result was a thirty-fold improvement in the sigma level of the order entry operation. Motorola employees also found that the very act of counting and recording internal defects led in most cases to their correction, so that a defective order was not transmitted to the factory, and an incorrect shipment was not sent to the customer.

### Changing Priorities and Incentives

Motorola's priorities have changed since launching the quality journey. In the past, top-level meetings began with discussions about financial data. Now the first topic on the agenda is quality. It takes precedence over everything else.

The quality message is continually reinforced companywide. For example, it's possible for employees to earn up to an additional 40 percent of their base salaries if they surpass goals set for their division or business group, goals based on team and individual accomplishments.

## Integrating the Quality Message Throughout All Systems

To ensure that continuous improvement endures, you must ensure that employees are willing to invest time to measure their quality improvements, that your training and development processes are in line with the continuous improvement message, and that communication initiatives are synchronized with the organization's continuous improvement focus.

### Applying Problem Solving and Raising the Standard

A focus on the concrete helps people learn how to begin their quality journey. *Measuring* their quality improvement efforts specifically helps them move past the theoretical into terms they can understand, and get excited about.

For example, the ISO 9000 standards can raise the quality consciousness of an entire organization. ISO 9000 can really bring this "quality thing" down to earth and define it step by step. In industries from Du-Pont to Square D, it has moved quality from a vague abstract concept to a frame of reference for managers and subordinates alike.

Employees in engineering, systems, and finance positions can get turned on to the idea of applying their deductive, logical reasoning to *all* processes—not just to their respective areas of specialization. They can enjoy the challenge in using the criterion of "value-added" to examine steps in procurement, for example, or even in processes as mundane as travel authorization—which is still quite labor-intensive in government. Employees can get just as excited about performing a not-so-new practice at a higher level than previously as about a totally new idea as yet untried.

### Employee Training and Development

Education and training have become integral parts of the worklife at Motorola, because of changing requirements. Motorola has between 800 and 1,000 people working full time on training, and each employee receives a minimum of five days of job-related training each year. More than 75,000 Motorolans have attended the course "Understanding the Six Steps to Six Sigma." Motorola also trains groups outside the company; in a typical year, more than 100,000 hours are devoted to training suppliers in quality-related subjects. As Bill Wiggenhorn, President of Motorola University, explains, the need for people at all levels of the organization to think and make decisions is relatively new:

> Ten years ago, we hired people to perform set tasks and didn't ask them to do a lot of thinking. If a machine went down, workers raised their hands, and a troubleshooter came to fix it. Ten years ago, we saw quality control as a screening process, catching defects before they went out the door. Ten years ago, most workers and some managers learned their jobs by observation, experience, and trial and error . . . then all the rules of manufacturing and competition changed, and in our drive to change with them, we found we had to rewrite the rules of corporate training and education. We learned that line workers had to actually understand their work and their equipment, that senior management had to exemplify and reinforce new methods and skills if they were going to stick, that change had to be continuous and participative, and that education was the way to make this occur.

Other companies that are back on track also recognize the importance of training in transitioning a culture. Procter & Gamble, for example, has a comprehensive training and development program to ensure that employees deliver value in products and services, and new customer service employees spend their first few weeks in a classroom learning how to solve customer problems. FedEx has developed curricula to teach quality theory and skills training to management and hourly employees alike, and its Leadership Institute offers training for management employees and quality facilitators on a variety of topics, such as the meaning of quality, the cost of quality, continuous improvement, and problem-solving processes. Its Quality Academy provides similar training to non-management employees. Since front-line customer contact people exert the greatest impact on day-to-day customer satisfaction, FedEx makes a special point of providing extensive job training to new hires about customer problems and service.

When Square D-Groupe Schneider, North America, stepped up its quality emphasis, to mobilize its employees it sent sweepers, dye casters, and vice presidents alike to training on customer service and empowerment. Management knew that in order to succeed, the quality initiative had to touch the individual lives of everyone.

Square D's training philosophy was that it would give employees the tools when they were ready to use them. Bill Fightmaster, former Corporate Quality Vice President, explains, "We set the courses up so they were broken into modules. So one of the metal clad team members might say, 'I have a process that isn't working. I know we must improve it $x$ percent, or we're not going to meet our customer's needs. We not only need to put the people from our group (because they can only do so much), but we need others who will impact the process and be impacted.'" Fightmaster explains that this laid the groundwork for the problem and who would participate.

Fightmaster explains further that manufacturing engineers needed to be involved to ensure that the training was useful and was appropriate. He offers a possible scenario. "A production team might be trying to change to self-tapping screws, so the members need a product engineer. Upon adding the product engineer as a member, the team requests classroom training. In the training the team identifies what the issue is. Team members have the instruction, resources (time), and a quality coach who is trained in all these tools. They elect a leader, and a facilitator. And they solve their problem *within* the training." Fightmaster continues, "They're learning and they are doing, by the time you get through this model. That way they learn the *process* while they are working on their issue. You're learning the steps as you go through."

"Training," Fightmaster summarizes, "provided the process to bring the input out. While ninety percent of all TQM training courses make problem-solving skill development one of the major components, often the actual training is not a part of the work process." In the case of Square D, the trainer and/or facilitator was asking participants to define the root cause of the problem. And as they thought through that question, they used cause-and-effect diagrams, for example.

Any time a work group focuses on a problem, it has to consider why it chose this problem over another one. Members must evaluate the impact that the problem is having on customers. And in terms of training, the only way they get training is when someone says, "We want to go fix something," and that item or issue has customer impact down the line.

Training, then, should connect the operational principles of Total Quality Management to the business strategies of the customers being served. People often find training seminars boring, with too much talk about "vision statements" and quality principles. They have heard too much verbiage and seen too little action to believe the lectures.

Trainers must work out case studies and application exercises within the customers' frames of reference. And that implies real research into their operations and systems before the actual training begins. It also suggests the need for a vision of where that customer will end up by the end of the training. And that outcome cannot be just acquisition of knowledge. It must move the participant forward either in that organization or in another one, enabling him or her to cross functions, get into a team leader's role, or even recareer into another organization.

Organizations must recognize that people get "turned on" for a variety of reasons: some from seeing new ways to improve otherwise mundane jobs they may feel stuck in; others from seeing new possibilities for transferring existing skills to new processes; others from realizing they may have the creative potential to do something new for the very first time.

For skeptics who maintain that they are in a service organization, not a manufacturing business, trainers can use quality problem-solving principles, such as the nominal group process or fishboning to resolve internal employee problems, such as low morale. If internal customers are not totally satisfied with the training effort, the trainer can use the tools to discover the real problem: Are the wrong people designing and conducting it? Is the content appropriate for the audience? Does the resistance have to do with job pressures? These tools are also appropriate to federal agencies, where trainers can use them to streamline the procurement or travel authorization process by pinpointing steps that don't add value.

Companies must develop systems and structures that allow employees to put into practice what they've been trained to do. One of the most frequent complaints I hear from managers and team leaders is that they are unable to implement customer service and continuous improvement concepts once they return to work because of a lack of senior leadership support. The message they sometimes get is, "Improvement sounds good, but we've got work to do around here."

Employees in the best organizations are trained in how to give and receive recognition and positive reinforcement for quality improvement.

### Appraisal Systems

When employees' performance evaluations make no mention of their customer commitment or their contributions to quality, they get the message that these areas are not something they really need to worry about. If, on the other hand, customer commitment and continuous improvement are factored into employees' performance objectives, employees must be measured on them. Living the message requires developing performance measures linked directly to components in a quality culture, including value creation for customers, continuous improvement, and teamwork. The entire performance measurement system at FedEx revolves around tracking the activities critical for creating a quality culture.

What gets measured gets done. That means organizations must have continuous improvement initiatives—product and product improvement—factored into their appraisal process. There is a tendency to think that continuous improvement is reserved for senior managers' development plans. But continuous improvement should be factored into *everyone's* operational objectives. For example, lock operators can, in conjunction with their leaders, determine an objective that would improve the maintenance of the locks. Project managers can define objectives that would relate to decreased cycle time of a project. Trainers can define objectives that relate to demonstrated improved performance of the person being trained.

Writing objectives and action plans to achieve them helps give form and structure to the quality initiative. "Customer service" is a good idea, as is "communicating effectively with internal customers" and "interfacing with suppliers." But these are ideas; you must bring them to life with concrete, measurable objectives.

To demonstrate belief that customer service is a central ingredient in the quality journey, managers must help employees figure out how to write objectives that will factor in "the voice of the customer." They might, for example, include in their objectives the design, administration, and use of customer surveys to determine product development over the next year. Or they might include the development of supplier relationships that result in a more desirable product for the customer.

Managers and team leaders must focus on setting exceptionally high standards. As they collaborate with employees about operational objectives and benchmarks, they must be certain to clarify not only average performance but also exceptional performance. Industry and government standards have traditionally been set at the "met" level. But if businesses do not define "A" level performance, they may get only "C" performance. And today's organizations cannot afford mediocrity. If they set objectives only at an average level, they contradict their message of continuous improvement.

Similarly, if businesses say in their mission statements that they value teamwork as a necessary ingredient in the quality imperative, then they must require team objectives, as well as individual ones. Even in the process itself, they need to demonstrate teamwork and rely heavily on employees' ideas about what will be needed in the future—in other words, how they see their mission fitting in to the overall mission. To help employees connect the vision statement with their work, team leaders and managers must first recall the vision statement and then help employees design objectives that will support it so that they are not operating in a vacuum.

During the 1970s and 1980s, our focus was strictly on individual performance. Self-reliance and competition—internal as much as external—were the rule of the day, and measuring performance based on individual efforts was natural. And actually, until the 1970s, that focus worked well. Now, however, some twenty years later, our philosophy has outrun our systems. Though organizations need team objectives to quicken the pace and compete internationally, many still focus only on individual performance in appraisal systems. Most of their mission statements include an endorsement of teamwork, but employees' operational objectives are still developed individually and primarily focus on individual outcomes.

It is true that appraisal systems must continue to recognize individual effort, since most innovations have been the result of individual thought. They should still promote what has been an historical strength—self-reliance and entrepreneurship. But organizations should also remember that entrepreneurism is not confined to the corporate office—lock operators and corporate planners alike may come up with new ideas to improve quality and add value to customers.

The existing culture developed, and is now sustained, by the present

set-up. Our rewards and sanctions must be consistent with the new corporate focus. But balance that reflects both individual and team effort is
key. Performance appraisals of corporations like Saturn Corporation and
Square D combine individual and team objectives.

Corporations need to alter their performance measurement systems
in another way. In order to enact the messages of Deming and Juran, they
should zero in on only those priorities that most impact the customer,
focusing employees on setting operational objectives that do just that—
impact customers most strongly. Otherwise, employees may work and
work to improve a process that doesn't make too much difference to
begin with.

When the concept of the horizontal organization truly takes hold,
performance objectives will be linked to customer satisfaction, rather than
to profitability or shareholder value or to internal functions.

Many employees have a tendency at the beginning of review periods
to pull out old job descriptions. These, however, may not reflect current
or future initiatives—especially those that most impact customer satisfaction. Job elements, which are written to be longer-lasting than objectives,
may still be relevant and are likely to remain constant. But if the organization is dynamic, that is, if it is expanding its markets as well as its product
offerings, then operational objectives (which are different from elements)
written years ago are probably obsolete. For example, an employee may
have in her job description an element such as "coordination efforts with
external and internal customers"; during this particular review period,
however, the focus or objective may relate to interaction with EPA officials, a reflection of a new focus on the environment. Similarly, objectives
written years ago for the federal government would not contain an emphasis on partnering as a way to reduce litigation costs.

Companies also need employees' input on the direction their jobs
should be moving in, since the employees are closer to the jobs and can
judge whether certain tasks should still be done at all. Instead of advising
that a process be revised, employees may believe that it should be eliminated entirely. Their managers should get their ideas on how their performance can be measured. They may be surprised at how high
employees set their own standards when given the opportunity.

Some companies have found that performance appraisals can contribute to developing a quality culture and need not be viewed with trepi-
dation. Eastman Chemical, for example, has adopted a Deming-based
performance assessment system that has eliminated employee labeling,
improved the focus on individual development planning, and encouraged employee involvement and ownership.

## Communication Systems

Communication efforts must reflect customer value. Leaders focused on customers find opportunities to listen to both employees and customers on what will have value for customers. Managers need to develop channels to communicate performance information throughout the organization. These may include newsletters, videos, bulletin board postings, and brown bag meetings with employees. Organizations from the U.S. Army Corps of Engineers to DuPont have newsletters that celebrate successes in customer satisfaction and quality improvement.

### Oral Communication

Every oral message delivered to internal or external customers should reflect continuous improvement. The "best" organizations today believe in a wide variety of ways to communicate recognition and reinforcement for quality achievements, ranging from simple "thank you"s to company-wide celebration.

Do you examine your department meetings or even your cross-functional meetings to see if they have value added *for the ultimate customer*? Or are they composed of deadwood to merely fill meeting time? Meetings should focus on what customers prefer, rather than what will be best for corporate functions.

### Written Communication

"Total quality" implies that we examine all our processes to ensure value added to the customer. This includes our communication efforts. Former Secretary of Commerce Malcolm Baldrige, for whom the Baldrige Award is named, emphasized the relationship between clear, concise writing and TQM. He urged that we scrutinize our written communications to see if they have value-added components and eliminate fillers and gobbledygook that dilute our purpose and waste the recipient's time.

Often we refute our talk of customer focus with pompous, overblown language, as illustrated by a job experience of mine many years ago. Shortly after I had begun working as a trainer, the partners in charge at Price Waterhouse asked me to take a look at their written communications to ensure that they were customer-focused. We agreed that if I correctly diagnosed those proposals that were successful in securing the prospective clients' business, I would receive a contract to conduct some writing seminars for them.

PW's proposals were like most accounting proposals written at that time, company- rather than customer-focused. Although at first timid about critiquing writing of the partners in charge, I did successfully pick out those proposals that had not been successful in securing clients. I smile now at the seminars I later led, in which senior level managers laughed at one another's overblown language and expressed relief at being liberated from this style.

Overblown language is found in government communications as well. In one of our government training sessions, I was shown a letter written by a woman whose property was being taken for a flood control project. The woman, who was at about a fourth-grade literacy level, was clearly upset about having to relocate. Not only was the written response to her letter legalistic, written in a pompous and obscure style, but it was written at the technical level of the sender, rather than the audience. The woman undoubtedly had to take the response to an attorney for interpretation. And certainly this kind of response is not unique to federal agencies.

Organizations need to ask themselves whether their written communications reflect a customer focus. Fortunately, organizations today are beginning to integrate continuous improvement principles into their writing and scrutinize it for value-added elements.

## Living the Message in All Businesses

Living the quality message is as applicable to service industries as to manufacturing. Instead of working to improve material variations, organizations can work to reduce the time it takes to award a contract, settle a land dispute, or answer customers' questions. It focuses on those factors that really create the major impact on customers.

## Requirements for Living the Vision

- *Determine what you value yourself.* Determine where the customer rates. Examine, for instance, how you spend your time. Do you conduct and analyze customer surveys only when you've finished with everything else? If you say you value empowerment, consider the extent to which you are still exercising a great deal of control and sheltering information.

- *Spend time with customers.* Find ways to stay connected with customers. Don't delegate this to the marketing department.

- *Sell your quality/customer vision in various ways.* Every time you make a presentation or hold a meeting, refer to it. Use bulletin boards and newsletters to celebrate successes of customer satisfaction.

- *Align your structures and systems with the quality/customer vision.* Ensure that your selection criteria and your performance evaluation systems reflect the values set forth in your vision statement.

- *Lead by example.* If you see trash that needs to be picked up, pick it up. Think about your language around the water cooler. Whom do you invite to play golf with you? Someone is always "listening" to your actions.

# 9

# More Than a Train Ride

## Commitment: Beyond What's Required

The legendary football coach Vince Lombardi once said that "the quality of a person's life is in direct proportion to his commitment to excellence." Commitment to excellence implies going the extra mile for the customer. Here are some examples:

Following the destruction of Mr. Morimoto's house and dry cleaning service by the 1995 Kobe, Japan, earthquake, Mr. Morimoto and his family slept on the street in front of the remains of their home in freezing temperatures to guard his customers' clothing from theft. Closer to home, a domestic news station aired the story not long ago of a recent fire that burned an apartment building where lower income people lived. One of the residents was a disabled veteran who managed to help rescue ten other residents from the burning building. As he was interviewed about his losses, his major concern—besides the welfare of the other residents—was for his customers' paintings (created by him), which were destroyed, and over which he was clearly grief-stricken. Considerably affected by the story, I forwarded him a small check to help him purchase some new art supplies. I received a letter from him, written in broken English, expressing appreciation for helping him meet his commitments to his customers, affirming that he had begun anew his customers' artwork.

When a malfunction in the powerhouse at Saturn Corporation interrupted the flow of crucial cooling water to the paint shop, a maintenance team worked thirty-six straight hours to fix the problem.

How many of us show this kind of commitment to our customers? Quality is primarily a function of commitment. It is impossible to achieve the goals that global competition demands unless the employees at each level are committed to continuous improvement. And commitment comes as much from the heart as from the head; it is a result more of passion than of technique.

## Quality: A Function of Human Commitment, Not Legalism

Even though he stressed statistical quality control, W. Edwards Deming believed that quality is primarily a function of human commitment. And if passion is absent—whether in a training class or on the manufacturing floor—then superior performance cannot be sustained. Ray Kroc's love of hamburger buns is evidenced by his famous remark, "You've gotta be able to see the beauty in a hamburger bun." Debbi Fields, founder of Mrs. Fields Cookies, is known to have once expressed, "I am not a business-woman, I'm a cookie person." Vince Lombardi once said, "I don't have to like my associates, but as a man I must love them. . . . Heartpower is the strength of your corporation." Love and passion play an important role in delivering sustained quality.

Those of us in the training business can write lesson plans to the nth detail and we can standardize schedules, but unless we live the principles we are espousing, the training we offer will be sterile and unbelievable. For example, if we teach the value of integrity to any quality initiative and yet pander to a customer-trainee whose positional level (title) is higher than those of the other customers, our training will fall on deaf ears. If we urge going the extra mile for the customer and then refuse to take participants' questions after the "scheduled" hours of training, the latter message will be heard much more clearly by our customers than any preceding.

Similarly, we can use control charts and scattergrams and other tools to plot our defects and diagnose the source of those defects, but if we don't back up those efforts with the determination to use that knowledge to prevent future defects, the activity will soon become an end in itself. We can preach effective communication, but if our written messages are pompous and filled with gobbledygook, our preaching won't be believed. We train our employees in teamwork, but if we refuse to partner with them in setting their performance objectives and treat them as if they were children, our lack of commitment will prevent employees from taking teamwork and empowerment seriously.

We can learn some lessons from the Japanese about commitment to a shared mission, which goes beyond decreasing manufacturing defects. In Japan, one of the first things a personnel department does is to teach new employees the company's basic business philosophy, which is often rooted in Confucianism. New employees are expected to exercise social responsibility; serve society; show respect for laws, elders, and community; and follow the company's rules. This commitment to the social good is sealed not by a written contract but by an implicit assumption of mutual commitment between the employee and the company.

Japanese employees are also expected to work for the common business mission. A business activity is undertaken only after total commitment is obtained from the group affected. While achieving this consensus takes patience and has its downside (including the greater demand on time), the emphasis on consensus promotes a commitment to a shared goal. There is some concern today in Japan that the rise in Japanese entrepreneurism may dilute this shared commitment to the mission, considered one of the reasons for Japan's leadership in quality in the past few decades.

Employees in U.S. industries are developing a similar commitment to mission and to each other. More remarkably, however, front-line employees demonstrate this commitment when they make great sacrifices for the good of the customer.

## The Origin of Commitment

A large part of employees' commitment stems from a belief in the quality initiative. As we said in Chapter 8, in order for that belief to translate into commitment to service excellence, it must be lived through policies and actions. During America's "derailment," employee commitment was a largely neglected aspect of American management, and this neglect played a large role in the U.S. loss of competitiveness. People took less pride in their work than they did in the 1960s, and that loss of pride showed up in their workmanship. Whereas only 9 percent of American workers felt left out of things during the 1960s, that percentage had increased overall to 50 percent by the early 1980s.

Within the last couple of years, however, employee attitude surveys have begun to reflect increased commitment again resulting in large part from greater employee satisfaction. And this employee satisfaction, in turn, is showing up in a quality product. High commitment to the quality initiative is demonstrated particularly in those organizations that are back on track.

## Commitment From the Top

Commitment shows up in management that is willing to develop structures, systems, and practices that sustain high quality. It shows up at companies like Hampton Inns, where employees are allowed to solve customers' problems on their own. It shows up in the Saturn Corporation, which designs its plant facilities around the employees' work schedules. It shows up at the Square D plant at Smyrna, Tennessee, where employees, realizing that the plant was going to have to lay some people off, suggested instead that all workers take one vacation day to save jobs.

Leaders demonstrate commitment by following through and designing processes that make high quality possible. That means that CEOs today have to do more than clearly articulate a new strategic vision. They have to follow through with practical policies and plans to implement their vision. And they have to be willing to rely on all the talents and initiatives of their employees to pursue their quality journey.

Commitment also means that leaders must provide every person in the organization with the resources and the support to do his or her own quality improvement. An occasional brochure or an isolated speech won't do the trick. Leaders have to live commitment every day, in all their policies and actions.

### Commitment From the Top at FedEx

FedEx officials insist that it is the company's "people" commitment and the willingness to act on it that won it the Malcolm Baldrige National Quality Award. That same commitment lies behind the practice of converting the annual Survey-Feedback-Action into a comprehensive "report card" by subordinates on management's leadership capability, accompanied by employee's recommendations for fixing any problem.

CEO Fred Smith, who is very popular with employees at FedEx, is a leader who transmits his commitment to customer satisfaction through his actions. Bob Brown, Manager of Global Personnel Programs, clarifies:

> Fred has always talked about customer satisfaction. He used to come in to the training classes and talk about customer satisfaction. He talked to everyone. We had courier classes in the beginning, where we brought the couriers into the corporate office, and Fred came and talked to them. The same was true with the sales classes. He was so good about getting the point across about how well we were doing in on-time deliveries. He always emphasized that 99 percent is not good enough. The average person sitting there was thinking, "How much better can you get?" Sensing that everyone wasn't on board with this concept, he then asked the people how many of them were

going to fly home after this class, and how many of them wanted to get on an airline that got them to their destination 99 percent of the time. He also asked, "How many of you want to bank with a bank that gets 99 percent of your checks correct?" According to Fred, there are just times when 99 percent is not good enough.

Brown adds, "People accused him and us of having this maniacal pursuit of customer satisfaction. Looking back, I guess they were right."

Smith's level of commitment drove the corporation to assemble one of the world's most extensive private television networks in order to foster prompt, open, two-way dialogue with employees on critical company decisions, goals, and performance issues. The company spends an estimated $100 per employee each year on both print and audiovisual programs. Perhaps the most impressive communications tool is FXTV, a $10 million investment in television broadcast technology that enables FedEx executives and managers to communicate quickly and directly with employees.

Each weekday morning at 4:30 A.M. an engineer inside the company's broadcast-quality studio in Memphis transmits a five- to seven-minute morning news program, "FedEx Overnight," via satellite to 1,200 downlink sites in the United States and Canada and six new facilities in the United Kingdom and continental Europe. At these sites the program is recorded automatically by VCRs located in lunchroom areas and conference rooms. As employees report to work, and from then on throughout the day, they can view prerecorded news features on company products and services; the previous day's stock prices, package volume, and service performance; and forecasts of the current day's volume. Only eighteen hours after allied war planes began bombing Baghdad during the 1991 Persian Gulf conflict, executives went live on FXTV to describe for employees the impact they expected the conflict to have on FedEx's Mideast operations.

"In general," says Smith, "the company is committed to going live as soon as possible after a major event or change to discuss the situation and open the phone lines to employees."

### Demonstrating Commitment Through Enabling Processes and Structures at Saturn

Beyond clearly communicating corporate goals, service quality commitments, and performance objectives, successful organizations provide their people with the knowledge, skills, and structures to demonstrate their commitment to quality and the customer. The Saturn Corporation believes that the front-line people "own" the process. Consequently, they must have access to whatever information—including financial—they need to implement ideas. And Saturn believes that enabling processes must be in place to allow that to happen.

Bob Boruff, Vice President of Saturn, explains that Saturn has put these enabling processes in place.

> In other words, if you change schedules so that people are working, say, twelve-hour shifts in the summer, then you have to change the working conditions, including the design of the factory—which may include air-conditioning the facility—to enable them to continue to produce high quality. There are many variables that go into this, but you can't change the requirements without addressing the conditions. Our structures, just as much as our daily actions, reflect also what's important.

To stress the importance of quality and to motivate workers further, Saturn ties a portion of pay to performance and training goals. Robert Palmer, Training and Development Coordinator, explains: "Employees earn a base salary set below the industry average. They can earn additional compensation to meet or exceed industry parity by meeting or exceeding goals in quality, productivity, and training."

Saturn's commitment to its employees doesn't end at the factory floor. The company forges strong relationships with its independent dealers, referred to at Saturn as "retailers."

Nearly all retailers and their associates throughout the country attend training programs at the Saturn plant, where they meet and train with the factory workers. One of the dealers spoke of the experience of going to the company's Spring Hill facility. "When you walk through the plant you can see the enthusiasm and can tell that the workers are proud of what they are making," he says.

The training focuses on teamwork and is intended to foster the critical elements of trust and respect. It stresses the interdependence between the dealers and the factory workers. Many of the exercises show that if either group fails, both will suffer. As Bob Palmer explains, "They [the dealers] rely on the factory to provide them with a high-quality product they can sell with pride; we in turn rely on the dealers to sell it better than anyone else is selling cars."

Saturn displays its commitment to its dealers in other ways. Most sales associates are paid a salary rather than a commission, to discourage the hard-sell tactics common among car dealers.

## Commitment From the Front Line

In visiting kill floors of sausage factories, I have seen the pride that those working to process meat have displayed in the quality of their operation and the opportunities they have been given to figure out ways to improve on that quality. I have listened to lock operators at dam sites speak with enthusiasm about a new and better way to maintain locks. I have seen the care and attention to detail that a hotel banquet staff displays in cleaning and setting up a conference room. None of these workers were being monitored by an inspector. Many of them were working in self-directed teams. Other examples of this type of commitment are contained in this section.

### Going the Extra Mile

Commitment to the customer shows up in some unique ways. Bart Clayton, a customer service representative at Jimmy Dean Foods, received a telephone call on Jimmy Dean's "800" customer service line from a consumer of Jimmy Dean Foods who had a problem. The consumer was from New York but had telephoned from Massachusetts, where she and her husband had taken their autistic daughter for medical treatment. Part of her daughter's problem was that Jimmy Dean hamburgers were among the very few foods she would eat. Having tried unsuccessfully to locate this particular type of hamburger in Massachusetts, the child's father was ready to return to New York for the burgers, when the mother decided to telephone Jimmy Dean's customer service toll-free number for help. Responding to her need, Clayton first telephoned various stores in Massachusetts to try to find the hamburger but found that the stores had only cheeseburgers. Clayton then FedExed several cases to the family to tide them over until they could return to New York.

Customer commitment didn't stop with resolving the immediate problem, however. A few months later when Clayton learned that that particular type of burger was about to be discontinued, he telephoned the family to inform them so that they could stock up to ward off a potential disaster.

### Overcoming the Odds Through Dedication

One of the DuPont Film Operation's plants at Old Hickory, Tennessee, felt the urgent need to increase the capacity of an air compressor that supplies air to one of their reactors. For some time, the plant had been having a difficult time meeting an increased demand for a special chemical, dimethylterathalate (DMT). This chemical supply shortage was affecting both internal customers, like some of DuPont Film's other plants, as well as external customers, like GE and 3M. The increased temperature during the summer months, which further reduced the compressor's capacity and intensified the chemical shortage, prompted engineers to tackle the project. Though the need for greater capacity had surfaced previously, environmental concerns had prevented engineers from acting.

Julie Rouse, project manager, explains the process for securing approval from the environmental engineers. "We knew their concerns and decided to involve them from the beginning. We thoroughly discussed our plans with them and how the change would have no adverse impact on the environment. Through communication and negotiation, we were able to secure their go-ahead."

Julie explains that once they secured approval for the project, the sense of urgency took hold. Julie recalls the great commitment displayed by all members of the cross-functional team, including maintenance and production workers and environmental, chemical, and electrical engineers. "Maintenance workers worked many sixteen-hour shifts—in fact, we all did. And we had to work through schedule and other changes."

The results were worth it. What normally would have taken from three to four months was accomplished in less than one month. And the plant achieved its goal of 10 percent increase in capacity.

### Commitment Even During Downsizings

Some years back, I had the opportunity (which I accepted with some ambivalence) to help with the re-careering of laid-off Sara Lee Meat Group employees after a merger between Rudy's Farm Sausage and Jimmy Dean Sausage led to the closing of several plants.

In one Little Rock, Arkansas, sausage plant slated for closing, I was asked to help some of the employees write resumés and learn some interviewing skills that would help them find other jobs. Many of these men and women had worked their entire lives for this company and were rooted in the area for one reason or another, meaning that they could not move to another geographic location. I was told ahead of time that their formal education was, in many cases, limited and that considerable time would therefore need to be spent with them. I welcomed the opportunity to help but anticipated that there would be some drudgery in the work, since I was to conduct career counseling sessions on three different shifts to a diverse work force. In addition, Little Rock was at that time depressed economically, and there were few job openings. As I began the assignment, I just didn't have a lot of confidence that the training would do much good.

I was wrong. While some of these employees might be described technically as functionally illiterate, I discovered they were far from unskilled and far from unintelligent. What surprised me most, however, was a display of characteristics and values I never expected to find in a plant that was closing down: team spirit, pride, creativity, and appreciation for a company that had given them opportunities for expressing their creativity to deliver a quality product.

Employees ranging from those who worked on the kill floor to those who packaged the finished sausage talked to me about ideas they had been allowed to implement to make their jobs more effective and less stressful. One told me about a rubber mat her team had devised to reduce back strain. Another talked about the opportunity to rotate jobs, which reduced monotony. Another said that her greatest joy was helping other employees feel good about their work. Still another spoke with pride about her low reject rate. Oh, they didn't use terms such as "creativity," "flexibility," "empathy," or "quality control" when I asked them what they considered their strengths that they might transfer to another environment. But they possessed those traits, nonetheless.

As I toured the sausage plant, I had the opportunity to see these characteristics exhibited from the kill floor where the hogs were killed and their insides extracted, to the assembly line where scrappy biscuits were pulled off the line. At each phase of the process, employees wanted to show me their quality charts and their safety records.

With the help of these workers, I pulled their transferable strengths—like pride of craftsmanship and commitment to quality—together, which enabled most of them to find jobs. As I talked to them, I found they were also committed to each other. If an interview were set up for one of the employees, almost inevitably that person would make sure his teammates got interviews, too.

### Going "Beyond the Scope" for the Customer

Leaders expect a lot of commitment, and they communicate that expectation. Robert Galvin, former CEO of Motorola and the man responsible for

Motorola's highly regarded achievements in quality, believes that workers are often victimized by expectation levels set lower than they should be, which affects their commitment to a quality product. He believes that workers as well as managers have learned to accept quality levels that are unworthy of their talents.

When I interview new people for one of our instructional staff positions, I always ask them to assess their level of commitment to the customer. Almost invariably they answer "total commitment." Then when I ask them the extent to which they are willing to demonstrate that commitment to the customer, I often get an answer like "How much does it pay?" When I do, I terminate the interview, because in my mind the applicant has just contradicted the previous answer.

Commitment is internal; it stems from passion for the customer and the work. It is a separate issue from receiving acknowledgment for one's efforts. If the trainer is unwilling to extend his efforts beyond the scope of work, I know he's of little use to the customer or to me.

"Scope of work" is a common phrase in the contracting business. Typically, federal agencies get a little concerned when training contractors go the extra mile; they fear the contractor will charge them for that extra work or time or that the agency will somehow end up in court. In reality, however, it is in going the extra mile that the contractor can create belief and trust in those being trained.

I have found that it's hard to get commitment from our customers if we don't show that ourselves. And demonstrating that commitment in the formal training is usually not enough. In reality, what you often have to do is train during the breaks, in unscheduled counseling sessions at night, or over lunch. Commitment means that you must follow up on how the training is impacting the organization when the customers return to their work sites, even though this may be technically beyond the scope of the contract. It means that you must stay in touch with the participants' supervisors and team leaders to be sure that their investment in the training is paying off. It means that you have to be willing to have your work measured long after the customer/trainee evaluation is completed on the last day of training. You have to be willing to be evaluated on outcomes—all usually outside the scope of work.

It is only by going this extra mile that you can be sure of staying competitive. While other consultants have often expressed cynicism about this extra effort, maintaining that it cannot possibly be a profitable course of action, I maintain that it is the *only* course of action if you want to play the long game. This willingness to go beyond the "technical scope of work" pays off not only for participants but for trainers and consultants—in the long run. When you increase your customers' value, you automatically increase your own by repeat business from those clients.

## Getting Commitment When Resources Shrink

Companies recognize that it's tough to get employee commitment today when resources are reduced and people have to do more with less. Downsizing and restructuring are continuing to produce increased stress and "burned-out" employees. As a small-business owner and consultant, I have faced this problem during the past few years as competitors continue to enter the consulting arena and low-bid us on contracts to get work. This requires us to keep lowering our own price, which in turn results in less money to pay our training staff.

Given these conditions, I have had to figure out ways to attract and retain trainers, including restructuring the relationship between them and me by giving them some authority to determine training objectives and content and then holding them responsible for their piece of the work. That includes not only their delivery of a particular segment of the training program but achievement of high success levels among participants, as demonstrated on post-training assessment instruments. I also frequently solicit their ideas—as well as those of my administrative assistant—on what should or should not be done. While allowing employees the opportunity to generate excitement in their work by making it more valuable never totally replaces guaranteed financial increases, it does go a long way toward increasing employee commitment.

Successful companies have dismissed paternalism and embraced self-reliance. They have shown commitment to employees by providing opportunities for self-improvement and self-management, and employees have responded with a willingness to take charge of their own work lives and a commitment to continue to raise their quality standards. Decentralizing authority enables employees to gain control over what they do. If employees decide a job is unsafe, they can either decide not to do it or exert influence to decrease the hazard. If they decide to change their shifts around, they can do so.

Companies that have a renewed respect for entrepreneurism are providing funds with which to recognize and support initiatives that will enhance customer value.

One effective way to increase commitment among employees is to give them the opportunity to perform high-quality work and satisfy the customers as a result. Virtually nobody wants to perform sloppy work, and employees don't like to be associated with a company that has a reputation for poor quality. I have capitalized on my company's credibility and used it to recruit trainers who could make much more money at a larger company but who would have to sacrifice job satisfaction to do so.

The most successful way to get commitment from your employees to the customer is to show it yourself. One thing is certain—you can't legislate human commitment. Nor can you get it by berating employees about their lack of it. And certainly you cannot get it by comparing your workers to the Japanese. But you can get it by knowing how to reach the human heart and showing service commitment yourself. If you roll up your sleeves and do whatever needs to be done, from moving furniture to typing certificates to counseling participants after the official class schedule, those around you will follow suit. Leaders like Martin Luther King, Jr., Winston Churchill, and Mother Teresa did not win the admiration of others because they had great titles; they were able to lead others because they gave of themselves.

## The Rocky Road Ahead

U.S. industry still has a way to go to build and sustain employee commitment. Many industries still resist sharing success with front-line workers. Although it is a fairly common practice in U.S. industries to have a performance-pay linkage for managers, gain-sharing is still not widespread for front-line workers. Research has shown that when employees are brought into the partnership with management—and that includes partnership in profits as well as in production—their commitment is increased.

Companies must continue to promote a shared sense of mission. The old centralism was based on the managers' participating in one loop of information and reward and workers in another. Each loop stayed separate and developed its own values and notions. This separation prevented a common purpose. Companies that are successfully competing today have managed to close the gap. All employees—managers and individual contributors alike—share in the company's success. Decentralized, team-based structures have reduced the possibility that values will develop along two separate tracks and promoted a single shared mission.

We pay a high price in quality when common purpose and commitment are missing because of management policies and practices. Kate Ludeman, in her book *The Worth Ethic*, observes that the work ethic is suffering in America because managers pay too little attention to creating an environment that encourages people to work from the heart. She finds a direct correlation between managers who dedicate themselves to building self-worth among their employees and employees who show high commitment and work from the heart. Moreover, she asserts, if managers neglect this duty and do not "walk their talk," employees will take a company for all it's worth.

Leaders today must learn to respect the importance of each person's contribution, even while working to promote a sense of group worth.

# 10

# Getting Out of Your Box (Car)

## Ensuring Continuous Improvement Through Measurement and Innovation

I attempt to play golf, but I always play badly. If there's a sand trap, I'm in it; if there's a lake, I'm in that. But even if I can't see the green (and from where I am, I usually can't), somehow I have to find out where it is. Without knowing where I'm heading, I have little motivation to move out of those woods, and I have no idea of what kind of club to use or how to swing. Also, I find I need my scorecard to see how bad I really am.

A lot of people say, "I know when I do a good job; I don't have to measure." Or "I've got some great people in my unit. . . . I don't have to write measurable performance standards." Or "Quality measures just take up a lot of time, and they're not worth it." Like the golfer who is reluctant to keep a scorecard, many people still resist measurement of their quality improvement efforts.

We need alarm signals to tell us when we're getting close to the sand or the lake. It's not enough to know that the shot sounded or looked good. And we can't tell where we are just by focusing on the guy we're playing with. He may not be all that great a golfer, either! We have to go beyond focusing on the competition. We have to raise our own bar, like a golfer who lowers his handicap by continuing to play better.

There's a lot of emphasis today on "golf management"—anticipating barriers ahead and figuring out how to use existing strengths to avoid them. To continue the golf analogy, if you're terrible in the sand, and you look ahead and see two sand traps in front of the green, you probably should play in front of them, rather than try to hit over them. You also must learn new techniques to keep improving your swing. It's not enough just to keep with the old tried and true ways. Yes, be it on the golf course or on the management field, you have to anticipate and stay creative to continuously improve.

Certainly competitive pressure can be an effective motivator for continuous improvement. Sometimes it's easier to get people to make changes when things aren't going so well and the wolf is at the door.

Until the mid-1970s American industries had little competition and were making record profits. They didn't have much on their instrument panels to tell them they needed to change. Even though quality was decreasing, businesses were still shipping products out the door. When they did measure quality, it was usually at the end of the line. While the emphasis on inspection instead of prevention resulted in a lot of scrap and rework, there was little effort to measure quality on the front end of the process, and the cost of that too-late "inspection" was passed on to the customer.

U.S. industry managed to sell what it made until the late 1970s because there was a pent-up demand and because, until that time, it had a monopoly in many products. Even in the late 1970s when foreign competition finally did get America's attention, the only signals managers received came from Wall Street, as U.S. companies began to lose market share in automobiles and electronics. Rather than prompting managers to focus on raising quality during the production process, however, those signals often prompted managers to increase an already developed short-term orientation and to manipulate data to make "this quarter's bottom line look good" to the corporate office.

The notion of measuring quality during—not after—the process didn't figure much into the equation, except on the manufacturing floor, where efforts were stepped up to reduce scrap to decrease production costs. Mediocre quality in employee performance became so commonplace that it was often rated as "satisfactory" and sometimes even higher than that. Industry didn't even realize that its standards had deteriorated to this degree.

Today, things are different. "Good" is not good enough. We know that if we're not using the best as our standard, we're not yet on track. Those organizations that are back on track have found the world champions in every process they measure, from customer service to design engineering, and benchmark against them. They also innovate to meet anticipated customers' needs.

Although criticized by some as unrealistic and not cost-effective, Motorola's quality focus has enabled it to attain superior quality and to market its portable phones successfully, in Asia, where its MicroTAC is now the best-selling cellular phone.

## Focusing Beyond Just the Competition, or Yourself

The need to compete globally has pressured companies to examine their quality from the front end and to figure out which processes are helping and hurting services and products. This shift in focus from inspection to prevention has resulted in higher quality. However, the force driving this higher quality can make the difference as to whether or not continuous improvement is *sustained*.

Higher quality that results primarily from efforts to turn back the competition can be almost as dangerous as mediocre quality resulting from a lack of competition. Focusing only on the competition can hurt us in two ways. First, when we actually do "beat" the competition, we can be lured into thinking that "we have arrived" or "we are ahead," lulling us into that same false sense of security we had in the 1970s when our products and services were uncontested. When, as a result of overcoming our competition, we start to think about how good we are, we start slipping. The spotlight turned on today's model companies may turn out to be their downfall if it lulls them into relaxing their quality effort. Success can become a business's greatest enemy if that happens.

Second, focusing just on the competition keeps us in a reacting mode. This philosophy says that if Jimmy Dean Sausage comes out with a fatfree sausage, then we at Oscar Meyer must come out with one, too. Or if Marriott hotels place fax machines in all guests' rooms, then we at Sheraton must do the same. That way, perhaps we can still hold on to our market share. Many companies operate this way. The danger is that the competition may be looking only at present needs and wants, overlooking future trends in consumer preferences. While this approach may be low-risk, it will keep us just hanging in there.

While focusing only on the competition may keep you in a reacting position, just raising your own bar can lead to a false sense of security. You may think that a 7 percent improvement in quality is great, compared to last year's standard of 5 percent, but your competitor may be improving by 10 percent. Even if your business is creating value for customers and you are raising your own bar, you may not be doing so better than your competitors. Internal focus and failure to conduct specific comparisons to "best in the class" competitors will cause your organization to remain ignorant of weaknesses and gaps in its quality and service. You may lose market share and not know why.

Since neither of these approaches—raising the bar on the basis of last year's achievement or raising the bar just enough to beat the competition—in and of itself is driven by customers' needs, you will ultimately fall short of success. In both being distracted by internally derived standards and trying to outwit the competition, the customer is viewed as a pawn to be manipulated or outwitted rather than as a partner in a mutually beneficial relationship.

## Continuous Improvement Driven by the Customer's Expectations

Unlike other approaches, continuous improvement is about what the customer's needs and expectations are today and what they will be in the future and then continuously improving quality to meet those needs and expectations better than anyone else and before anyone else. Since you are focusing on both existing and future customer needs, both continuous improvement and innovation are required. Together, they will enable you to lead the market, perhaps just by a little, but by enough.

Although we hear and read a lot about meeting customer expectations, merely meeting them is usually not enough. If you are merely satisfying customers, they will probably continue to compare your product or service to the competition's. To outdistance your competition, you must raise the quality of existing products and services so that they exceed your customers' requirements and expectations, and you must also innovate to meet future needs of customers before anyone else does. Even if you're currently leading the market (which usually implies that you are meeting customers' expectations), that doesn't guarantee that you will lead it tomorrow. Customers' expectations are constantly rising, so you must continually raise your own bar so that you can stay at least a notch ahead of your customers' expectations.

That translates into many different business requirements. For one thing, it means employees who deal with customers must have greater skills and knowledge. Jim Ellis, Vice President of Technical Services for Jimmy Dean Foods, cites the example of the salesperson today who has to possess more than just the "people skills" required ten or fifteen years ago. Salespeople must know the product and the product possibilities and be able to match those up with the customer's needs.

## Continuous Improvement Through Innovation

Continuing to recreate value for your services and products requires not only improvement of existing products but also innovation. You must continually anticipate what your customer's needs will be and meet that need with a benefit, regardless of whether the competition is on your heels. This requires examining trends and fractures on the horizon and continuously trying to anticipate future needs of customers and potential new markets and products. A big part of improving quality service, then, is anticipating customer expectations and changing your operations if those requirements change. That may mean redefining what business you're really in.

### *Motorola: Continuously Improving by Innovating*

Motorola knows what it does best and provides investments that promote continuous renewal. But Motorola doesn't just work to improve existing products and processes. The company spends over three quarters of a billion dollars annually on research and development. It has become much admired as a role model for American business because of its ability to continually move out along the curve of innovation, to invent new, related applications of technology as fast as older ones become everyday products. Unlike IBM, which faltered when its business entered a new phase, permitting upstarts to dominate the market, Motorola moved speedily from conventional two-way radios to cellular radio and to paging. The company's current goal is to expand into wireless data and advanced dispatch systems.

Motorola has a long history of using self-obsoleting tactics, dating back to its original amplitude modulation (AM) car radio business. Motorola's founder, Paul Galvin, in 1940 lured to the company University of Connecticut Professor Daniel Noble, a pioneer in a new transmission technique called frequency modulation (FM). FM became a hot competitor for AM and led Motorola far beyond car radios into the two-way radio business, selling Handie-Talkies to the Army to enable soldiers in World War II to talk to one another without stringing wires in the field, and, after the war, installing radios in police cars.

Cellular phones and pagers are all modern descendants of the battlefield and police-car business at Motorola. In 1993 its cellular manufacturing arm did over $4.6 billion in sales, and its paging business did $1.6 billion, with $190 million in operating profit. Motorola also has a computer chip division, which contributed a third of sales in 1993. The company has practiced the art of moving beyond commodity businesses. Apple puts Motorola chips in its PCs; specialized chips control everything from car engines to home appliances. With $6 billion in semiconductor sales in 1993, Motorola has become the world's number three producer of chips, behind Intel and NEC.

The company constantly spins off technology and capital into new businesses. Edward Staiano, President and General Manager of the General Systems sector, says that Motorola is one of the few big companies where you have a pretty good chance of starting up your own business and running it.

Motorola's newest startup is wireless data communications for people on the go. Wireless data include the use of computers to transmit memos, data, faxes, and pictures among users who are away from their desks.

There is a relationship between Motorola's new messaging strategy and its pagers. In industrially advanced countries, pagers are used to alert people to call a particular phone number, using the air waves as an adjunct to wired communications. But some of the world's largest potential markets are in less industrially advanced countries than ours, such as China, which has primitive phone systems. The market there for pagers has exploded—but not to prompt phone calls. The Chinese use them to send coded messages. Combining the message capability of pagers with portable PCs led to development of a product being used today by drivers in the United Parcel Service, who transmit package tracking data from their trucks. Motorola's risk taking, its entrepreneurship, and its rapid cycle times worked together to serve a new market.

### Eastman Chemical's Talent for Solutions

Perhaps no sector is more closely associated with environmental issues than the chemical industry. Aware that they need to regain the public's trust, the nation's leading chemical producers have embraced the multifaceted "Responsible Care" program adopted in 1990 by the Chemical Manufacturers Association. This program is responsible for continuous improvement in the safe manufacture, transportation, storage, use, and disposal of chemical products.

The Eastman Chemical Company has taken several initiatives to encourage recycling. After a local recycling company went out of business, the company's Tennessee Eastman Division approached Waste Management, Inc. (WMI), and proposed a novel partnership. The result was construction of a 50 million-pound-per-year recycling plant on Eastman's property in Kingsport, Tennessee.

The facility, known as Recycle America, handles paper, plastic, glass, and aluminum. Operated by WMI, it was designed to handle both waste generated within the huge twelve-thousand-employee Tennessee Eastman complex and recyclables collected by nearby communities. Not only has the recycling plant reduced the amount of waste the company must send to incineration or landfills; it spurred the city of Kingsport to adopt a curbside recycling pickup program. The WMI facility, which serves a region covering parts of three states and a population of 500,000, won a national award from Keep America Beautiful and now receives all the plastics collected in the Great Smoky Mountains National Park.

On the R&D side, Eastman engineers have developed and applied for a patent on an automated sorting system that could revolutionize plastics recycling. The breakthrough technology combines advanced chemistry and sophisticated electronics to make it easier to identify particular types of plastics.

The automated sorting technology could pull from the waste stream over 600 million pounds of plastic soda bottles, more than double the amount currently being processed for recycling, according to Earnie W. Deavenport, President of Eastman Chemical.

Eastman Chemical regards environmental management as one of the "core competencies" that give it a competitive advantage.

## Quality—Still Conformance to *Customer-Driven* Requirements

Historically quality has been defined as "conformance to requirements." In this definition, quality is measured by how closely the product or service meets the specifications set for it. In the functional organization of the 1970s, in manufacturing, quality was conformance to engineering requirements; in engineering, quality was conformance to marketing. Only in marketing did quality mean conformance to customers' requirements.

Conformance to requirements is central to Motorola's goal of six sigma (3.4 defects per million parts) and to FedEx's goal of 100 percent defect-free deliveries. But even within Motorola and FedEx, this standard is driven by customer requirements. Today the commonly held view is that this quality standard must originate from the customers' expectations, and consequently quality is evaluated by how well the product or service conforms to customers' expectations and preferences.

## The Importance of Measurement

Americans don't like math, and judging from our students' math scores, they're not very good at it, either. But when people talk about whether something is good or bad, the question always becomes "As compared to what?" Without measurement, people cannot know if they're improving. It's that simple. Also, people tend to exaggerate their successes if measurements aren't in place. Or people think they're measuring when they're really using indirect, unreliable measurements (e.g., "orders are ahead of last year's," "we're not getting a lot of complaints," or "I haven't been chewed out lately by my boss").

If you're going to kill the alligators, you first have to find them. You have to identify your problem areas. Where are the complaints coming from? What is the real source of that defect in your hardware? After you find the problems, then you have to decide which ones you're going to tackle. To answer that question, you must ask yourself which ones are causing customers the most difficulty. Answering these questions requires analysis and measurement.

Measurements should be clear, quantitative, and indicative of what the customer thinks is important. Measurement also implies that you go beyond fixing problem areas. If, for example, you focus solely on solving the rough spots to the exclusion of improving all aspects of the business, the quality of those areas being ignored will soon begin to deteriorate or, at best, will stay constant. In other words, if it isn't broke, you must make it better, anyway, because if you are standing still, you are losing ground.

Today we recognize the necessity of appropriate statistical tools and measurements and systematic process improvement, as long as they are integral parts of daily operations and as long as we are measuring the right things. Industries that are doing the best have not shied away from measurement. Even the best service organizations, which have a harder time formulating quality indicators, collect data on features of customer satisfaction, such as responsiveness, reliability, accuracy, and ease of access.

Some of the U.S. Army's arsenals have achieved significant improvement in quality and productivity through analysis of work processes. And the U.S. Air Force has put great effort into training its personnel on tools for analyzing and resolving problems from control charts to pareto charts.

### Measuring the Right Things

Measurement for the sake of measurement is useless. By answering some questions, you can identify the product and service attributes that determine customer satisfaction and value:

1. Which product and service characteristics are important to your customers (e.g., using less fat in the sausage patty or developing a sausage patty that can cook fast in the microwave)?
2. What is the relative importance of each of their wants (e.g., which is more important, health or speed?)?
3. What level of performance on each product and service characteristic will meet or exceed customers' expectations (e.g., will 80 percent fat free and six minutes in the microwave do it?)?

## The Importance of ISO

DuPont believes that a quality mindset among employees is not very useful unless you define quality in specific, measurable terms. For that company, "continuous improvement" is not just an ideal. It represents a detailed program designed to encourage the continuous upgrading of products and services through active communication and interaction with customers. DuPont measures its success in terms of leadership, information gathering and analysis, strategic quality planning, valuing of people, quality assurance of products and services, quality results, and customer satisfaction. DuPont's operations have also implemented programs based upon the company's certification as an ISO 9000 supplier.

ISO 9000 is a series of five international standards, developed by the International Organization for Standardization, that establish requirements for the quality systems of organizations. The standards have been adopted by the European Community and by the individual nations of that community. As trade barriers fall and Europe becomes economically unified, ISO 9000 will have even greater significance in ensuring cross-border quality. At least thirty-five countries around the world have adopted ISO 9000. According to Donald Marquardt, the head of DuPont's Quality Management and Technology Center, the ISO 9000 series is the best accepted standards in the history of the International Organization for Standardization.

Being registered with the ISO 9000 gives companies a competitive advantage internationally, since most European companies have met ISO 9000 requirements and since the European Community has come to equate this certification with quality. According to DuPont ISO team members, there are also other advantages. They believe that ISO 9000 has enabled DuPont to gain insight into all of its operations.

ISO 9000 doesn't tell you what to measure to improve quality. You determine what systems you want to document. At DuPont, ISO 9000 forced employees to address the following questions:

1. What system did DuPont want to document?
2. What were the current quality trends?
3. What error rates could DuPont afford to institutionalize?
4. What did DuPont have to do to bring each aspect of the system up to a level that it would be comfortable with?
5. What customers did DuPont want to reach?
6. Who did DuPont want to compete with?

Billy Joe Hinson, an ISO team member at the Old Hickory plant of DuPont and a veteran employee, recalls how intense and rigorous the ISO 9000 training was. Hinson explains that team members attended class eight hours a day for five days and then had case studies to review at night. He affirms that the results were worth the labor. According to Hinson, the effort provided DuPont's Old Hickory business with an opportunity to construct a solid quality foundation.

For DuPont as a company, ISO 9000 has brought quality down to earth. DuPont ISO team members attest to the benefits that have accrued from certification at various plants: an increase in on-time delivery from 70 to 90 percent; a drop in cycle time from fifteen days to one and one-half days; an increase in first-pass yield on one product line from 72 percent to 92 percent; and a reduction in the number of test procedures from more than three thousand to two thousand.

According to Ronnie Pugh, a safety team leader and also an ISO team member, one of the great advantages of ISO 9000 audits is that new people can use the documentation to continue making the product or providing the service as before, even if all personnel have to be replaced.

The ISO team members at DuPont affirm that the ISO process has forced a discipline that has benefited the entire organization. It has forced them to consider critical success factors and the main elements in achieving these factors, and it has increased workers' pride in their product as they achieved and exceeded their quality goals.

### How to Be Defect Free

Thirteen years after launching its quality campaign, Motorola remains a model of how to use TQM to reinvigorate organizations. It continues to raise its own bar in pushing quality, cycle-time reduction, and teamwork. Some of its factories begin their day with manufacturing directors requesting which records factory supervisors had broken the previous day. The philosophy is that if they aren't breaking records, they aren't improving. The company strives to measure every task performed by every one of its 120,000 employees and calculates that it saved $1.5 billion by reducing defects and simplifying procedures during 1993. Motorola has found that quality is "better than free": It controls an astonishing 85 percent of the global pagers market, besting a field that includes NEC and Panasonic. Today, more than fifty years after the company invented the Handie Talkie for American soldiers to lug through the battlefields of Europe, portable wireless two-way communication is finally becoming a medium for the masses. And Motorola is the preeminent supplier of this equipment to a global industry with some 100 million users.

Motorola defines quality as defect-free performance in all products and services provided to the customer. Defects are any failures to meet customer satisfaction requirements, and customers are anyone involved in the process, culminating with the consumer. The measure of quality, then, becomes total defects per unit of work measured through the entire process.

By 1985 Motorola had begun to realize that if you have to identify and fix defects incurred during manufacturing, then you will miss defects that affect the customer during the early life of the product. On the other hand, if your designs are robust and your manufacturing procedures are controlled so that virtually everything works right the first time, you are likely to ship products that will be free from failure in their early life. Clearly, the objective is to eliminate the cause, not to identify and repair defects. They have found that this process also reduces defects in nonmanufacturing operations, such as order entry.

Reducing total defects per unit of work is the goal of Motorola's Six Sigma initiative. Sigma is a statistical unit of measurement that describes the distribution about the mean of any process or procedure. A process or procedure that can achieve plus-or-minus six sigma capability, even allowing for some shift in the mean, can approach a defect rate of no more than a few parts per billion. This initiative not only slashes cycle time per unit of work, it also results in fewer delivered defects and fewer early-life failures.

According to Motorola, the way to achieve lower defect rates is through robust design, the primary focus of Six Sigma. Robust design results in products which function at 100 percent despite variation in the parts used, the different processes employed to put those parts together, and the different ways in which the product might be used or misused. The late Bill Smith, former V.P. and Senior Quality Assurance Manager, cited the example of a robustly designed product surviving a four-foot drop to concrete and still working. "Designers envisioned that users might conceivably drop the product and accounted for that foreseeable misuse. The more robust the design, the better the product will be able to withstand variations in stress without breaking."

Smith explained that traditional "good design practice" dictated that designs have tolerance limits for parts and processes of plus-or-minus three sigma (standard deviation). This three-sigma design yields a defect rate of 2,700 defective parts per million (PPM). Therefore, a product design with 10,000 characteristics, either parts or manufacturing steps, yields 27 defects per finished product. That, Smith believed, is completely inadequate for a company aiming to design products with the lowest possible number of defects. Accordingly, in 1987 Motorola engineers were required to create all new designs with plus-or-minus six sigma tolerance limits.

Some critics have argued that once a company begins to average fewer than 100 defects per million, then further improvements are uneconomic. In response, Smith gave the following scenario:

> A product with 10,000 parts or processes, each of which is 100 PPM defective, will contain an average of one defect per unit. In fact, only 36.79 percent of the units will go through the entire process without a defect. Out of every 1,000 units made, 632 will have to be repaired at least once; of these 368 will have one repair, 184 will have two repairs, 61 will have three, 15 will have four, three will have five, and one will need six repairs.

Smith contended that making designs more robust and reducing the opportunity for defects to creep into the final product is a one-time expense. "If it's not done, the cost of repairs, excessive scrap, and unhappy customers will continue through the life of the product."

Smith explained that even when we think we have "arrived," our customer might not agree. Even at reducing defect rates to 3.4 per million, the same product of 10,000 parts or processes will contain .034 defects per unit. Smith claimed that this improved yield (96.66 percent) is still too high to permit a "lights out" factory [where the workers go home because the efforts to improve quality are finished]. Smith affirmed that 17 defects out of 10,000 units sounds good, unless you happen to be one of those customers receiving a defective unit.

Smith snubbed traditional wisdom once held that higher quality costs more. Motorola's experience demonstrates that the higher the quality (or fewer defects), the lower the costs of prevention and appraisal, as well as the costs of failure. Each time Motorola has improved quality, the manufacturing costs per unit have declined.

Smith maintained that neither the "we're no worse than anybody else" mind-set or the "our quality is good enough" mind-set will win you first place in the global marketplace.

At some Motorola factories quality is so high that they've stopped counting defects per million and have started working on defects per billion. Overall, the company aims to reduce its error rate tenfold every two years and to increase the speed of its processes—cut its cycle time—tenfold every five years.

### Measuring Beyond the Factory Floor

Motorola understands that reducing process variability in manufacturing is only one part of building a world-class company. From the beginning, Motorola believed that the measurement of quality was not strictly a manufacturing function, but should be applied to all functions, including human resources and accounting. Every sector/group/staff organization and business unit develops its own supportive policies, and the details are oriented toward every phase of the business. Each establishes and maintains regular improvement programs in product quality, reliability and services, customer driven satisfaction indices, and responsiveness.

Achievements are targeted for a 10 times reduction in defects every two years. Specifically, each sector/group organization has documented and installed a quality system detailing responsibility for achieving its quality goal, and each has a formal process for planning and achieving continuing improvements in quality and reliability of its products and services. By the beginning of 1993, Motorola could point to the 170 times improvement that they had made in reducing cycle time and improving the quality level of their products and services.

A reexamination of accounting methods led to millions of dollars in savings for the company. Says Richard Buetow, Quality Director, "It used to take them about two weeks to close the books; now it takes about four days and saves us $20 million a year."

In one of Motorola's order processing operations, analysis of the way work was being done revealed several glaring opportunities for error. At one step the mistake-proofing solution was a simple matter of instituting a five-by-eight-inch notecard filing system for recording key customer information. At another step the computer program for initial order entry was revised to make certain input errors impossible. As a result of these and several other measures, return material requests due to order entry errors dropped from 525 to 63. This reduced costs due to returned orders from $1.8 million to $132,000.

## Only 100 Percent Is Good Enough

FedEx has proved that quality measures do not apply only to manufacturing processes. Since its beginning, FedEx has measured progress against its quality goals of 100 percent customer satisfaction after every interaction and transaction and 100 percent service performance on every package handled. FedEx has always recognized the danger of settling for anything less than this standard. To those who suggest that 98 percent is as good as it can get, FedEx is quick to point out that if each person, department, and division within a service organization handles its assigned task at this 98 percent level, the end result won't be a 98 percent service level for the entire system, but something closer to 94 percent.

In other words, problems, mistakes, and delays get passed along from one operation to the next, in linear fashion. For that reason FedEx established what might seem an unrealistic standard; a 100 percent service level goal for all deliveries to be within the time commitments pledged to customers.

But today, FedEx has gone beyond merely counting defects or delays. In the early days of FedEx's operation, the primary gauge was percentage of on-time delivery: the number of packages delivered on time as a percentage of total package volume. By the late 1980s FedEx officials began to recognize that the percentage of on-time delivery was, in reality, an internal measure of customer satisfaction, using the company's own standards. Even though the standard might be met, the customer, for one reason or another, might still be dissatisfied for a number of service related reasons. They also came to realize that complaint lists and customer surveys didn't tell the whole story.

Over time the company developed some key components of a feasible approach to measuring customer satisfaction. In addition to defining service quality from the perspective of the customer, rather than by internal standards, these included developing a means for measuring actual service failures, rather than simply overall percentages of service achievement; weighting each category of service failure to reflect its relative impact on customer satisfaction; continually tracking and measuring performance against the 100 percent customer satisfaction and service performance goals; and providing accurate, immediate feedback so that employees can spur action and innovation toward the company's 100 percent customer satisfaction and service performance goals. FedEx now has a twelve-item statistical measure of customer satisfaction and service quality from the customer's viewpoint.

In explaining FedEx's statistical quality indicators (SQI), Bob Brown,

Manager of Global Personnel Programs, explains that FedEx measures its own service against itself. The SQI list came about as the company tried to discover what irritates customers the most. Brown refers to it as the "yell" factor—what do customers yell the loudest about? Brown explains:

> We look at things like late deliveries, but we break it down into same-day delivery "late" and "wrong-day" late. On a weighting factor, the same-day late is given a numerical factor, and wrong-day late is given a numerical factor. For each incident of wrong-day late, we would count that many points against us. Another thing that is a highly weighted factor is a missed pickup. We count those things ourselves and measure against our own performance. If we carry 2 million packages a day, the potential number of points is astronomical. We hold ourselves accountable [to our customers]. Our continuing goal is the continuing decrease in the number of SQI points while volume is rising. For each of those factors, there is an officer of the company who is responsible. For example, for the number of wrong-day lates there is an officer who is in charge of getting that number down. A large portion of their income is tied to this.

## Measuring Across the Border

Eastman Chemical uses data and information at all levels and in all dimensions to plan, control, manage, evaluate, and improve quality. Highly developed electronic manufacturing information systems collect inputs daily on millions of process and product data points. These data are collected as close to the source as possible and are used extensively to control and improve business and support processes.

Access to databases is provided through strategically located work stations and off-site locations. Computer terminals are located in key locations, rather than in one central location, enabling Eastman employees to respond to customers more quickly and reduce cycle time. Reliability and dependability of major computing environments are monitored and summarized regularly.

Eastman uses interlocking management and process teams to analyze the data and benchmarks that are that team's responsibility. Computer systems provide a large amount of data and data summaries to evaluate each situation. Standard problem-solving tools such as run charts, histograms, control charts, flow charts, scatter plots, check sheets, cause and effect diagrams, and regression analysis are used to analyze the data and processes.

One of its MEPS (Make Eastman the Preferred Supplier) teams has worked to make at least 90 percent of the International Competitive Price Reports (ICPRs) prepared in Mexico error-free. The changes speed response time and improve customer satisfaction.

This ICPR is required to satisfy a legal requirement on pricing. If one of Eastman's competitors wants to sell a product below list price and Eastman wants to match that price, Eastman must prepare a ICPR that justifies its price. The customer in Mexico must fax that ICPR to the corporate office, which reviews it and sends it back to Mexico. "Through our customer satisfaction survey form, customers were telling us that we were slow to respond with that information," says Bob Kearns, leader of the MEPS team. He explains that since much of their product is sold through competitive pricing, any errors or incomplete information that delays response to ICPRs contributes to customer dissatisfaction. "Since the response time averaged around five-to-seven days—and in some cases as many as twelve days—due in part to Mexico's less than state-of-the-art telecommunications systems, the best way to provide faster service to customers was to ensure that the ICPRs were clean and error-free," explains Kearns. A MEPS team was formed, including representatives from Eastman Chemical Mexicana (ECM) and Eastman's contract representative.

The team set a target of 90 percent clean ICPRs and began monitoring the documents along the way. In the project they flowcharted the ICPR process from their offices and began to measure more than just the number of errors. Other data obtained and charted monthly included the percentage of ICPRs that met the requested approval date, the average number of days taken to approve, and the number of ICPRs entered by each office each month.

As the number of clean ICPRs increased, the number of days required to respond to the customer decreased. The result was that for about 80 percent of the ICPRs, service is now obtained in less than three days, and many are answered in one or two days. Response time was reduced by more than half since the team began its work.

According to Bob Kearns, the most important benefit for the customer is that he will receive faster information regarding Eastman's ability to meet a price already offered by another producer. "With clean ICPRs being entered, there will be no need for additional questions from product support specialists or the business organizations and faster results will be obtained on approvals or rejections," Kearns says. The accuracy and timeliness of ICPRs in the Mexico City office are now being monitored quarterly, so that Eastman's international operations can continue to improve and will not drift backward.

## Measuring Government Operations

The federal government, like private industry, has learned an expensive lesson about the danger of monopolies. Our government, built around a complex cluster of monopolies, insulates both managers and workers from the power of incentives. Consequently, until recently, there was not a lot of focus on outcomes or quality measures. Many federal agencies have had strategic plans, but they have not defined targeted results. This is changing, however. Facing the threat of privatization, and recognizing that they actually have customers too, federal agencies have begun measuring their current quality levels and launching quality improvement initiatives.

At the Air Force Combat Command, for example, units doubled their productivity over five years because the command measured their performance everywhere. Squadrons and bases competed proudly for the best maintenance, flight, and safety records; top management empowered employees to strip away red tape and redesign work processes. A supply system that had once required 243 entries by twenty-two people on thirteen forms to get one spare part into an F-15 has been radically simplified and decentralized.

Another government organization that has accomplished dramatic quality improvements because of its willingness to measure quality is the New Orleans District (NOD) of the U.S. Army Corps of Engineers. NOD, with a budget of approximately $400 million and employing 1,300 people, is responsible for federal participation in water resource projects such as navigation, flood control, and environmental initiatives. The activities of the district are evenly split between the operation, maintenance, and improvement of existing water resource projects and the planning, designing, and construction of new projects.

NOD stepped up its quality initiative in the early 1990s. Although the district admits that the paradigms and skills characteristic of a mature TQM program are not yet imbedded in its culture, it has achieved dramatic improvements in both the quality and the cost-effectiveness of services provided to its customers, in large part thanks to its dedication to measurement of current quality level and its efforts to establish a process to raise that level.

Early in its quality improvement journey, NOD identified fifteen business processes and decisions that have major customer impact on both internal and external customers. Lock operation and maintenance was one area seen as having significant-enough customer impact to warrant spending time and resources to improve it. (Navigations customers are greatly affected by the length of time the lock is closed during the year.) One question dominated in the beginning: "How many days will a lock be closed?" In turn, there was one major cause of lock closures: lock dewaterings for scheduled maintenance.

After the lock business team identified three major groups of customers—navigation, environment, and taxpayer—Mike Park, Chief of Locks, realized the importance of establishing good quality measures for the twelve locks operated by the district. For example, navigation customers require safe and reliable transit through the locks. According to Park, "Based on the adverse economic impact on our navigation customers and the significant cost of repairs to the district, we decided to focus on our quality improvement efforts on the lock dewatering process."

The Algiers Lock dewatering process was chosen as a target for study and action. A summer's closure of this lock—a critical link in the inland navigation system—was estimated to cost the towing industry $93,000 per day. The quality measure for reliability was established as the number of days of partial and total lock closure, and the measure for safety was the number and type of accidents.

The lock business team searched for the best opportunities for quality improvement and found that the lock gate dewaterings caused the largest number of total closure days and constituted the largest annual maintenance expenditure.

The dewatering team first analyzed the dewatering process to establish a baseline from which to measure quality improvements. Because the duration of lock closure was the most significant quality measure, the team identified tasks that had the greatest potential for improvement. Work scheduling, gate sandblasting and painting, gate-bay dewatering, and environmental compliance process teams were established to develop recommendations for improvements.

The work schedule process action team found that unanticipated problems with hinge repairs were a common cause of closure extensions. Jacking the gates off hinges had to be done late in the dewatering process in order to prevent damage to exposed hinges and lock machinery from sandblasting. Shop mechanics, however, found a way to protect the exposed hinges and machinery so that the jacking could be done earlier in the operation, allowing workers to identify potential hinge problems earlier.

Sandblasting and paintings are labor-intensive activities, so the gate sandblasting and painting team determined optimal procedures, location, equipment, supplies, and staffing to maintain a high quality level of workmanship while maximizing production. The team found that changing the equipment made a significant difference. Using air-coolers on the sand-blasting pressure lines and hydraulic man-lifts improved the quality and speed of their painting. Says Marvin Creel, Field Foreman, "With the man-lifts we were able to sand-blast the exterior of the gate in about the same time it used to take us to set up the scaffolding."

Other improvements included improving seals to decrease leakage and improving procedures for containment, storage, testing, and disposal of industrial wastes generated by gate repair. Ultimately, the Algiers Lock dewatering initiative produced a total closure reduction of twenty-two days, with resulting savings to the district's navigation customers and taxpayers of $2,050,000 and $230,000, respectively.

## Benchmarking: Measuring Yourself Against the Best

Though I contend that it is more important to measure your operation against your own potential rather than against the competition, no customer satisfaction research can be considered complete if it does not include measuring against the "best in the class." Following World War II, the U.S. economy grew so smoothly that most companies took profitable growth for granted and dismissed new ideas that didn't originate within. They felt that their own work was so good that they had nothing valuable to learn from outsiders, especially from those who had been devastated in the war. This smugness made us ignore Japan's strengths. Although we blamed market-share losses on cheap goods or unfair trade practices, the truth is that our quality deteriorated while that of those "cheap" Japanese goods got better.

Today, however, both public and private sector organizations measure themselves against the best. Continuous improvement companies go everywhere to find the masters.

Strictly speaking, a benchmark is a number that represents a measure of quality, response time, or some other performance indicator. In his book, *Competitive Benchmarking, What It Can Do For You*, David T. Kearns, CEO of Xerox, defines benchmarking as "the continuous process of measuring products, services, and practices against the toughest competitors or those companies recognized as industry leaders." You can benchmark against a company that produces products or delivers services similar to yours, or you can benchmark a particular function, such as customer service, against that function in another company of any type. IBM benchmarks its warehouse operations against the renowned catalog retailer L.L. Bean. To make the most of this operational benchmarking, you need to determine which function has the greatest leverage in your industry, that is, which would most improve your strategic position if you could exceed "best in class" performance. Too often inexperienced benchmarkers get caught up in the numbers game. You must first decide **what** to measure. Find out how the company you are benchmarking got its good numbers.

When a benchmarking project is launched, it should have a customer—the person or work unit that will make use of the information obtained to take action.

Operational benchmarking includes cost benchmarking, in which data are gathered about other companies to find out how they operate specific functions at lower cost or with fewer people. Another type of benchmarking measures support functions (e.g., human resources, research and development, and legal) against other "best-in-class" performers. These functions are particularly pressured today to justify their costs, and benchmarking against similar functions in other organizations gives them ideas on how better to serve their internal customers and justify their staff and budget.

### The Benchmarking Process

The benchmarking process involves the following steps:

1. *Identity what is to be benchmarked.* Although you can benchmark any function of the business for which an output can be defined, you should attempt to benchmark only key functions which set your organization apart from others. Rather than begin with a helter-skelter research effort and then try to link your findings to bottom-line objectives, start with the business objectives, from the strategic level down to the work groups. Then decide what types of benchmarking activities will produce useful information. Benchmarkers who haven't done their homework and who aren't quite sure what they're looking for often impose burdensome requests on their partners by asking them to fill out lengthy detailed surveys. It's easier to motivate participants if the subject they are dealing with is closely related to their normal work responsibilities. Subjects that are too ethereal tend to exceed the scope and authority of the team members to implement real change.

2. *Identify who should conduct the benchmarking.* Rather than hire consultants to do your benchmarking, it is usually better to have your own employees do the background research and participate in site visits. Benchmarking is more likely to stimulate employees to take action if they have themselves observed a "best practice" as it is carried out in another company. About six or eight people should be on each benchmarking team. In putting together a team, it's important that the members represent a blend of functional expertise and credibility. It takes a certain level of expertise to recognize a "best practice" in another company; you can't send your junior person off to talk to the senior engineer at a company like Hewlett-Packard. Team members need internal credibility as well, because the recommendations that flow out of their work are likely to challenge the status quo and encounter resistance.

3. *Identify comparable companies or organizations.* These should be the "best in the class," those organizations that you can learn the most from.

4. *Determine the data to be collected.* Variables here include cost and overhead comparisons, customer satisfaction levels, quality levels, service levels, market share, brand leveraging, and profitability. It's important to identify the processes and practices that were used to achieve these results.

5. *Determine how the information is to be collected.* Many customers resist lengthy surveys. Focus your questions as much as possible. Consider how much of your information can be obtained by telephone. Then arrange site visits to see a particular operation firsthand.

6. *Determine the current performance "gap."* Measure your own performance, and compare it to the performance at the company being benchmarked.

7. *Communicate benchmark findings, and sell them.* Sell senior leadership on the credibility of the findings, and communicate them to all areas of the organization that must support the changed practices.

8. *Establish operational goals.* Translate the findings into operational goals and standards. These should be a part of employees' performance plans.

9. *Develop action plans.* These plans can target either strengthening identified weaknesses or introducing practices that are superior to those being benchmarked. The action plans should include milestone schedules and should identify who will be accountable for what.

10. *Reset benchmarks periodically.* While you are improving your operations, those you are benchmarking against are improving theirs. Benchmarking is a dynamic process.

### Benchmarking the Benchmarking

Eastman Chemical benchmarks a number of international companies selected for competitive and value-chain analysis on the basis of their innovative, financial, and strategic successes in the marketplace; the similarity of their benchmarks to Eastman's; and their industry leadership positions. Data from these companies form the basis for Eastman's strategic planning and goals.

The company has established a central benchmarking coordination function to disseminate the strategic targets to employees and departments throughout the company. This function trains people to use a formal eleven-step benchmark corporate model, developed by benchmarking leading companies. The central benchmark coordination function is also charged with improving the benchmarking process and its use through the Quality Management Process.

## The Advantage of Quality Measures

Measures enable managers and employees to know how close they are to their targets and how to make the right decisions for improving work processes. Measures support improvement. They enable you to know if you are spending the right amounts on the right things and in the right way.

One great advantage of quality measures is that employees themselves can track their own progress, eliminating the need for inspectors and freeing up the managers and team leaders for forecasting and product and service development. When employees have input into setting measurable indicators, they can track their own progress. Unfortunately, in many organizations the only areas that have good quantifiable performance data are manufacturing and customer service. Indicators should be developed for every business unit and process in order for total quality to be viewed as integrated throughout the entire organization.

As a contractor with the U.S. Army Corps of Engineers, I have received weekly feedback from the Huntsville Training Division headquarters on participants' ratings of our training programs. That feedback enables me at all times to track KHA's performance and to know the "scores" we are getting from our customers. It also saves the government's technical proponent (content expert) and contracting official from having to "give us a grade."

The training headquarters also does a six-month follow-up to measure transferability of the training to the work site and then passes the results on to us. This is perhaps more significant than the end-of-week or end-of-month evaluation, because it assesses ways in which managers and team leaders have been able to put the training to work and which processes have improved.

Measurement can go a long way toward overcoming the dread associated with handing out "grades" at performance review. If employees track their own quality, they don't have to wait until after the process is completed to get their score. They always know where they are in relation to their quality goals, and they have the opportunity to close quality gaps during—not after—the process.

## The Continuing Challenges of Continuing Improvement

There is a great challenge in trying to get better when you're the best already. More than a decade after launching a quality campaign, Motorola stands as a loud retort to those who would minimize the TQM initiative. It has demonstrated how constancy of purpose can invigorate an organization. One of the biggest challenges for Motorola in the future, however, may be to keep its workers energized, motivated, and continually reaching up. It may require their forgetting how good they really are. According to Motorola's vice chairman and CEO, Gary Tooker, "Fame is a fleeting thing." He maintains that companies must always find ways to be better.

Businesses face other challenges as well, such as the financial cost of aligning organization and resources to support long-term improvement efforts while taking care of current demands. Also, constant revision can cut into the psychological satisfaction and the feeling of control that comes from finishing something. Similarly, delaying delivery of a product or service because of an inability to attain zero defects can cause a business to miss the chance to get it to the customer altogether. Employees are always torn between the conflicting quality priorities of meeting scheduling demands and satisfying quality demands. Sometimes, timely delivery is more important to the customer than having a product with no defects.

Service and manufacturing industries echo the frustration of continuously changing priorities, as front-line leaders struggle to come up with operational objectives that won't have to be continually rewritten during the performance review period. It's tough to hold people accountable when the mission and objectives keep changing. While a certain amount of chaos and unpredictability is inherent in dynamic and continuously improving cultures, too much change can cause immobility.

The training business faces special challenges of continuous improvement as it tries to respond to the continually changing business needs of customers. Since training should be developed around the mission and strategies of the customer, trainers find themselves constantly having to redesign training in response to customers' changing needs and priorities. Naturally, their ability to deliver training with panache and confidence is thereby lessened. For trainers to be believed, they have to reflect authenticity and passion about the subject. To move audiences to action, they have to create inspiring visions. That's tough to do if they have just learned the material ourselves. About the time trainers feel comfortable that they can deliver a program with energy and enthusiasm, the organizations they are serving change their missions or their mode of operating, compelling trainers to revise their material as well. Trainers also often run across new research that requires additions and deletions of material and application exercises in order to keep the training current.

Since missions of most organizations are constantly evolving, there is absolutely no such thing as finishing a training program. As the speed with which customers must respond to their changing markets quickens, so too must trainers and consultants respond more quickly. As greater time has to be devoted to research and development, it becomes difficult for a lean, small training operation to continue to make a profit and stay in business, because the development effort takes away from the delivery time.

With federal government clients, continuous improvement also has consequences for technical proponents in Washington and agency coordinators. Every time the contractor redesigns the training, that means more work for the technical proponent, who must review and approve the work. Continuous revision thus has an impact on immediate customers, as well as on ultimate customers.

Businesses also face the challenge of targeting both current and future needs of customers. Continuous improvement implies more than merely exceeding customers' current expectations; it implies anticipating what their future preferences will be and responding to them before anyone else does. That's difficult to do for a couple of reasons. Your customers may have a tough time defining who their customers will be in the future or what their mission will be, thereby increasing the challenge of designing products and services around their future needs. Second, even when you're able to anticipate their needs, customers may feel you're too "blue-sky," not targeting needs they have identified themselves.

Trainers often face this problem. Customers sometimes immediately reject ideas and skills that they see as unrelated to their current identified needs, however critical they may be for their future work. We have to be willing to accept that the appreciation for that training may not come until some future time, offer the training anyway, and just accept the immediate evaluations. If we offer customers more than they demand, they will ultimately raise their expectations for future training and reject any training that doesn't meet that higher standard.

## Overcoming Employees' Fear of Continuous Improvement

During the 1970s continuous improvement was seen as threatening. Even today, some workers worry that they will not be able to meet the new performance standards. Others don't want to throw away skills they have spent a lifetime developing.

To offset the "threat" of continuous improvement, companies must first diagnose who will be threatened by the improvement and then offer a payoff to them for joining the effort. Culture change is impossible unless people see a benefit for behaving differently. Companies have to lobby the resistors: Explain how their involvement is critical for moving the organization forward. Involve them in raising the bar and formulating quality indicators. Let them determine which companies to benchmark against and perhaps even have them act as mentors for newer persons in the organization.

If this more positive approach doesn't work, management must re-move rewards for following the old culture. The entitlement mind-set has to be destroyed. Sometimes the only way to get people's attention is to put all rewards out of reach of those workers who refuse to contribute to the new culture and raise their quality level. If no one qualifies for the rewards, no one qualifies.

## Ensuring Your Success in Today's Marketplace

If customers perceive your service or product to be exceeding their expec-tations (this is different from having a lot of "bells and whistles" on a product), if they believe that the product is preparing them for the future at a reasonable price, they will rarely look at the competition. Remember, though, a lot of characteristics—both tangible and intangible—can be in-cluded in that customer's notion of value. Response time, product durability, flexibility—all of these are considered by the customer as quality components. To be assured of keeping their share of the market and to have any hope of increasing that market share, companies need to do three things: raise their standard of quality for their products and services by measuring against their own potential; beat the standard of the "best in the class" for existing products and services; and create products to meet future needs of customers.

# 11

# Let the Porter Decide

## *The Front Line Can Make a Difference If We Enable It To*

Before the derailment, we Americans marveled at the skills of steelrollers, carpenters, pipefitters, and mechanics. And then for a couple of decades, taking our cue from industrial leaders, we completely ignored them. Today, however, U.S. organizations are once again lauding such workers as the answer to getting American industry and government back on track and keeping it on track.

The legacy of Sam Walton may very well be his "servant leadership." Walton believed that the role of the executive is not to dictate but to provide workers with whatever they need to serve the customers and then to get out of the way. Empowerment means that employees feel the internal authority to act in the absence of the "leader." Organizations that are doing better with their bottom line have turned the organization chart upside down so that it shows the increased significance of and increased respect for those closer to the customer. They have put into place enabling technology and systems that help employees make decisions. This freer access to information has eliminated the need for hierarchical management.

The centralized organizations of the 1970s and 1980s had far too many managers because, as it produced more layers of hierarchy, the system needed more people to chase inputs and ensure conformance. "Normal work" became administrivia and the management of managers, much of which had little to do with either the external customer or those on the front line. Not only was sharing information with employees down the line considered threatening for many managers in corporate America, but listening to those on the front line was considered dangerous practice.

Unions were beginning to lose much of their power, and management feared that listening to the front line could reverse the process. Consequently, managers gave their subordinates only that information they deemed it necessary for them to have in order to deal with immediate assignments, which rarely was enough for employees to feel confident about making judgments about how things could be done better. That kept employees in a tentative, reactive mode of operation.

Similarly, employees generally had no real way to communicate their candid views to senior leadership. Even though front-line employees had occasional formal "meetings" with senior managers, they usually were allowed to ask only "acceptable" questions they had submitted ahead of time. Had senior leadership interacted more with the front line on a daily basis, it would not have needed these formalized communication vehicles, since it would have "heard" employees' views by observing their actions and behaviors. Management had not learned a valuable lesson: You go to the front line not to issue directives or give a speech but to gain insight.

Even today some managers are still challenged to give due weight to the front line. From some managers' perspective, inverting the organizational pyramid—giving the greatest significance in the organization to those closest to the customer—can be threatening if they interpret it as implying that managers are subservient to employees. The word "empowerment" still sends chills up some managerial spines, especially if they see it as making them more vulnerable. For every empowered employee on the front line there is a manager cowering in the office feeling less valuable than before.

Competitive companies today, caught up in the struggle to regain global competitiveness, have recognized that they must turn the world of the middle manager and supervisor upside down. Aware that the people closest to the work may have the best ideas on how to improve things, top management increasingly is encouraging front-line workers to use their brains.

These cultures recognize the negative consequences for product quality of having layers of bureaucracy between the front-line employees and the customer and, conversely, the positive effects of bringing the employee closer to that customer. They also understand the advantage of giving those people on the front line authority to make decisions that affect the customer, since they have the greatest impact on that customer. Successful organizations also recognize that employees on the front line have to be just as inspired to succeed as those in management.

Delighting the customer may be the only primary competitive advantage a company has, and the ability to produce that delight almost always originates from the front line. Banks and financial institutions realize now that people do business with them primarily because of the attitude and accuracy of the tellers, not because of the return on investment, which usually varies very little from bank to bank. Hotels recognize that guests return because of the promptness of their wake-up calls and the cleanliness of their rooms more than anything else—a result of responsiveness of the front line.

## Recognizing Those Who Have the Most Impact on the Customer

We read today about the best managed hotels, like the Ritz Carlton and the Hampton Inn. "Best managed" means very little management, outside of employees themselves. These hotels have been able to spot in prospective employees the capacity to demonstrate initiative, an ability to communicate, and a commitment to quality.

Of all the people on the hotel staff, housekeepers probably have the greatest impact on customer satisfaction and probably create the most lasting impression. At one of our conferences held at the Red Lion Hotel in Sacramento, California, all the housekeeping staff smiled and greeted all seminar participants during the entire week; each day they delivered handwritten notes to them asking about their satisfaction with their room service. Some of these notes were written in broken English, but what an impression this effort made on all of us!

The Ritz-Carlton Hotel has very few managers, and yet it is considered one of the best-run hotels in the world. It has empowered its housekeeping staff—as well as its other staff—to make decisions that impact the customer, including the power to make purchasing decisions for the customer's benefit. Clearly, Ritz-Carlton hotels recognize the impact of housekeeping on customers' satisfaction.

At Hampton Inns, everyone, from maids to front-desk clerks, is given the authority to grant refunds to customers. Partly as a result of this empowerment, staff turnover at the chain fell to 50 percent in 1993 from 100 percent in 1990. Hampton also listened to its front line about some very basic, and relatively inexpensive, needs of guests, such as having irons and ironing boards in every room. The chain has profited handsomely from paying attention to the front line.

In a hospital, the workers who clean the rooms and the hospital aides who cheer up patients probably have as much effect as the physicians on patient compliance with outpatient treatment and recovery. Housekeeping staffs are beginning to be moved out of the hospital basements, which have hardly been an appropriate symbol for the value they add to the patients.

## Removing the Barriers to Front-Line Empowerment

Eastman Chemical's CEO and Chairman of the Board, Earnie Deavenport, affirms that the challenge of leadership is to remove the barriers that keep people from doing their best and to unleash employees' potential by providing a work environment that fosters a "want to" attitude instead of a "have to" attitude. He believes management must guide by believing in principles of trust, honesty, and integrity, instead of ruling the workplace with rigid regulations.

This liberation does not mean an absence of structure or goals. It simply implies a new organizational structure that creates new roles, responsibilities, and relationships and a recognition of the utility of teams as the basis for permanent structural design.

While there are indeed times when employees need some management, particularly when they are new on the job, for the most part they prefer to be given the overall picture, clear expectations, and guidelines and then to be allowed to determine for themselves how to fulfill them. Most people in business and government prefer being led to being managed. Those managers in our training classes who feel compelled to "call the office" each day to check up on things are not those who have clearly communicated values and priorities that enable employees to reconcile competing demands without the manager's intervention.

## Listening to the Front Line at Square D

Eugene Martin, a member of the metal-clad work unit at Square D, relates how bussing fabrication, a team within metal clad, was given a chance to solve a problem that once only management would have worked on. Ordering and getting copper used to take two or three weeks because the supplier would not manufacture the copper until Square D ordered it. As a consequence, Square D had to keep enough inventory to last at least this much time, and usually it felt it needed to keep an additional two or three weeks' supply as a safety net. But that became a problem when, explains Martin, the unit:

. . . got into a situation where our storage racks were cut, and we didn't have the space to keep this inventory. So we had to speed up our ordering process. We were given the opportunity to go to the supplier and make a proposal. We would guarantee the supplier that we would buy $x$ amount of copper, if they would keep it for us. They agreed, and it helped us to speed up our process, besides resolving the space problem. Due to that interaction with the supplier, we solved a problem that helped both the supplier and us.

Catherine Bradford, also a member of Square D's metal-clad work group, speaks enthusiastically about the latitude management gives employees to make decisions and resolve work problems: "If there is a bottleneck, the team, using problem-solving tools such as cause-and-effect and pareto diagrams, determines what it is that is hurting the process or product. It brainstorms about the best solution and then takes its proposal to management." She explains that management doesn't just give the unit total discretionary power; it requires a plan, including a cost-benefit analysis in which the team compares the cost of the present system with the cost of the proposed new equipment and the accrued benefits. Bradford cites the time the unit wanted to buy a lowering table so that members wouldn't have to use ladders to go down into the ground. The unit justified the purchase by arguing that the existing process was cumbersome on the basis of ergonomics. Management bought the decision.

All the team members speak about the benefits of using problem-solving tools to trace the real cause of a defect. Bradford explains that these tools have enabled the team to realize that the real quality problem isn't always the most obvious problem; many times the problem turns out to be a lot simpler than the team members thought it would be. She cites the example of a sticker that was left off to identify the coating. The specifications called for tin plate over copper, even though copper was normally used. A failure to identify this type of coating produced the real source of the defect, which their problem-solving process helped them to locate. These tools have enabled teams to identify problems at the beginning, or *during* the process, and thus save down time later.

Jim Jackson summarizes the opportunities in empowerment:

Management gives us the knowledge and education to do our own tracking and measurement. By graphing them out, we can see on a regular basis our defects per unit. By management allowing us to do our own tracking, we have a lot more interest in those figures. We also set our own vacation schedules, budgets, and performance reviews.

According to Jackson, management considers the team members to be the "experts," since they're closer to the problem.

## Turning the Organization Pyramid Upside Down at FedEx

Even though FedEx is still a vertical organization where one can still find functional silos, it has recognized the significance of the front line and has empowered it to take care of the customer. The company has actually turned the organizational pyramid upside down to reflect its corporate philosophy: customer satisfaction is a by-product of employee satisfaction. The pyramid reflects FedEx's philosophy that the role of each successive level of management is to lead even as it simultaneously serves the next highest level on the inverted pyramid. The concerns of those who handle the mail, for instance, are given the greatest priority.

The company commits itself to creating a workplace environment that empowers people and continually taps human potential. Jean Ward-Jones, Corporate Quality Director, stresses that the job of the courier is to work directly for the customer. "Likewise, a front-line manager's job is to make the courier's job easier, and the front-line manager's manager is to make the front-line manager's job easier, and so on until you get to the executive suite. . . . If I'm not practicing quality responsibility, then the people on the front line cannot make the score. . . . In other words, if I don't give my best effort, then employees will not give discretionary effort." FedEx wants everyone in the company to be viewed as the CEO's customer.

This respect for internal customers shows up in training efforts in areas like ground operations (pickup and delivery). Recognizing that front-line customer contact people exert the greatest impact on day-to-day customer satisfaction, FedEx makes a special point of providing extensive job training to new hires in this category. Customer service agents complete a five-week course before fielding customer calls on their own, and couriers receive semiannual training in customer service.

FedEx realizes the relationship between satisfying its internal customers and satisfying its external ones. Its commitment to inverting the pyramid shows up in employee attitude surveys, which are treated seriously and acted upon. Rather than try to cover up what might be viewed as "negative responses," companies like FedEx use these surveys to demonstrate that employee opinions and ideas really do matter.

Ward-Jones explains the importance of the survey-feedback-action. "Certainly, if I'm not doing my job, this affects employee satisfaction, which in turn shows up in customer satisfaction." Elements on this survey range from "I feel free to tell managers what I think" to "My manager finds ways to help us do our jobs better." Other questions relate to pride in working for FedEx, communication from upper management on company goals, and the degree to which employees think FedEx is doing a good job for the customers.

Ward-Jones speaks with openness about the evolution of these measures of employee attitudes, and the evolution of her own awareness. She explains that the surveys helped her discover negative actions and behaviors of her own that were impacting employees' perception of her willingness to listen. While it has become commonplace in most organizations to administer employee attitude surveys, at FedEx they function as a management evaluation tool and a work-group problem-solving mechanism.

After survey results are tabulated and distributed to managers, managers and their employees meet in formal feedback sessions to discuss survey findings and to develop action plans to solve problems diagnosed. The survey is also used as a leadership evaluation tool and consequently affects managers' compensation.

## Doing Without an Executive Dining Room at Saturn

When I'm doing training at Saturn and lunch with some of the management there, we don't eat in the executive dining room. There *are* no executive dining rooms at Saturn, just as there are no reserved parking spaces for senior management. When I talk with and watch Bob Boruff, Vice President of Manufacturing, I'm always struck with how much this guy lives Saturn's philosophy of empowerment and how he conveys it to others. From one-on-one interaction to speeches to the entire organization, he focuses on the people on the front line and their contribution to continuous improvement, the foundation of Saturn's success.

Saturn has given new meaning to turning the pyramid upside down. There are no manager prerogatives for decision making. Decisions are made by all the stakeholders, with UAW Local 1853, a co-manager at Saturn, sharing fully in that process. Because employees elect representatives who are fully seated members of every decision-making body, management at Saturn has gone beyond traditional participative management.

By giving people challenging jobs and workers a voice in all decisions, Saturn has created an enthusiastic and proud workforce rarely paralleled in U.S. industry today. The company has taught other automobile manufacturers that there is more to quality than body design and manufacturing equipment. Partnerships with the workforce and with external customers also make a difference. That difference has shown up in the quality of the Saturn automobile.

## Enabling Innovation Throughout Eastman Chemical

One of the many reasons Eastman Chemical earned the 1993 Malcolm Baldrige Award is that it encourages those on the front line—the real experts—to innovate anywhere in the world to solve customers' problems.

Earnie Deavenport, Eastman's CEO and Chairman of the Board, cites as an example what happened at a warehouse in Singapore. Eastman's product labels kept falling off. "The warehouse folks would come out and these labels would be laying on the floor . . . they couldn't tell what to ship, and it was getting to be a big hassle. The puzzling thing was that we ship this product all over the world, and we weren't having this problem anywhere except in Singapore. . . . Now back in Kingsport [the corporate office], where we have another large warehouse operation, one of our stacker operators figured that it must be the moisture and humidity peeling our labels off. So we tried a new kind of adhesive and it worked great."

Eastman is able to compete globally by providing a work environment that enables innovation to come from anywhere in the company. It also offers an employee stock ownership plan that makes every employee an owner in the company. Deavenport claims that "ownership changes behavior in a way that work takes on a whole new meaning."

## Giving Them the Necessary Skill to Do Their Jobs

After two decades of organizing for quality, business knows one thing for sure: You can't just go off and empower employees carte blanche. You have to give people the skills to work as teams, use new computer software, interpret financial information, communicate with people, take risks, and manage change. Today's worker understands that the most important task is to continue learning and to apply new knowledge to the challenge at hand.

As Bob Brown, Manager of Global Personnel Programs at FedEx, explains, "Exceeding the customer's expectations revolves around what makes for an empowered employee, and we [FedEx] believe that a knowledgeable employee is an empowered employee." According to Brown, an empowered employee is someone who has both the inclination and the ability to satisfy the customer. That implies a couple of things: (1) that they have the inclination, the attitude that says "not only is it OK to satisfy customers, but I actually want to do it" and (2) that they have the skills, the necessary training, and the atmosphere that give them the ability.

FedEx spends a lot of money and effort communicating to its employees what satisfying customers really means. It has its own television network, with daily programs on various subjects. These programs show the company's operations and special situations that require problem solving. Says Brown:

> We have different programs for different departments—sales, customer service, marketing. The advantage of this television communication is that you can get information to employees immediately so they can become proactive in problem solving. For example, in our "Flying Tigers Program," we had a live TV show with Fred Smith, and we opened it up to phone calls—not prescreened phone calls, either—and allowed employees, such as couriers, to ask how such and such a program is going to work.

The U.S. Army Corps of Engineers recognizes that if employees are liberated from regulations (and, indeed, federal agency employees, not just taxpayers, complain about too much "red tape" and the cost of running government), they will then have to make decisions themselves. They will not be able to depend on a policy or "rule" for every action they take and will need skills that will enable them to make good decisions. Consequently, much of the managers' training today is focused on issues such as problem solving and continuous improvement.

### Twenty Thousand Trained Consultants

Square D-Groupe Schneider has successfully reduced cycle time and rejects and has increased its market share as a result of an intense quality focus that assumes that every employee has the right and the responsibility to raise quality levels. Whereas reengineering usually assumes that the way to higher quality will come from a group of "experts" outside the organization, Square D recognized that it had access to its own intelligence. It also realized that if it involved only reengineering teams, rather than the whole organization, reengineering wasn't going to work. When it launched its quality program, therefore, the company actively enlisted every employee in the effort.

Bill Fightmaster, then Vice President for Corporate Quality, explains how the initiative worked:

> This initiative was launched in 1987 when twenty thousand people (when asked how many consultants we have, I love telling people we have twenty thousand internal consultants) were brought together for two and a half days of intense orientation at Vision-Mission College. The training included three principles: (1) quality is a way of life; (2) customer satisfaction is key; and (3) every one is accountable for improving quality. We wanted everybody to feel they were empowered to speak up for improvement. Square D wanted to involve the expertise and experience of everyone in the organization.

Fightmaster further explains that this was a major change, since:

> Square D's top management had reflected a top-down style, and decisions had been made mostly by management. A change which said that anyone could make suggestions of improvement was a radical departure. But a third dimension was added, and that was that anyone could make a suggestion without fear of reprisal. So we [corporate management] were working on what we called the "3 P's": power to make changes, the permission to do it, and the protection to do it.
>
> This philosophy was reflective of our new CEO at that time, who was participative in approach and wanted everybody to realize quality was their business.

In the company's enthusiasm to get the front line empowered, however, Square D learned that, in addition to authority to change things, people also need guidelines and training on how to do it. Fightmaster recalls a valuable lesson:

In our enthusiasm about getting everybody involved, we failed in our planning to think through all the consequences of empowerment. . . . The first one was that we did not set parameters. Here we had all these fired-up people, who left those three days at Vision-Mission, went back to their work sites, and, charged up that they were, wanted to go kill something right now and make something happen immediately. Here these Vision-Mission teams were going back to their work sites, painting the walls different colors, and if someone disagreed, they would respond, "Vision-Mission."

Both Bill Fightmaster and Jim Clark, Vice President of Engineering Products of Square D-Groupe Schneider, North America, smile a bit ruefully at the memory. As Fightmaster recalls:

Yeh, we had all these Vision-Mission vigilantes. . . . The worst thing about it was that everything they worked on was creature-comfort-type things, rather like what our quality circles were in the 1970s. We had to go back to them and say, "Now we don't want you to rebuild the building, but we want you to work on improving those things you have the authority to do and things that impact the customer." We tried to tell them to concentrate on their own world, to make something happen within their own work groups.

## The Generals Listening to the Lieutenants: Empowerment in the Feds

Even the military, the granddaddy of the chain of command, is stressing the need to listen to its front-line workers. Air Force literature and senior leaders stress the core elements of the Quality Air Force philosophy—in a quality culture, individuals are the process experts, vital to the continuous improvement process. The Air Force realizes that because front-line workers deal directly with the customer, they know better than anyone what's required to satisfy the customer. It urges senior and midlevel leaders to involve the front line in developing metrics and estimating process capability.

The Air Force also stresses that process workers are the key to identifying training and resources necessary to effectively execute the strategic plans. It urges that senior leaders get them involved in turning the vision, mission, and strategic plan into living documents tied directly to customer and process requirements.

General John Michael Loh, Commander, Air Force Combat Command, recognizes the contribution of those closest to the work; young mechanics are taking parts from B-1s, F-15s, and F-16s—parts that can cost $30,000 to $40,000—and fixing them for as little as $10, instead of discarding them or sending them out to the depot to be repaired. The savings, according to the 1993 *National Performance Review*, were expected to reach $100 million in 1994.

As early as 1988 the U.S. Navy saved $1.8 billion by reducing paperwork and by purchasing spare parts directly from subcontractors. Says a boatbuilder-mechanic who was quoted in a 1991 *Business Week* article, "Even Uncle Sam is Starting to See the Light": "Before total quality management, the common view was that mechanics check their brains at the gate when they come to work . . . now if there's a problem, supervisors often go up to the mechanics and ask for their solutions."

At the Robbins Air Force Base, the 1926th Communications-Computer Systems Group cut its supervisory staff in half by organizing into teams.

The need to respond to major disasters like Hurricane Hugo and Hurricane Andrew gave senior leaders at the U.S. Army Corps of Engineers, Mobile District, the opportunity to learn from the actual experiences of the front line and to document and formulate guidelines for similar future disaster relief operations. The district selected field personnel experienced in various response procedures to develop guidelines for specific missions, such as debris removal, life support, contracting, logistics, and financial management. These field personnel provided the draft guidance to the division and to headquarters, which reviewed the draft. Some of the procedures developed are being incorporated into the corps's regulations.

Suggestions developed at the field level have filtered upward to headquarters and are now becoming policies that will result in substantial improvements in the corps's ability to respond quickly and efficiently following a disaster and consequently improve the ability to satisfy the customer.

## Empowerment in Other Federal Agencies

Organizations are beginning to define those processes and people that most impact the customer and to rank highest in importance those who most directly take care of the customer. For example, the U.S. Postal Service is turning the organization pyramid upside down with a basic question: "Do they touch the mail?" in recognition of the fact that front-line workers have the most customer impact.

The Social Security Administration's Atlanta field office has shown the wisdom of empowering workers to fulfill their mission. Because the office has experienced a 40 percent jump in disability benefit claims since 1990, workers were asked to come up with ways to speed up processing. They realized that if they asked customers to bring along medical records when filing claims, workers could reduce the time they spent contacting doctors and requesting the records. That idea alone saved sixty days on the average claim, and it saved taxpayers $351,000 in 1993.

Ranchers, allowed to graze their cattle in Missouri's Mark Twain National Forest, must move their herds regularly to avoid overgrazing any plot of land. In the past, ranchers had to apply at the local Forest Service (USDA) office for permits to move the cattle. Typically, the local office sent their applications on to the regional office for approval, which, in some cases, sent them on to Washington. Approval took up to sixty days—long enough to hurt the forest and starve the cows, to say nothing of annoying the rancher. Thanks to an employee suggestion, local staffers now can settle the details of moving the herd directly with the rancher, sometimes taking no more than a couple of hours. Everybody is happier because local workers now make decisions within their area of expertise.

## Using Your Own Resources

Many times it seems easier and quicker for organizations to call in a consultant to get things rolling in their quality improvement initiative than to rely on their own staffs to develop strategies and practices for improvement. A catalyst is not necessarily a bad idea, as long as organizations realize that the ultimate success or failure depends on their own people. The challenge is to keep the interest from waning and, before the consultant leaves, ensuring that employees understand how to move their new knowledge to their work units. If this is not done, there is a tendency to relegate quality advancement to quality improvement teams, which can become mired in process rather than outcome.

It's more effective to involve your own people, your own "consultants," from the beginning, with or without an outside consultant, so that they will "own" the process of quality improvement from the outset. Only when all employees are working and problem solving to enhance or improve the quality of service and products in their areas of responsibility will any organization see consistent and significant improvement. That means that even when there is an outsider who provides the tools and techniques needed for quality improvement, employees must develop their own personal training plans to use their newly acquired skills.

## Overcoming Resistance and Responding to the Challenge

Clearly, all this empowerment can produce a particular threat to middle managers and even to first-line supervisors as they begin to question what will be left for them to do. They may have worked for years to attain their position in the company, and now they see that slipping away. In the past, their job description consisted primarily of checking quality and ensuring compliance. With empowerment of the front line, this role is diminished. In discussing Square D's quality journey, Bill Fightmaster explains this downside of empowerment.

> The supervisors weren't quite ready for that [empowerment]. Virtually in all industries, the one group that feels the most caught in this quality movement, and in this change, the one that feels it stands the most to lose, are the first-line supervisors. They felt we were undermining their authority. We had to go in and figure out what to do with that. We were not able to react as quickly as we should have, and that probably hurt us. We had done all this; it was great, but we had this gap. We had to go back and fix it.

To overcome resistance to front-line decision making and empowerment, both managers and supervisors must realize that there is still much they need to do. Ownership and responsibility are not zero-sum games. Leaders must realize that they can transfer ownership and get other people to assume responsibility without diminishing their own ownership and responsibility in the situation. For example, leaders are responsible for designing the context within which the desire for ownership takes place. If employees are refusing to put their best effort out for the customer, or to take accountability for a project, leaders must figure out what in their work climate is keeping them from doing that and fix it, whether it's a system that tolerates mediocre performance or encourages dependency or a supervisor who doesn't care about the customer and is spreading that lack of concern.

Supervisors, managers, and team leaders must continue to organize data and systems to encourage great performance for the customers.

In our training business, I've had a very difficult time relinquishing the actual training to my training staff—partly because I love it so much myself and hate administrivia, and partly because of my fear that others couldn't do it well enough. I have finally come to the realization, however, that if the systems are in place to engender great performance—and I am responsible for seeing that they are—I won't have to do it myself. It means, for example, allowing them to define what "great training" looks like and what it takes to execute it and then holding them accountable for achieving it.

Supervisors and managers must remember that they are still responsible for determining strategy and driving it throughout the organization in order to shift the culture to a continuous improvement culture. They must recognize that their systems depend on inputs from the organizational environment that must be managed and on outputs that fulfill needs of various constituents, including suppliers, investors, government regulators, and end users. These leaders have the responsibility for improving systems that provide value for users. And their own employee development objectives should reflect this critical component of their jobs.

To improve those systems, senior-level leaders and managers should have broad knowledge about the organization and the environment, but that knowledge must come from the front line.

A major remaining challenge is to convince senior leadership that there's more to empowerment than moving out of functional silos, although this is a good start. American business has recognized the drain on quality and productivity that is created by centralism. And it has again remembered the importance of the human spirit in producing a quality product. But it still has a ways to go to develop organizational structures that facilitate empowerment and ownership. Organizations like Saturn, Square D, Eastman Chemical, Motorola, and various federal agencies have moved in that direction and consequently have realized the competitive advantage of listening to the front line.

# 12

# Uncoupling the Cars

## Reducing Layers and Boundaries to Create Smallness

Historically, the bigger the organization, the more complex the organizational structure. And the more complex the structure, the more people you need to keep track of the complexity. And on and on it goes. Throughout the 1970s, the United States built large, top-down, centralized bureaucracies to do its business. These were hierarchical structures in which tasks were broken into simple parts, each the responsibility of a different layer of employees and each defined by specific rules and regulations. With their rigid preoccupation with standard operating procedures and their vertical chains of command, these bureaucracies were slow and cumbersome.

Bigness and complexity have become even greater problems today because things need to be as simple as possible for people to be able to respond creatively and quickly to the customer with a high-quality product or service. With tough global competition and demanding customers, most corporate cultures today know they can't afford the negative consequences on product quality of layers of bureaucracy between the front-line employees and the customer and between the top and the bottom of an organization.

Today we see the costly effects of too many layers in the federal government, and this layering inhibits the local agencies' ability to respond to their customers as well. Take the Department of Defense, for example. After Congress passes a law, it is passed to the DOD, which writes regulations to interpret it for that organization; it is then passed to the army, which adds regulations to interpret it for the army; and then eventually it makes its way to the Corps of Engineers, which in turn writes regulations to define application for the Corps. It may take as long as a year before that initial law is actually used to make decisions in the field. In some cases, it may take a law like the 1994 Streamlining Regulations Act, which is intended to streamline the federal government's procurement process and save millions, a year or more to be implemented in the field. Meanwhile, the taxpayer must pay for the costly, labor-intensive, and obsolete process of procurement—all because of a layered bureaucracy. Wouldn't it be great if that law, intended as it is to be a guiding principle, could pass directly to the field and the employees in the local agencies be given the authority to use their judgment and discretion to apply it to their situations? In a smaller and leaner government, that is what would happen.

The fewer layers between senior management and staffers in any given process, and the more invisible the lines between functions, the less ambiguity in quality expectations. So companies are continually trying to restructure to engender entrepreneurism but at the same foster team unity. Although you still occasionally see engineering do battle with manufacturing, or marketing compete with sales, successful companies today are beginning to bring the top and bottom closer together and to reduce the functional fiefdoms. Saturn Corporation isn't run the way General Motors was.

Tom Peters, in his books *In Search of Excellence* and *A Passion for Excellence,* reminded us some years ago that the most successful businesses operate like small businesses. It's no coincidence that in the 1960s, when America's quality and productivity were high, organizations were leaner and offered less opportunity to "delegate" quality. Even company owners and presidents were integrally involved with the product and the processes used to produce it. Because people were more directly tied to their work, they felt more passion about it.

Twenty-five years ago, before they became so fat and layered, most businesses acted like small businesses. Business managers talked directly to presidents of companies, and managers talked directly to employees. In-between translation losses were avoided. Bill Hardison, past corporate vice-president of the Sara Lee Meat Group, remembers this time, when the president's quality vision could be transmitted clearly as there were few layers to dilute it.

Managers had the authority to act at the local or field office. Most people worked in smaller groups, which facilitated direct communication. If they wanted something done, they generally didn't write a memo about it; they either telephoned or, better still, went to see the person about the request. If there was an impending problem, everybody felt it;

it was considered everybody's problem. People just didn't have the luxury of protecting turf or of delegating. The few managers that did exist rolled up their sleeves and worked alongside those they supervised. Consequently, they were connected integrally with the processes and the product. More than anything else, they set the model in intensity about quality.

During this earlier time there was virtually no training on "leadership" and "management" skills, but still there were leaders who inspired others to great performance and managers who were pretty good at planning the day-to-day operation. They were effective primarily because they were close to those they were leading. While certainly some of these were "theory X" style managers, those they were supervising expected this behavior, and actually some preferred it. With few staff, there is little time to "collaborate," and simply telling is more efficient.

During the late 1970s and 1980s, however, corporations became so bureaucratic that sharing information directly with employees became next to impossible. Layers have a way of producing paranoia, and sharing information with employees down the line was seen as threatening. Many managers truly believed that they knew best what employees needed to know, gave them only that information, and guarded the rest. One of the most frequently heard criticisms that surfaced on employee surveys administered during those years was that employees were not getting enough information to do their jobs. Employees were often given piecemeal tasks, and consequently, they had to stand around waiting for the "head guy" to show up and deliver their next assignment. This paternalistic attitude fed the rumor mill, which tended to run rampant. In some corporations, when two people were seen together discussing anything, managers feared that they were planning some sort of uprising. Virtually everything was micromanaged.

When employees are denied access to information, however, there is no way they can be proactive and entrepreneurial.

Certainly today's workplace is more complex, and there is no way for companies to operate small exactly as they once did. Geographic distance alone provides one significant barrier, as U.S. industries compete globally and secure markets outside the United States. Even for domestic companies, lines of communication are long and slow, often because of geographic dispersion of company offices. Those companies that are back on track, however, are using modern technology to facilitate communication between the corporate and the local offices.

Organizations from auto manufacturers to the Department of Defense are slicing themselves into more management pieces, farming out all but essential functions, and sharing risks with new partners. The best are seeking something quite basic: to make their companies operate like small companies. They share a realization that maintaining the flexibility of a small enterprise is the real measure of their long-term success.

## The Virtues of Creating "Smallness"

Consider that because of their leanness, smaller businesses do not have the option of operating in a top-heavy fashion. They are forced to give employees responsibility and authority for their actions. There is no such thing as fragmenting the work. There is no such thing as "staying in the box." And failing to use every person's knowledge and creativity and understanding of process is not an option.

As GE's Jack Welch has insisted, having fewer layers forces people to move from administration to execution. Budget cuts and consolidations force managers and leaders to create new operational systems or improve existing ones to enable the local level to act.

Fred Smith, CEO of FedEx, likens it to an agrarian society, when work and rewards were very closely related. If you didn't plant, you didn't sow, you didn't reap, and you starved. There was that immediate feedback. And smaller businesses operate in a similar fashion.

## Taking Initiatives to Bring People Closer Together

Organizations are trying to reduce their layers of bureaucracy. Corporate America recognizes that flatter, more fluid organizational structures encourage empowerment because the workers are closer to the customers. Tools like e-mail, teleconferencing, computer networks, and groupware enable people to regain some of the spirit of the small business. They bring people together despite distance and time, regardless of departmental boundaries.

One of the qualities behind Motorola's innovative success is its ability to run a giant business like a small business. Its trained engineers in senior management remain integrally involved with technology and contribute to this ability. Motorola is dominated by what has been called "engineering entrepreneurs"; all but two of Motorola's top dozen or so senior executives are engineers who are heavily involved in the business and who enjoy starting up new projects. Motorola's senior leadership believes that there is an advantage in having the leadership of the company comfortable with technology. Informal communication is a mark of Motorola, and the chain of command is not allowed to interfere with efficiency and speed of cycle time. If the chief executive officer has a question, he's likely to pick up the phone and talk to the engineer directly involved, not to the engineer's boss. That informality has been institutionalized so that everybody understands how the company works, and nobody's toes get stepped on when a senior leader calls an engineer to find out how something really works or what his opinion is.

Bob Brown, Manager of Global Personnel Programs at FedEx, says that when you are working in the "bowels of a finance department someplace," you're likely to forget where the money comes from. "In large part what managers are responsible for is making sure that everyone knows that their paycheck comes from a satisfied customer," he says. Brown explains that on the envelope of every FedEx employee's paycheck is the statement "This check comes as a result of a satisfied customer." This is one way FedEx keeps the customer continually in the front of employees' minds.

Some senior leaders believe that the best way to get around monstrous size is to structure around product lines or discrete businesses. They believe that such moves can unleash a tidal wave of payoffs, including releasing the pent-up creativity of their employees. Companies like Emerson argue that the best companies push the planning and control of profits down to product lines and open communication channels so that crucial information flows down to the shop floor and suggestions flow up from there to the chairperson.

## Moving Toward a Horizontal Organization

The horizontal organization goes much further than merely downsizing. Not only does it eliminate hierarchy; it also eliminates functional or department boundaries and organizes around core processes for the sake of the customer, as in the case of new product development.

DuPont has begun moving along horizontal lines. Craig Binetti, General Manager and Business Director of the DuPont Film Operation, explains that organizing around processes moves people away from an internal perspective and forces them to focus on the customer's needs. DuPont, he adds, is trying to do away with the "disconnects" that are common between functions and departments.

Eastman Chemical Company replaced several of its senior vice presidents in charge of key functions with "self-directed work teams." Instead of having a head of manufacturing, for example, the company uses a team consisting of all its plant managers. Eastman's president, Earnie Deavenport, claims that it "makes people take off their organizational hats and put on their team hats. It forces decision making down at least another level."

In creating the new organization, Eastman's five hundred senior managers agreed that the primary role of the functions was to support Eastman's business in chemicals, plastics, fibers, and polymers. Deavenport insists that a "function does not and should not have a function of its own . . . they shouldn't exist for themselves." Virtually all of the company's managers work on at least one cross-functional team, and most work on two or more on a daily basis.

Reminiscent of organizations before the "derailment," companies like Jimmy Dean Foods are now beginning to bring various functions like marketing and sales together with R & D in new product development. Jim Ellis, Vice-President of Technical Services at Jimmy Dean (Sara Lee), explains that "these alliances have speeded up our process."

## Overcoming Bigness by Acting Locally

In large organizations, those at the corporate office simply cannot know what occurs in the field. Only those in the field know their work, how to solve problems surrounding it, and how to improve it. With all the talk about the vision being promulgated from the top, it is at the local level where culture change really occurs. Acting locally enables huge organizations to operate as if they were small companies.

Large organizations can overcome the effects of largeness and layering by decentralizing and enabling local operations to formulate clear, forceful statements of what they aspire to be. In the case of the U.S. Army Corps of Engineers, an organization of more than 40,000 people, it may be what a local district aspires to be. The New Orleans District has a very different mission from that of the Portland District, those missions being driven by different customers and geographic conditions. In the case of Sara Lee, a huge multinational, diversified corporation with autonomous companies, each company mission reflects where the individual company (Isotoner, Jimmy Dean Foods, Coach, and others) is headed and what business it will be in. Certainly, it is easier if the corporate office or headquarters endorses this effort, but managers and individual contributors can act even if it doesn't.

It is at the local level that multidisciplinary teams are formed. It is there that managers can initiate brown-bag lunch meetings to share thoughts about quality improvement. It is there that process action teams are developed to measure current quality levels, establish means to raise that level, and then celebrate quality successes. It is there that the quality indicators are developed for all processes. Last, it is there that senior managers—including the CEO—can participate in the design process.

Certainly local missions need to complement the corporate mission, but the local level is where the action is. That is where you must formulate understandable, visible, and doable strategies that complement the overall mission and corporate vision statements. That is where, for example, you develop operational objectives that factor in continuous improvement. Sam Walton's philosophy was to lead from the top but run from the bottom. Grass-roots change is more long-lasting, anyway.

## From Washington to Local Communities

Nowhere are bigness and complexity bigger problems than in the federal government, where "bigness" resulted from control systems piled up to minimize the risk of scandal. The budget system, the personnel rules, and the procurement process were all designed to prevent missteps. Because there have nonetheless been scandals, the government has assumed that none of its employees can be trusted to make the right decisions, and federal agencies have spelled out in detail how employees must do virtually everything. Employees are then audited to ensure that they have obeyed the rules. Simple travel arrangements require endless forms and numerous signatures. Purchases take months and even years so that by the time equipment is finally acquired, it is obsolete.

The federal government, like the private sector, is now emphasizing smallness, empowerment, and accountability at the local level. The Council on Excellence in Government has worked to decentralize government and to give individual agencies the opportunity to use discretion, choice, and innovation to make government operate better for the taxpayer.

The Louisville District of the U.S. Army Corps of Engineers recognized that in Operations, the time spent on processing all the correspondence and documentation required for the Regulatory Branch was preventing some managers from doing their real jobs. Consequently, senior leadership in that district delegated authority to sign correspondence, permits, environmental assessments, and statements of findings from the district engineer and the chief of operations to the branch chief, section chief, and project managers.

Nowhere is grass-roots involvement more apparent than in the Resource Conservation and Development (RC&D) mission of the U.S. Department of Agriculture. Coordinated by the Soil Conservation Service, the RC&D illustrates entrepreneurism at work in the federal government. RC&D coordinators organize local leaders—farmers, ranchers, bankers, homemakers, environmentalists—who volunteer their time to improve the area's economy, environment, and living standards and who really do "make things happen" in their local communities. Reducing cropland erosion by using no-till planting methods, improving water quality by more effective use of animal waste, protecting large areas of fish and wildlife habitats, and helping farmers diversify their crops are a few of the objectives of these RC&D councils.

When these coordinators talk about accelerating tree planting on marginal open land to ensure a future supply of high-quality timber products or creating a way to use the by-product of sawmill operations as pellet fuel, a listener can feel their energy and enthusiasm about having the freedom to seize opportunities and figure out ways to get around federal red tape. Although technically a part of the Soil Conservation Service, these "entrepreneurs" have been given the latitude to maneuver around traditional processes and find the shortest way to get things rolling.

Developing farmers' markets, expanding forestry seedbanks, building wooden bridges, developing rural fire protection programs, controlling erosion, and building community centers are just a few of the specific initiatives successfully completed. The Tallgrass RC&D council in Pawhuska, Oklahoma, has improved the 1.8 million acres of native tallgrass prairie used for livestock grazing, wildlife, and recreation. The RC&D council in Idaho coordinated efforts to raise funds for a senior citizens' center. The first state RC&D council in Delaware helped a local citizens' group establish a halfway house for recovering alcoholics and drug dependents.

The strength of RC&D councils is in the commitment of local people to solving their own problems. Critical to this commitment is the freedom to find the best sources of help without outside review or approval. They may get technical and financial help from federal, state, or local governments (often in the form of grants), but such support can also come from private citizens or nonprofit organizations or from cost-sharing arrangements.

In a day when citizens are sometimes challenged to find evidences of creativity and entrepreneurism in the federal government, one is refreshed to observe these RC&D councils in action. They appear to encompass all the major ingredients of TQM: continuous improvement—in this case, of natural resources; meeting or exceeding customer requirements—in this case, residents of rural areas; and total workforce involvement—seen in the use of the talents and energies of those whom the projects most directly affect. And this work complements the overall mission of the Soil Conservation Service—improving and preserving the natural environment.

The U.S. Air Force is flattening its structure and moving from a vertical to a horizontal organization. The number of layers between major commands and unit levels is being reduced, and major commands themselves are being consolidated, to reduce parochialism.

When I talk to Air Force personnel, I am struck by the similarity between the movement in corporate America toward a return to a simpler structure and that in the Air Force, which is leaning toward a structure similar to the one that prevailed during World War II, when, to quote one Air Force officer, "the big guys ran the major commands, and you had one or two stars at the bases." Just as corporations began to get too large and layered and middle and top managers began running businesses from behind the desk, so did the same problems beset the Air Force. Says one major, "By the time the 1970s rolled around, Deming's ideas about management were real threatening to us. . . . If we took him seriously, then that might mean the 'big guys' would have to come back to the field—to the operations level." This echoes Corporate America's "deafness" to the prophets during the 1970s when senior and middle managers became further and further removed from "the trenches." And the Air Force initiative sounds remarkably like the effort today to bring senior and middle managers close again to the operation of the business.

## Changing Notions About Career Advancement

In order to convert people into believing in flat organizations, corporate leaders have to reinvent their organizations to recondition people about success. Part of this implies rethinking ideas on career advancement. For many years, this term has meant promotions up the corporate ladder, with their accompanying perks. Today, although there is little corporate ladder left, some employees still think that success comes only from "moving up." People must learn to think of success in terms of satisfying customers, and companies must bring their classification and compensation systems into sync. The efforts of some industries that have moved to a horizontal organization are beginning to pay off.

The trend is definitely toward smaller, even singular organizations, where most, if not all, employees come together in small teams to complete a project, then disband and regroup for a different project. Even if organizations don't go the route of this "virtual corporation" entirely, they are heading away from the vertically integrated giants of old, propelled toward smaller organizations by information technology. In the future, managers may well command no premium in status or compensation compared to the people whose work they coordinate. Managers, therefore, need to begin to operate as if they didn't have the crutch of hierarchy or the corporate office.

## Overcoming the Threat of "Headquarters" Policies

To people working in any large organization—public or private—the term "headquarters" often has a negative connotation. In people's minds, it's some vague entity where "policy" is created, along with corporate rituals to go along with it. In many employees' minds, headquarters never understands the dilemmas at the local level.

Decentralized organizations (decentralized execution of centralized policies) have been the rule of the day for some time now, for decentralization implies that the local level has a great deal of autonomy. That autonomy is particularly significant to an organization's ability to satisfy its customers as diversity of customer preferences increases with the opening of more markets outside the United States. Companies recognize that the demographics and preferences of customers are known best at the local level and are thus better addressed there.

One way to eliminate people's stereotypes about the corporate office is to get "headquarters" closer to the local offices. When the corporate office people get together with the local people, the negative aura surrounding the "corporate office" often disappears. When people start actually communicating with each other, they are forced to see each other as humans, not as abstract entities.

Project management is one initiative that has used direct communication to decrease hostility between corporate and field personnel. When project management was first introduced into the U.S. Army Corps of Engineers, its purpose—to facilitate integration of functions and to reduce internal competition—was not explained completely to Corps members in the field. Consequently, engineers greatly resented this movement from "engineering" to "administrivia," as they saw it, and believed it was done primarily to reduce their power and authority.

In one training session I conducted, attended by members of both headquarters and the field office, I made the mistake of mentioning project management as a "progressive" move within the Corps to promote a more integrated organization. After first taking issue with me, the field office representative, who clearly had not understood the original intent of life-cycle project management, transferred his anger to the headquarters representative, who had not previously dealt with the field personnel. Each began verbally attacking the other. Eventually the headquarters representative conceded that the concept had not been clearly communicated to the field, and the local guy admitted that moving from functionality could, indeed, be a good thing.

Corporate offices will probably continue to provide planning and direction for the future. That is their job. But more and more, the input for that direction will come from the local level as corporate offices make it easier for individual companies and field offices to communicate more directly with them.

## The Urgency and the Challenge

One thing is certain. Bureaucracies enable people to hide. When you remove layers, people can't hide in the system. Small-business owners have nowhere to hide. They have to be accountable.

Bill Hardison, formerly of Rudy's Farm Company of Sara Lee, acknowledges the financial burden of owning and managing small operations. "I think that big corporation managers do not understand the financial burden that start-up companies go through," he comments. "Financial managers in a large corporation can write up a detailed capital expenditures report and make the data show a good return on investment. That in no way approaches going before a banker, having him tear you up, and making you sign a personal guarantee on all the loans."

The bureaucratic structures of the 1970s and 1980s—like those structures today—enabled people to hide mediocre performance and made it difficult to pinpoint accountability. Corporate management did not feel the need to unleash the power of existing staff, since it could "create" another position and had the funds to pay for it. Furthermore, managers were not convinced that it was safe to relinquish power. Today, we don't have that option. There is an urgent need to reduce the effects of bureaucracy and to more clearly communicate quality expectations to the local operations.

Altering workplace structures is certain to alter titles, career paths, and individual goals. Asking people to resist thinking of themselves as marketers or planners can be very unsettling and threatening. And there is a great challenge in getting people who've fought each other for years to want to collaborate.

But organizations have found that mere downsizing or streamlining hasn't produced the gains they had hoped for. They are seeking other ways to increase their competitive edge in the marketplace. Those ways are varied, but most of them focus on reducing the effects of functionality and layering so that the company can focus more on the customer and less on itself.

# 13

# The Ties That Bind

## Back on Track Through Teamwork

The ability to cooperate may be one of mankind's tools for evolutionary survival. For many years, people have known the benefits of working in teams, where everybody's strengths are valued. We can assume that even in prehistoric times, those who were good hunters hunted; those who were good scouts scouted. And everyone shared in the result—the meal. Before America's economic derailment, before memos, before e-mail, before teleconferencing, people interacted with each other, one on one. Senior leadership worked alongside employees and was vitally connected to the daily operations of the business. People didn't emphasize status or positional power much, and employees seemed to understand the interdependence of everyone's work. Competitive? Yes. Companies competed against outside competitors, and sometimes companies within corporations competed against each other, but only if the competition led to increased quality and not to confrontation and lack of cooperation. Indeed, a key strength of American society has been its love of competition and individual achievement for the sake of the overall good.

Even during the derailment, people talked about the benefits of small-group interaction. In 1973 John Naisbitt in his book *Megatrends* alluded to the benefit of teams as he observed that hierarchies slow down information and networks speed it up.

U.S. industry didn't heed such advice, though, and during the 1970s it got off track for a while. It let bureaucratic layers separate people from each other. It forgot the impact that one-on-one interaction can have on an organization. Corporations tended to compete internally as functions fought for resources and employees came to guard their turfs and their particular areas of expertise. Businesses particularly forgot about the impact on quality that teams can bring to services and products.

It was during this time that I entered corporate America. I came to understand that being a good team player in the 1970s meant something quite different from what it had meant in my soda fountain days. It meant that you played the position you were assigned, and you certainly didn't run all over the field performing assorted roles. You were happy to "warm the bench"—just sit or perform meaningless tasks—until you had earned the right to play real ball. Moreover, you did those dull and boring tasks very well if you hoped to ever get to first base. And during your rookie year you were never, never allowed into the real players' planning meetings. Even the real players competed against each other for the possession of the ball.

By these standards, unfortunately, I was not a very good team player, because my idea of teamwork had to do with cooperation and networking. I still believed people to be more of a cooperative animal than did most of my corporate colleagues, who saw people as self-seekers whose every move is an attempt to gain an edge over the other fellow. I had understood survival of the fittest, but mostly as it related to outside competitors. I had been programmed in smaller businesses, when the key to a winning game was the harmonious integration of the various positions, not one player competing against another.

## The Return to Real Teamwork

Today, the term "team player" has taken on a meaning similar to the one it had before the "derailment," and U.S. businesses are reaping the benefits. Organizations recognize the value of cooperating so that team members can bring meaning to information faster than if they were operating independently and can capitalize on each other's strength. On successful teams, all players work cooperatively for a clearly defined goal—the satisfaction of the customer. Senior leadership in these organizations recognizes the value of crossing functions to achieve that goal. Consequently, today's teams are enabling organizations to produce a higher-quality service or product than they would be able to do otherwise.

There is even team playing among competitors. Unlike the derailment era, when game theory mostly applied to shark-eat-shark situations and helped executives plot a strategy for eating rather than being eaten, today's game theorists have learned from genetic biologists that eating the other fellow is not necessarily the best path to long-term survival. They have learned that cooperative behavior may enhance survivability and that killing the competition isn't always the best way to succeed. Wal-

Mart, which has frequently obliterated the competition because it gives consumers a better deal, is becoming more cooperative as local residents come to the defense of hometown merchants. IBM, since its loss of significant market share in the 1980s, has begun an increasing number of joint ventures, cooperating today with onetime competitors, such as Apple.

## Forms of Teams

Teams take many forms. Some are process action teams that work to reduce process cycle time or the number of defects or to create entirely new processes. Others are multidisciplinary teams that incorporate customers' preferences on the front end of the process to reduce change orders down the line. Still others are self-managed teams that hire, fire, procure equipment, and do their own performance appraisals. All are focused on the customer.

At Sara Lee Knit Productions in Gretna, Virginia, some teams are like the work teams, whose members are judged by their team's overall accomplishments, rather than by individual achievement. These teams have less supervision than before, and, according to Barry Yeatts, Plant Manager, they have managed to cut the rejection rate by about 60 percent; annual employee turnover has dropped from 60 percent to 22 percent. Yeatts explains that these teams set their own quality and production goals and that often their goals are even higher than those set by management. Says Yeatts, "As teams mature, they have the opportunity to become more self-directing." There are team "facilitators" who give direction when it is needed. Yeatts believes that one of the primary jobs of the leader-manager is "to continuously keep awareness up about how we're doing, in terms of the department, and in the overall business. . . . Of course, since they track their own performance, they know on a daily basis where they are."

Some companies have formed supplier teams for customer value. Wal-Mart and Japanese auto makers have tried not just to extract the best price from their suppliers but to help deliver the best possible product at the lowest price to the consumer.

In-house teams are used in various ways to create added value for customers. Team leaders are able to facilitate discussion, bring out diverse viewpoints, and ensure that teams are working on those processes that most add value to the customer. At times the leaders are part of the teams; at other times, they must be willing to step out and coach from the sidelines.

## Overcoming the Barrier of Functionality

When teamwork proves difficult to achieve in an organization, the reason usually has to do with the systems in place. As mentioned earlier, traditional hierarchical structures have a tendency to degenerate into vertical silos in which information flows up and down but not out to the rest of the organization. Many companies have attempted to move people out of functionality by creating business units that include employees from various functions who focus on customer value. Engineers are found in traditional "marketing" roles; a pipe fitter may be called in to respond to a customer problem.

To reduce functionality and promote teamwork, U.S. managers have also found it useful to stress internal customers. Kaoru Ishikawa, one of the quality gurus, first introduced the concept of "internal customer" in 1950 when he was working to reduce defects in a steel mill in Japan. He asked one department to talk to another about the problems it was having because it was receiving poor raw materials from the other group. The workers refused because they didn't want to talk to their "enemies."

Today, companies like FedEx and DuPont and federal agencies like the U.S. Army Corps of Engineers and the Department of Agriculture stress the importance of responding to the next group on the production or service-delivery "line"—their internal customers. The importance of considering the value of these internal customers has been facilitated by cross-functional work teams and process action teams that get members from different functions to communicate with each other. These mechanisms have fostered a sense of shared responsibility and accountability—responsibility and accountability for the customer.

Ishikawa dismissed the view that line workers exist solely for the purpose of carrying out staff departments' orders. He stressed that the line departments and workers were the "true customers." In other words, the role of the accounting department is to provide data to the line departments to enhance their work methods so that the external customer ultimately receives a higher value.

## Saturn: A Cultural Revolution for GM Employees

Most people have heard or read about the success of Saturn Corporation's self-managed teams. All employees are a part of at least one team. On the production floor, workers are formed into teams of eight to fifteen people who manage themselves, from budgeting and scheduling to hiring and training. They are a model of team success. But this success didn't happen overnight.

In the beginning of the enterprise, before the mile-long plant was built in Spring Hill, Tennessee, when employees were still housed in mobile units, I did some training for powertrain team members. Saturn and I came to realize that there's more to developing a team culture than just having an aptitude for it.

## Too Much, Too Soon

Saturn had hand-picked its workforce from among current and laid-off GM workers. Its initial strategy was to select its blue-collar employees entirely from within the GM ranks—but only those it considered adaptable, capable of working well in teams, and possessing good communications skills. These workers were considered the "cream of the crop" at General Motors and were culled in a highly selective process that included measuring propensities for autonomy and self-directedness.

Applicants for the jobs were asked to complete a twelve-page assessment that asked for specific information on skills and probed for attitudes and behaviors. Most of the questions took the form of case studies that asked applicants to offer solutions to problems. Not only was Saturn looking for people who demonstrated ability to work in teams; it was also looking for people who would support its mission: "To market vehicles developed and manufactured in the United States that are world leaders in quality, cost, and customer satisfaction through the integration of people, technology, and business systems, and to transfer knowledge, technology, and experience throughout General Motors."

They identified workers with an aptitude for teamwork. But that, Saturn learned, was not enough.

The crafters of the Saturn experiment anticipated that these workers would create the new organization. In their zeal and enthusiasm for self-directedness, Saturn executives sculpted a plan that would compel employees instantly to become team players and to make their own decisions regarding their work. Theoretically, this sounded like a good idea.

The GM culture the workers had come from, however, was too drastically different from that at Saturn for even these highly talented workers to make the transition without help. Historically hierarchical and top-down, GM had given its employees their goals, objectives, and benchmarks. Although they might have possessed the capacity for teamwork, these former GM employees had not had a chance to use their team skills. Yet now they were expected to create their own organizational culture—

vision statements, strategic plans, and operational objectives. And to do it all in a self-managed team atmosphere. It was too much of a radical adjustment.

Many of the employees expressed frustration; they believed in the philosophy, but some of them felt that they had been "thrown on the wall" and were operating in some kind of maze that they couldn't get a handle on. They were concerned that many of their skills and abilities, which had been useful in an autocratic hierarchical, were viewed now as nonvaluable and useless. They liked the idea of setting their own goals, but they were not entirely comfortable with it and didn't know exactly how to go about writing the standards for performance. They were frustrated with Spring Hill, and they were frustrated with General Motors. They didn't care too much for me, either. This was too much change all at once.

The heavy demands placed on employees to adjust probably had some part to play in the bottlenecks Saturn experienced in the beginning. When production began, the drive-train operation had some difficulty in meeting an unexpectedly high demand for automatic transmissions, and there was some unevenness in the quality of the paint system. Even though these employees had gone through a rigorous assessment of their ability to fit in with the new culture, their frustrations about the changing paradigms no doubt showed up in the early days. Even when structures and systems supporting a culture are in place (and they were at Saturn), it takes time for workers to believe in them. Some workers were unable to adjust and ended up leaving.

In retrospect, some seven years later, Bob Boruff, Vice President for Manufacturing, and Bob Palmer, Training and Organizational Development Coordinator, both admit that they should have given employees more training in the beginning. Palmer recognizes that aptitude, while important, is not enough. It is true, he says, that "it all starts with selection of the right people. If they don't have team skills and traits of listening, problem solving, and the humility to say 'I made a mistake,' then you have to develop them." When asked if he thought humility could be developed, Palmer responded: "Even though we think of humility as inherent in a person, we do know that people can change. But the desire to change must be present."

Palmer looks back on the beginning of the Saturn experiment:

> Probably, we should have had more structure and more direction in the beginning than we did. It's somewhat like situational leadership, when we can gradually reduce the direction

and loosen the reins as individuals gain maturity and readiness in their jobs. We treated the teams as if they were already high performing teams . . . already in the fourth quadrant. And that just wasn't the case, however much potential team skills they are diagnosed as having. And after six years, it's tough to go back and try to impose structure and direction on a body of people who are not used to it.

## A High-Performing Team Today

Saturn seems to have ironed out most of the glitches. Today, the pride at Saturn is obvious, and workers exhibit a strong commitment to their company and appreciate the opportunity to make their own decisions.

It took time to build, but the partnership between Saturn and the auto workers' union is in some measure responsible for the cars' high quality ratings. A revolutionary labor agreement makes partners of Saturn's blue- and white-collar workers and gives everyone the authority to solve quality problems. Now employees truly believe in the culture.

## Preserving the Intent

From the beginning Saturn has recognized that for teams to be successful, there has to be a clear declaration of purpose to keep the enterprise on track. Saturn's team structure pushes the intent of the quality vision and value structure throughout the organization, from the corporate office down to the teams (of which there are six hundred) where policy is actually executed and the product is produced. Beginning with SAC (Strategic Action Council), down through MAC (Manufacturing Action Council), business team units, modules, and, finally, the teams themselves, the system ensures the transmission of the company's expectation by having one person from each team participate in the team immediately above. For example, Bob Boruff, Vice President of Manufacturing, is a member of the corporate council on quality. He is also a member of MAC. One member of the MAC team is in turn on the business team, and so on.

Every aspect of the business is addressed at the top and at the bottom. This ensures that the real intent stays intact, the language doesn't get muddled, and all people have meaningful access to the decision-making process. In addition, team members are responsible for thirty working functions. The Saturn experience illustrates that a chain of command doesn't have to be a barrier to an open communicative process, when total involvement is a part of the making and execution of policy.

## How Saturn Operates

Saturn employees work in high-performing work units and are charged with making a lot of decisions about their jobs. They track their own quality performance, draft maintenance schedules, manage their budgets, and coordinate team training. Each team is responsible for screening and hiring its own new members. Line workers who encounter defective parts can telephone the supplier to recommend a fix; members of a Saturn machine maintenance team can order many of the tools and parts they need, speeding up repairs and getting rid of time-consuming bureaucratic purchase orders.

The teams monitor themselves to make sure they're performing as well as they can. For example, one person checks scrap and receives weekly reports on the amount of waste. If the line on the chart is rising, she reminds everyone during a team meeting that they need to be more careful. Since team members know the cost of each part, they know how much money their scrap costs the company. Once a year, the team forecasts the amount of company resources it plans to use in the coming year. Each month team members get a report on what they budgeted and how much they actually spent. Teams also get a monthly breakdown of their telephone bills.

Each team member knows the other members' jobs, receives the same salary as other members, and rotates jobs regularly so that no employee performs the same task for weeks on end. Each team's function is to add value to the product, and the work is designed so that the results are always measurable.

Within the teams, there's no such thing as a democratic vote. Decisions are made by consensus. If the team cannot come to a decision, the team counselor intervenes and helps out the process. According to Palmer, people in the team need to get 70 percent comfortable with a decision, but when they leave the room, they must support the decision 100 percent.

### Bringing People Together

Saturn has tried to deemphasize the difference between management and workers in different ways. There are no executive dining rooms and no reserved executive parking spaces.

Each module has two advisers (team leaders), one of whom is a United Auto Workers representative and the other a nonunion employee. The system is designed so that decisions are made in partnership between

UAW employees and management, which gives the employees a sense of empowerment.

Work unit counselors within the teams themselves are chosen by team members to help coordinate and integrate work to help ensure that team goals are met. To say that management is totally absent is an over-statement, since there is an appointed team leader who manages a num-ber of teams and a Saturn UAW representative to complement each team leader. These leaders, who act as unifiers, intervene when the teams are not able to come to a consensus and resolve conflicts or dilemmas. But the goal is for these leaders to be needed less and less as the teams mature.

### Emphasis on Training

Saturn also demonstrates its commitment to a quality culture by its em-phasis on continuous improvement and team training. All Saturn em-ployees are expected to spend at least 5 percent of their time in one of the company's more than 650 training programs. Here again, though, Saturn has learned some lessons. Bob Palmer says that Saturn forgot that there are some basic components of team development, such as trust, that need time to develop. He discusses some experiential training given early on when employees hardly knew each other, much less cared about each other. "This was pretty scary, when you think about this," says Palmer. "Here these guys were scaling mountain ledges, depending on others to catch them when they fell back, and they didn't even know or like each other at this point, much less have any trust developed."

Palmer continues, "It is also quite a different situation to train in classroom or vestibule settings from the actual assembly of an automobile on the line. And it is also dramatically different when you are making ten cars a day, versus sixty an hour. You just can't have that sense of urgency."

By 1990 Saturn had realized that workers needed basic skills training. Each worker was given from three hundred to seven hundred hours of schooling in basic skills such as conflict management and problem solv-ing. Now every team member is required to take ninety-two hours of training a year; some of this training is technical, while some is more human-resources-oriented, focusing on skills such as problem solving and listening. Every team member has some eight or nine functions to perform in the team, including maintaining safety and industrial engi-neering. As a team member adds roles, he or she must incorporate sup-porting courses into his or her training plan. For example, an operating technician may have to take courses not only in engine assembly but in problem solving. The teams themselves are continuously changing as new people are added, so workers receive a great deal of continuous training in problem solving, including collaboration and consensus skills. The plant's Workplace Development Center allows engineers and teams to try out new processes on a simulated assembly line. Engineers videotape the workers in action and look for wasted motion—but the team must decide whether to accept the engineers' suggestions for improvement.

### Saturn's Continuing Challenge

Saturn's advantage in the quality initiative is that it was founded on a philosophy of continuous improvement; from its beginning, teams were expected continuously to raise the benchmarks of their work. But great expectations can sometimes be a company's albatross.

Like Motorola, which continues to wow the world with its nearly defect-free products and must continue to benchmark against itself, Saturn must live up to its reputation for high-performing teamwork. Bob Boruff is quick to suggest that "we are not there yet. We are still evolving." Try to tell that to a Saturn automobile owner, who is quick to remind you that the car's performance proves the benefits of highly developed teamwork.

## Putting the Team Concept into Practice at Square D

Other companies are integrating quality components like teamwork into the overall operation. Square D-Groupe Schneider has managed to reduce cycle time as a result of teamwork, contributing to increased profitability and market share. One local plant that was nearly closed is turning itself around by processes put into place to set up internal audits and to improve supplier quality, internal operations, and engineering. According to Bob Sheffield, Plant Manager at Middletown, Ohio, at the time of the near closing, Square D now knows that improving quality involves a lot of employee commitment, a team-centered approach, and employee involvement beyond traditional line inspections. Employees at Square D are trained to audit the quality program's effectiveness internally and even to audit others plants' progress in achieving high levels of performance.

At the Square D plant in Smyrna, Tennessee, team leaders' efforts brought the plant from a defect rate of 6.8 defects per unit in 1989 to 1.8 defects per unit in 1993.

The STAR team concept, which has been in place since 1990, is in large part responsible for the company's quality achievements. Employees in different functions, such as metal-clad (an assembly operation), are divided into teams like bussing (electrical conductors installation in switch gear). As Rick Agee, Manager of the Metal-Clad Unit, explains, on each team one person is responsible for each of the five points in the star: director, human resources, quality of work life (QWL), productivity, and quality. These teams have responsibility and authority over many of the major decisions that affect their own quality and productivity, such as a change in a quality checklist, an addition of a one-time operation for quality, work schedules, and development of team goals. On decisions affecting other departments, such as purchasing of major equipment, the teams can make recommendations and have more limited control. They have no authority over decisions related to company policy or benefit changes.

Each member of the STAR team has specific responsibilities. Bussing has a director who coordinates team meetings, sets up work schedules, and is more or less a control point for all reports. The human resources person schedules training, coordinates vacation schedules, coordinates peer evaluations, and tracks overtime. The QWL person organizes safety topics, evaluates housekeeping, maintains tool inventory, and is responsible for maintenance planning and coordination. The productivity person tracks production and schedules, provides production information, and reviews team progress, including goals. Last, the quality person issues monthly quality reports, gathers and maintains quality data, and coordinates with other teams on quality issues.

Teams look at root causes of defects and determine the necessary corrective action, who should take it, by when, and what the impact will be. These plans are posted where team members can refer to them. Team members track their own progress. Defects are not classified as major or minor; all defects are considered unacceptable.

As team members are interdependent on each other, so are all teams interdependent as they work to achieve a high-quality product and to maintain high productivity. "We've worked hard not to have lines of demarcation," says Agee. "We're all accountable for the quality of our final products." Each team understands not just where it fits into the Smyrna plant but where it fits into the global mission.

Agee explains that it took a lot of time and patience to get the teams to perform at the level they're performing at presently. Even though the idea of teams was not new to the culture, self-direction was. Some of the managers were skeptical and somewhat resistant in the beginning. "It meant learning to coach, rather than direct, and that is always slower," says Agee. With the reduction in reject rate, it has obviously been worth it. As testimony to the success of the STAR concept, Square D team members were able to design, build, and deliver the switch gear for the World Trade Center in less than six weeks, defect-free, whereas the estimated time before the introduction of the new structure would have been closer to six months!

## From the Factory Floor to the Office at Motorola

Motorola's dedication to quality shows up in its teamwork. In 1990 the total customer satisfaction team process was formalized in a problem-solving team competition, called Total Customer Satisfaction Team Competition. By 1992 the number of teams had increased to thirty-seven hundred, with twenty-four teams competing at the corporate level for the gold. Since that time the number of teams has grown to include more than 30 percent of Motorola's employees. The most recent competition drew more than five thousand teams from Motorola offices around the world. Teams are judged on the basis of seven criteria: teamwork; difficulty of the problem the team had set out to solve; quality of analysis; remedies; results; institutionalization; and presentations. Improvement processes have ranged from asset management to environmental responsibility. As a result of these improvements, Motorola has saved millions of dollars and significantly improved quality of products and services.

Some of Motorola's plants are moving toward self-directed teams. At the cellular equipment plant in Arlington Heights, Illinois, for example, self-directed teams hire and fire members, help select their supervisors, and schedule their own work. In 1993 the factory's 1,003 workers also assembled 168 special teams dedicated to improving quality, cutting costs, and reducing cycle time. General Manager Rick Chandler maintains that "teams help America use one of its great competitive advantages, the diversity of its people. They bring together people with different backgrounds, different cultures, different ideas."

Motorola is now pushing the concept of quality teams, so successful on the factory floor, into the office. Quality Director Richard Buetow estimates that the company will reduce overhead by $2 billion annually by having office employees work more efficiently.

For example, two years ago Motorola's property rights department was extremely backlogged in filing applications for patents on products and processes invented by company scientists. Engineers were spending days filling out disclosure forms. Patent attorneys spent still more hours rewriting those disclosures into legalese.

Working together, a team of lawyers and engineers reduced the standard invention disclosure form from fifteen pages to two, and reduced the backlog without adding staff. The streamlined disclosure process saved the company the equivalent of forty-four years of engineering time last year.

Motorola has started pushing suppliers to analyze how much quality defects add to their own costs. It gets its suppliers to help from the very start in designing parts and figuring out how to make them. Motorola realizes that suppliers sometimes understand better than customers how to design specialized high-tech parts to minimize their material and manufacturing costs.

Motorola has come to value its suppliers' inputs so much that it has established a council of suppliers to rate Motorola's own practices and to offer suggestions for improving the accuracy of such internal outputs as production schedules and design layouts.


## Teams Can Include Customers, Too

DuPont Films has become more cost-competitive and is better able to respond to its customers because of a team structure that has built a partnership-oriented way of doing business, with the customer at the center. The company is organized into strategic business units, each an autonomous but well-connected business team consisting of business, marketing, manufacturing, supply, service, and R & D experts.

The change from a functional to an integrated structure at Mylar (an operation within DuPont Films) began in 1987 because of the results of the first Mylar customer satisfaction survey.

According to Kelli Kukura, DuPont's Manager of State Government and Public Affairs, "Our results weren't good enough, so we knew we had to reengineer the business to reduce cycle time and produce higher quality. Today, by moving people out of functionality, they think less internally and focus more on the customer's needs."

The teams include members from what used to be called "functions," or work areas, such as research and development, marketing, and business management. These teams have helped Mylar make significant improvement in meeting ship dates from the plants to their customers.

Mickey Williams, an ISO team member, explains the impact of eliminating titles and levels in the plant.

> When we're working on a problem on the line, there will be a bunch of people out there and you won't be able to tell the business unit manager from an engineer from an operator . . . since we're all communicating freely. Titles are a little fuzzy. Here you just call who you need; everybody's on a first name basis; if it's a marketing person, you just call him or her. And nobody gets hung up with titles or functions. Roles mean nothing; what matters is the customer.

It used to be that only DuPont managers made customer site visits. Today, explains Williams, "DuPont customer teams share with customers on a monthly and quarterly basis all their quality data." Kukura explains the benefits of having team members actually interact with the customer. She asks, "Who better than a DuPont packager who knows the process to interact with that person who unpacks the product at the customer site?" Having built these partnerships with its customers for more than a decade, DuPont finds that the level of trust is now so high that customers don't sample the truck.

To quantify the success of the customer team program, Sam Bogle, Manager of Customer Service, points out that, out of the DMT (dimethyl-terathalate) plant's shipment of more than ten thousand loads of product to customers, in addition of transfer of product to its on-site customer, DuPont has had only one customer concern.

### Flexibility and Diversity as Key Ingredients in Team Development

One factor responsible for speeding the process at DuPont is the diversity of skills and the flexibility exercised by the employees. ISO team members explain that "it's not in my job description" is a banned phrase at DuPont. According to one ISO team member, Billy Joe Hinson, in the past, when there was a problem with maintenance at 3:00 A.M., workers would call in the pipe fitter. Now, because employees have been cross-trained and work together so closely, the person on the line just fixes the problem and keeps the line running.

Ronnie Pugh, safety team leader, explains the flexibility in the DuPont culture.

> Our structure used to be one supervisor over the whole shift; now we have what we call "process people." The wage person-

nel, who have taken on a lot of responsibility to run the line, set the team up to work on the lines. In other words, you check the line to see where you're working that day. In 1987 volunteers were asked to go to line four; approximately thirty-six of us volunteered to go. We went down there as a team. We set this line up. We made suggestions.

Pugh cites an example where the team creatively solved a space problem: "Back in Dacron days, we needed an office—a cubicle. One of the operators suggested a cubicle in Shipping that wasn't being used—it was idle. We tore the cubicle down, we saved money on both ends, and everybody won."

DuPont Films has realized a number of benefits from its customer team initiatives. Any member of the team now feels empowered and takes a leadership role when talking about customers' needs. Levels and functional "turf" have passed away, as the organization has moved toward a horizontal operation. DuPont team members have been able to make significant improvement in meeting ship dates from the plants to the customers. Quality has been improved by the installation of new and sophisticated computer interfaces that allow team members to measure their efforts against the final product and by the integration of a supply process that tracks critical areas from the customer's order back to the raw material. Finally, the customer service operation has achieved ISO 9001 certification and has enhanced the performance of the entire chain.

## Using Teams to Benchmark and Improve Processes at Eastman Chemical

Teamwork is the foundation for employee involvement at Eastman Chemical. Eastman leaders work alongside other company personnel to make decisions, find new and better ways to manage, and see that customers receive full value for products and services. Their "let's work together" philosophy has motivated men and women to commit to quality as a way of life.

The people on teams are chosen on the basis of some special expertise they can contribute.

### Improving Products and Services

At all levels, interlocking teams constantly look for new and innovative ways to increase customer satisfaction. These teams enable employees to develop objectives and measures that are integrated with company and organizational goals as defined by the Strategic Quality Planning Process. Through these teams, employees are able to improve processes and to manage their part of the business for continual improvement.

This interlocking team structure involves all employees through their natural unit teams and provides a direct link from operators to senior management. Earnie Deavenport, CEO and Chairman of the Board, chairs a weekly all-day meeting of what is called an interlocking team, actually a type of steering committee. The agenda includes only quality-related subjects. As at Saturn, the members are senior managers who in turn are leaders of teams made up of people who report to them, and so on down the line. Conversely, from the bottom up, the leader of every team is in turn a member of a team one step higher. Also as at Saturn, this ensures that the quality vision moves up and down.

Each team uses the company's Strategic Quality Management Process to understand and anticipate the needs of both internal and external customers, to define key processes and measures, and to continuously improve. Other teams are formed to improve specific processes, tackle projects, or build long-term relationships with suppliers and customers.

In its supplier improvement program, Eastman employees team with key suppliers to improve the quality and value of purchased materials, equipment, and services. Eastman's supplier program in 1994 was named one of the ten most copied supplier relations processes in U.S. industry by *Purchasing* magazine. Eastman has more than twenty-five supplier teams.

Eastman encourages innovation and provides a structured way to link ideas for new products with corporate business plans. Through the Eastman Innovation Process, a team of employees from various areas, such as business, sales, research, engineering, and manufacturing, shepherds a product idea from inception to market. Customer needs are considered early and then are validated and revalidated throughout the innovation process. Each design's plan is developed by a project team and reviewed with an innovation committee, led by the vice president of the business organization sponsoring the project and comprising a cross-functional representation of business, research, development, and functional managers.

As a result of the Eastman Innovation Process, the time to bring a new product to market has been reduced by 50 percent since 1990.

The work of the interlocking teams has also had major impact. The teams precipitated a major internal reorganization of the company in 1991, allowing only four levels of management. Quality improvement teams are credited with raising the first-pass yield on plastic for beverage bottles to 95 percent.

One of Eastman's quality improvement teams found that maintenance problems that resulted in shutdowns, breakdowns, and installation of equipment were a source of product variation—a much unwanted source of variation. The team worked on the linkage between maintenance and the manufacturing operation, resulting in a system that had production workers do light maintenance work and that trained maintenance workers in second and third skills so that jobs were not held up waiting for a specialist. The improved maintenance program at Eastman Chemical is credited with saving $24 million since its inception in the early 1980s.

Mike Warner, Total Productive Maintenance Coordinator and a twenty-five-year veteran at Eastman, explains one team initiative of which he's been a part. The initiative requires sharing skills between two crafts. Warner explains that craft people from different "natural unit teams" (teams employees work in during their daily operations) come together to share their skills.

> One team member, from, say, Electrical, will define some process that they want to improve and define who they rely on for support in that process. They will then either go to members of that other craft, say, mechanical, and express the interest to share their skills to improve the process. Or they may indicate this interest to the coordinator to facilitate the process.

Warner explains that often what workers choose to work on has been influenced by the Employee Development Program (a performance appraisal and development plan), which encourages employees to look continually at what needs to be improved. It is a process in which representatives agree on what they want to share. This process is supported by senior management, but it is driven by the teams.

One problem addressed by this process was the downtime that resulted when a motor had to be replaced. After the motor was pulled, there was a delay until an electrician showed up to do his job and then another delay waiting for the mechanic to resume his job. By the time the electrician had completed his part of the job, the mechanic was working on something else, so there was another delay as the mechanic finished the second installation. This downtime resulted from the fact that different work orders were required for each phase.

Mike Warner explains how the process works.

> After a problem is pinpointed, the coordinator then gets the members together to decide what they want to share. Electrical

says, in effect, we're going to relinquish "our job" on this process, to make it more efficient for the overall mission, but we will guide the process, for the sake of efficiency.

With the beginning of the new process, the first question asked the craft members is, "If you were running this company, that is, if you were the owner and had the responsibility to make this process better and more efficient, what tasks would you select to do in this process?" Craft members then determine selection criteria and narrow tasks down, analyzing them and doing a cost-benefit analysis. The electricians stay with the process and work with the mechanics to guide them in a breakout of the tasks. The electricians write the lesson plans and actually conduct the training.

This partnership has produced amazing results. When asked about why they do this, craft members responded, "It makes my job easier."

Last year Eastman's shift crews alone completed fifty-six hundred tasks, with an average of eighty-three minutes gained from each task. We're talking about *years* of time saved here!

## Making Things Happen through Teams in the Community

Teams are not confined to the private sector. In the U.S. Army Corps of Engineers, for example, teams are changing the way the Corps does business, proof that people who get together can make continuous improvement happen.

One example is seen in partnering initiatives in the Corps. Partnering is a relatively new mechanism in the construction industry. It started as a venture in private industry, as owners seeking construction services decided to adopt the practice of using sole suppliers for services that were being initiated in the manufacturing industry. This idea is based on the belief that a sole supplier will produce a better product or service over time when a strong personal relationship has been developed with a client. Although the basic practices followed in partnering have been well established for years, it is only recently that government agencies have begun employing those practices. In the Corps of Engineers, team partnering efforts have translated into significant improvements in morale, delivery, cost, and quality. In 1993 the Louisville District had more than thirty-three working partnerships in projects totaling almost $300 million. So successful have been its team efforts that the Canadian National Defense Headquarters used the district to benchmark on a $25 million project in 1994. (For more information on the Corps's partnering results, see Chapter 18.)

As discussed in Chapter 12, teams are also used by the U.S. Department of Agriculture, where Resource Conservation and Development (RC&D) coordinators from the Soil Conservation Service team up with volunteers in the community to care for and protect their natural resources in a way that will improve the area's economy, environment, and living standards. These RC&D coordinators help reduce cropland erosion and preserve historical and scenic sites, primarily by funding grants. They develop goals, objectives, and strategies for accomplishing everything from creating a market for wood pellets (made from compressed sawdust) in Missouri to providing technical assistance in farming methods to Native Americans in Arizona.

## The Challenge Ahead for Teams

Teams aren't new, but most employees working in U.S. companies had very little experience with them until recent years, because they were conditioned during the derailment at a time when hierarchical management reigned supreme. Internal competition is antithetical to teamwork, and during the 1970s most managers discouraged teamwork when they promoted functionality by allocating resources and goals to functions. These hierarchical managers assumed that by overseeing the functions through locally defined measures and controls, they would help the organization compete successfully. They managed toward specifications and standards within functions.

Companies starting getting off-track as functions became more and more inwardly focused, busying themselves with thinking up ways to compete against each other, rather than focusing on how the functions related to each other and to the overall value stream for the customer.

Although the idea of a virtually classless organization remains alien to many corporate hierarchies, companies that are back on track recognize the benefits of teamwork. Even with outsiders, they are beginning to recognize that the real key to success is not defeating an opponent but cooperating to manage a continuously changing environment.

Successful organizations are beginning to initiate structures and systems to enable teams to work together for the good of the customer. Whether they're in the form of customer-supplier teams or cross-functional teams or strategic business units, all teams stress flexibility, adaptability, and integration of skills for customer value. And most are headed by team leaders, chosen by their peers, who must depend more on persuasion than on rank to move people to action and who recognize the strength that each individual worker can bring to the team.

# 14

# The Conductor's Creed: What's Really OK to Do

## The Role of Values in Developing a Quality Culture

Former Speaker of the House Sam Rayburn was once asked by a journalist, "Mr. Rayburn, you are asked so many questions by so many people. How can you remember who you've said 'yes' to and who you've said 'no' to?" Speaker Rayburn replied, "If you tell the truth the first time, you don't have to remember."

Values are principles that keep people centered and give them strength in periods of self-doubt. They provide perhaps the only possible security in periods of great change and turbulence, and they also unify across diverse cultures, life phases, and functions.

Every time I talk to Judy Baines, Manager of Customer Service at Jimmy Dean Foods (Sara Lee), she alludes to integrity. She says that if you do what's right all the time, you don't have to remember whether or not it's politically expedient. According to her, employees must not jeopardize a relationship with a customer by failing to return telephone calls, nor can they fail to treat internal customers as they would want to be treated.

Knowing where you're going and what your ethical boundaries are enables you to make the right decisions on a daily basis and to withstand the pain that those decisions sometimes bring. Stephen Covey, in his book *The 7 Habits of Highly Effective People*, encourages readers to begin "with the end in mind":

> By keeping that end in mind, you can make certain that whatever you do on any particular day does not violate the criteria

you have defined as supremely important, and that each day of your life contributes in a meaningful way to the vision you have of your life as a whole.

Although a few managers still consider values and ethics to be a purely personal matter between individuals and their consciences, most successful leaders believe that wrongdoing and ethical breaches are management issues. High-performing organizations have a well-defined set of guiding principles that govern policies and actions.

## The Historical Emphasis on Values

For years many management leaders have acknowledged the importance of organizational values in achieving high quality. They have known that the quality of employees' minds will do them good only if it is supported by the quality of their integrity.

Alfred P. Sloan, the former GM president, who created GM's original management system, said in his 1941 book, *Adventures of a White-Collar Man*, that industrial management must expand its horizons of responsibility and "recognize that it can no longer confine its activities to the mere production of goods and services. . . . It must consider the impact of its operation on the economy as a whole in relation to the social and economic welfare of the entire community. . . . Those charged with great industrial responsibility must become industrial statesmen."

Tom Watson, the first president of IBM, wrote an entire book, *A Business and Its Beliefs*, about values, in which he affirmed that the most important thing about an organization is having a sound set of beliefs on which it premises all its policies and actions.

Others have affirmed the importance of values for achieving high quality. In *In Search of Excellence*, Tom Peters insists that excellent companies are clear on what they stand for and have a well-defined set of guiding beliefs. Steven Covey, in his book *Principled-Center Leadership*, emphasizes the important role that values play in keeping people centered in periods of turbulence. And in the early 1990s, various business periodicals published articles on organizational ethics, emphasizing that those companies that have been honest with their customers have benefited in terms of market share.

## Derailed From the Value of Values

Like so many other things we seemed to drop by the wayside, during the 1970s corporations didn't pay much attention to values and ethics. Large multinational corporations viewed success and failure strictly in terms of earnings per share of stock. If earnings were high, the business was considered good. If they were low, business was considered a failure. In one sense, businesses did define what they valued—the bottom line for the short run. But people generally did not enter the equation except to the extent that their performance hurt or enhanced market share. In that climate, unethical business decisions were considered justified. The devotion to the bottom line prompted ethical compromises, and American business during the 1970s in the most part accepted them.

Then I watched senior executives, in blind pursuit of the bottom line, force talented men into early retirement, falsify facts to make themselves look good to the corporate office, and lower product quality standards. Largely, these actions were the result of a blind devotion to a system that was, for the most part, unchecked. In quality meetings, rarely did I hear comments about the impact on internal or external customers of the decisions to lower standards.

In the corporate world of the late 1970s, many employees had a tough time figuring out what some of the managers stood for. It seemed that values were dictated by the crisis of the day. It may have been zero defects; it may have been camouflaging employee attitude surveys so the responses would look good to headquarters. Because of an absence of shared values, employees often had to wait around for the head guy to show up to define the value and the priority for that day. In his absence, they simply could not determine what the primary value that day was and therefore could operate only in a reactive mode.

## Affirming Shared Values

Organizations are paying more attention to the connection between values and sustained high quality. "Though integrity strategies may vary in design and scope, all strive to define companies' guiding values and aspirations," according to Lynn Sharp Paine in an article that appeared in HBR for March-April, 1994. Those values form the bedrock of a leader's vision. If that vision means shading or hiding the truth to improve the bottom line, those values will infect the entire organization.

Many participants in our training seminars note that their "shared values" have been announced from their corporate offices. This approach may have worked in the command and control structures of an earlier time, but it does not work in today's diverse work environment. If leaders don't want their goals sabotaged, they must seek to get all employees involved in affirming what they value. Developing shared values is as much about asking people for their involvement as it is telling them what's important.

Two questions are critical to developing shared values: "What do we really value?" and "Do these values guide us in our daily actions?"

## Communicating Values Throughout the Organization

People at FedEx have internalized CEO Fred Smith's values about 100 percent customer satisfaction. Just how deeply employees have internalized this corporate value to quality was evident at a meeting of new hired hourly workers, one of whom questioned the standard and was abruptly interrupted by a senior employee. The employee gave Smith's response by asking, as Smith would have, "How many of you would like to fly on an airplane that guaranteed 99 percent defect-free flights?" Smith believes that if values are to be institutionized, management must repeat them through visible, understandable policies, procedures, and programs and then be certain that employees really share them.

Bob Boruff, Vice President of Manufacturing at Saturn Corporation, says that effective leaders clearly communicate what's "really OK to do." They are clear on what they stand for. Boruff is an example of a manufacturing executive who is involved at the top with setting the vision but who also stays connected to the bottom of the pyramid where the product is actually produced. He is a member of the Saturn Action Council, that policy-making body at the helm of the organization, as well as a member of the manufacturing action council. In talking with Boruff, I am struck by how much the long-range vision means to him and by the importance of the organizational values that guide the activities at Saturn. The first time I met him, I was expecting someone who would talk only powertrain and camshafts; instead, he talked almost exclusively about the role of values in organizations.

Boruff explains the role of values:

> Our particular society, as it pertains to industrial America, has always been one-dimensional. We've tended to focus on just the short term, the bottom line, and everything we've done has been directed at that. And we've tended to forget everything else. Our vision has not been long term, and consequently, we are constantly in search of the easy answer or the silver bullet. We ask, "What can I do today which will by next week effect

radical change?" That's not the nature of human behavioral change. It is a matter of the change in culture which in general terms leverages the human capital of your enterprise.

He explains that the focus workers bring to their quality effort, whether it's engineering or hanging fenders on a car, is the "manifestation of what can I get out of my chair and do today that will result in customer satisfaction?"

Boruff came from General Motors, as many of the managers and senior leaders at Saturn did, where the culture was top-down and hierarchical. He explains that the focus at General Motors, like that in most of corporate America, was short term. He says that now "we've rediscovered 'Poor Richard's Almanac' ": in other words, the company has rediscovered some very basic principles that it had tended to forget for a while. He ruefully explains how corporate America is often in search of the latest "mecca." Boruff uses a metaphor to explain the U.S. tendency to grab the latest trend or label to stay on top of things. "If we stand back and look, we see the more traditional theorems that say 3 + 3 equals 6, others who say the square root of 36 is 6; we just need to recognize a 6 when we see one and bring discipline to that. Labels don't change the principle or the value." He explains how Saturn resists this urge. "I think the Saturn difference is understanding human beings, what they value, their behaviors, and what elicits certain kinds of behavior."

Boruff stresses the importance of communicating to people what's really "OK to do":

> We as human beings act out what is near and dear to our hearts. Our values modify our behavior, whether it is business teams or Saturn as a whole. Whether it's called mission, credo, or operational philosophy, companies often dutifully pin it to the wall, and then people go about their regular work and operate outside of that. This is what's on the wall, but what drives this behavior are our real values, meaning what's really OK to do. That's what we have to be clear on and practice.

### The Impact of the Leader's Actions on Employees

Boruff believes that the degree to which what's "really OK to do" is communicated across and down an organization will come to define the culture: "People will not generally act outside their value system. Everything a leader does and says in his demeanor should indicate 'OK' behavior. The leader describes the value."

People at all levels are "boss" or "leader" watchers. People sometimes pay more attention to remarks you make around the water fountain than they do to those you make in training sessions or team meetings. If the leader is preoccupied with quality, they will be, too. The leader must ensure constancy of purpose and avoid shifting values. If leaders themselves seek to control information or cover up facts, so will their employees. More than they sometimes wish, leaders play an extensive teaching role and must therefore model the type of behavior that is expected of everyone else in the organization.

Boruff believes that the number one responsibility of a leader is to be the keeper of the value system. Explains Boruff, "I used to listen to eloquent speeches about quality in GM. And then in that split moment after the guy sat down, when I saw his expression implying, "glad that crap is over with," in that moment he communicated more to me than a whole hour of flip charts."

Boruff believes that leaders manage themselves each day to be and to do what really matters most.

> This is a tough step, because you have to look in a mirror and say, "I'm not nearly as great as I thought I was." You don't have to go far to find what this value system is; the people in the organization can tell you precisely what that value system is. People go through dozens of mission, vision, and value statements; they say, "We did everything the consultant said." I say, "Yeah, but you didn't do anything *different* in your day-to-day operation."

Boruff maintains that there are five simple principles of quality leadership:

1. Determining what's really OK today
2. Determining what you want that OK something to be
3. Examining policies and procedures and processes to see if they are aligned with that ideal
4. Changing policies to enable people to get to that state
5. Having the courage to stay on course.

Saturn's employees believe in these principles, which, according to Boruff, enable Saturn to predict their contribution. There are no inspectors at Saturn. Everyone has the responsibility to produce good quality. Boruff defines some assumptions Saturn makes about human beings:

1. People want to do a good job.
2. People are trustworthy.
3. People want to be successful.
4. People want to be associated with high-quality products.
5. People's behavior reflects how they are treated.

Boruff says the team culture at Saturn illustrates the role of structure in backing up Saturn's mission statement: to clarify what's "OK to do." This clear declaration of purpose, he adds, keeps the enterprise on track. He explains that Saturn's team structure pushes the intent of the quality vision and value structure throughout the organization, down to the teams (of which there are six hundred) where policy is actually executed and the product is produced.

Boruff explains that Saturn's belief that the front-line people "own" the process must be backed up by enabling processes and systems. According to Boruff, "they [employees] must have access to whatever information—including financial—they need to implement ideas." Saturn, he says, believes that enabling processes must be in place to allow that to happen.

## Shared Values as Guiding Principles for Actions

Articulating a set of values isn't enough; the values have to be integrated into quality decisions on a day-to-day basis. They should guide the search for opportunities and the designs of new systems and processes. Managers have a responsibility to help shape organizational ethics; those who ignore that responsibility are shunning one of the primary responsibilities of leadership. Managers, for example, must communicate that it's OK to share bad news in a business meeting but not OK to control information.

The Tylenol scare of 1986, in which a Peekskill, New York, woman died after swallowing a cyanide-laced Tylenol capsule, has often been cited as an example of how a shared set of values can get a company successfully through troubled waters. The decision to recall all Tylenol capsules on shelves around the country in order to avoid further loss of life was made swiftly and cohesively, largely because the Johnson & Johnson culture had a companywide policy of putting ethical conduct foremost in all its business and management decisions. It therefore didn't have to sell employees on its decision. Tylenol simply came off the shelves. And that was that. The pervasiveness of the value of being honest with the customer ensured that everyone would buy into the decision.

Although integrity is a bit tough to define, for many it means behaving as one would expect others to behave and treating people the way one would want to be treated. People are not willing to follow someone they can't believe, who doesn't walk his talk on quality and customer satisfaction.

Judy Baines, Director of Customer Service of Jimmy Dean Foods, shares all the responsibilities with those she supervises. I have personally watched her over the years roll up her sleeves and do whatever needs to be done, sometimes on an assembly line production to get the product out, without regard for her rank or title.

## The Historical Emphasis on Values in the Military

The military has always stressed the importance of values like integrity, both for daily operations and for its future success. The military is now stressing values to help design and build a Quality Department of Defense for the future.

Integrity is stressed by an Air Force manual on leadership as a "life-essential element of every job, from filing work order requests to launching combat sorties." "Courage," proclaims the Air Force, is often needed in the pursuit of long-term improvement: "The temptation may be to apply a quick fix that gives fast results, but offers only short-term gains." Similarly, the Army encourages all managers to consider organizational values in measuring employees' performances.

## The Key to Withstanding the Struggle

Knowing what's really important can help you believe that your decisions are truly correct and enable you to withstand the financial and emotional pain that often accompanies those decisions. Several times in my career, I have been confronted with job-threatening situations where I was asked to do something unethical. At GE, I found it just as impossible to change findings to make them "look better" to the corporate office as I found it to change students' grades at a university to look better to the administration. Both those decisions were values-based, and both, although they hurt me financially in the short run, enabled me to gain in the long run.

I discussed the first of these incidents in Chapter 5. The second occurred many years ago, when I had been a college professor for only two years. I had a student who never came to class, never turned in work, despite my repeated attempts to motivate him, and consequently did not pass the course. He was known to have quite a lot of charm and power, which he leveraged with both students and faculty. During this time a lot of pressure was placed on the faculty to pass students in community colleges, since the number of FTEs (full-time equivalencies) generated in large part determined funding.

After I turned in my class's grades, the academic dean called me into his office and, along with the chairman of my department, asked me to change the grade. Having nothing to base any grade on, I replied that I could not do that. I was therefore asked to resign, which I did, and went to work in a donut shop for $1.40 an hour. But I had the peace of knowing I had done the right thing. A couple of months after that, I was awarded an assistantship to work on my doctorate, an honor that I probably would not have received had I been known to award undeserved grades to students.

It is liberating to see higher quality and continuous improvement valued today in colleges as well as in industry. For some people, the same ethical care that led to pain in an earlier time today reaps its reward.

# 15

# Who's Driving This Train Anyway?

## Leadership Required to Stay on Track

Organizations in virtually every era tend to produce men and women who seem to have so much of an impact on an organization that it is never quite the same again. It may be a positive or negative influence on quality and productivity, but it is an influence, nonetheless.

### And the Difference Is . . . Leadership

The 1970s made it clear that management practices really do make a difference to the bottom line. It was not just the abundance of management but the absence of leadership that significantly hurt America's quality initiatives. In its overmanaged and underled state during those years, U.S. business learned that the leadership gap had a lot to do with the lack of commitment companies received from employees. Since leadership has to do with providing a vision and management has to do with carrying it out, managers in the 1970s and early 1980s were caught up in administering the status quo and stretching it for all it was worth, for there was no overarching vision beckoning them to do otherwise.

Business has learned from its mistakes. A multitude of books and articles over the past decade has admonished corporations to groom leaders, not managers, for it is the leaders who shape organizational character and culture. By their own dynamism and caring spirit, they move organizations forward.

Today business leaders debate the specific characteristics required to keep organizations competitive and on track in their quality journey. There is a lot of discussion about the need for charismatic leadership, and yet some of America's greatest leaders—those who got things done—were not particularly charismatic. Men like Abraham Lincoln, Harry Truman, and Dwight Eisenhower are certainly not known today for their charisma, but they accomplished a great deal. Conversely, John Kennedy, whose charm appealed to the hearts of young and old alike, inspired people, but many observers insist that he actually accomplished very little.

The most successful organizations believe in leadership as a primary ingredient in making things happen. They don't dance around the concept but choose leaders who are willing to accept responsibility and accountability. And these leaders are found in every business unit and level of the organization.

There's nothing magical about leadership. It is not the special province of the CEO or senior management. The sheer speed of change in manufacturing and marketing makes it impractical for one person in any given unit or team to make all the decisions needed for industries to be competitive. Individuals must be empowered and willing to step forward in situations that call for their specific mix of skills and judgment. For people on the factory floor, that means having the confidence to speak up when they have the best information or a solution to a problem, rather than waiting for the "boss" to come up with the answer. For managers, it means throwing off old ideas about exercising absolute control over every situation.

FedEx's Fred Smith and the Air Force's Bill Creech are charismatic leaders with customer-focused visions who have been able to energize organizations and people. But even leaders like this will tell you that service leaders aren't always born. They can be developed.

## A Return to the Basics of Leadership

What separates a leader from a nonleader? Basically, it's the ability to get things done. When we're talking about the quality imperative, there are a few basic characteristics that are required, and they transcend specific times and settings.

Until about twenty-five years ago, those who had the most impact on business were those who sacrificed self to cause, were vitally connected to the product and process of the business, and did not let themselves get separated from the factory floor. Because of that connection with product and people, a quality consciousness was automatic. They set clear missions, made their goals consistent with those missions, and ensured that systems and structures were in place to accommodate that mission. They took responsibility for whatever went wrong, but they did not let ambition corrupt their sense of mission. Many of these same leadership characteristics are resurfacing today, characteristics that were significant to producing quality products before companies became layered and mechanical and before the "golden age of management" set in.

Senior and middle managers and individual contributors alike respect those who persistently communicate a commitment to quality through actions, attitudes, and behaviors. This commitment requires courage, patience, tenacity, involvement, and integrity. These characteristics are possessed by those who most inspire and influence others, in both large and small organizations. While they are not yet appreciated by some of the leftover "positional" power brokers conditioned and nurtured during the "derailment," most people today believe that men and women who possess these characteristics will carry the organization forward.

Successful leaders today, like those in earlier days, have a vision of a better future—a future to which the entire organization has a right and of which it can be proud. They demonstrate the courage of their convictions through self-sacrifice, sometimes by working long hours and, if need be, for little money. They have great confidence in their followers—and high standards. They are driven not by money or power but by the satisfaction of building the organization, seeing people develop, and accomplishing things through others. They don't try to sell their vision as much as they help others buy it.

## A Constancy of Purpose: What Are We Trying to Become?

Warren Bennis in *Leaders*, his study of 150 corporate leaders, found that today's successful leaders share a vision and a sense of purpose that are communicated throughout the organization. From commanders in the military to CEOs in private industry, they must clearly define and communicate that purpose and what they want the organization to become. Even the most brilliant vision is worthless unless the leader can articulate that vision to all members of the team and get them to direct their energies toward fulfilling its promise.

The foundation of effective leadership, then, is thinking through the organization's mission (why the organization exists) and defining it clearly, at the same time making sure that the mission is compatible with the overarching vision (what the organization is trying to become). Through their words and actions, leaders move the organization from where it is to where it should be. While they recognize the importance of planning and strategizing for the short term, they also recognize that if they don't define the future and create a unified vision that everyone can get excited about, the organization may have no future. But leaders also recognize that the vision may be modified as events warrant.

Jack Welch's drive to reshape GE began with a vision that GE wasn't truly competitive—a vision that few GE insiders shared in 1980. He made an effort to communicate his vision of GE to everyone in the company, an effort that was difficult to accomplish, and one that took a while to take hold.

Vince Lombardi was able to develop in the Green Bay Packers a shared sense of identity with his goals. The powerful chemistry that developed between the team members and the coach transcended, in Lombardi's view, individual talent and prior professional experience.

There is little question that those who are able to exercise charismatic leadership are able to lead in the creation and articulation of a corporate vision and mission that all employees can get excited about. The entire FedEx operation views as critical to leadership this ability to see what is really important and to transmit that sense of mission to others. Like that of the Green Bay Packers, FedEx's success is, in large measure, due to the vision and tenacity of its leader, and his ability to transmit his own quality vision throughout the organization.

Though some people may tire of hearing about this "vision thing," it certainly is not a new phenomenon. Long before the current leadership writings, the *Army Field Manual* contained this statement: "No successful project is possible without a vision of how it shall conclude." Since then, writers like Stephen Covey, who has had a profound impact on organizations from Saturn to the Department of Defense, has upheld the need to "begin with the end in mind," a clear understanding of destination. As Covey has articulated so well, having this clear vision enables leaders to know that the steps they take are always in the right direction. Adherence to that objective helps keep projects on course.

Clarity of vision can empower the organization. To the extent that senior leadership has been clear about purpose, vision, and values, people will be better able to reconcile competing priorities and ambiguities. If employees hear the message that quality is the most important priority, but find that on a particular day scheduling becomes more critical, they get confused. If they are told that customer responsiveness is at the heart of the business but see that actions are being driven by an internal view, they don't know how to act. If, on the other hand, they celebrate integrity and acknowledge those who continually try to improve the system, employees feel empowered to act even when the "boss" is away.

Constancy isn't just repeating the same thing; it's illustrating it in our policies and actions.

## Illustrating Constancy of Purpose Through Actions

Strong leaders set an example. They understand that their actions demonstrate their commitment to quality and customer service. They are the first to do what has been agreed to and learned.

Leaders are able to communicate their visions in various ways. Some do it quietly and collaboratively, through facilitating and coaching and much behind-the-spotlight work. Jack Smith, CEO of General Motors, has a large stone on his desk with a copper plate attached that reads, "A leader is best when people barely know he exists." Smith gets things done without screaming and barking. He's largely invisible to the public eye. An unassuming man and not the most dynamic speaker, he's edgy in the spotlight. Still, Smith has made great strides in simplifying the kinds of organizational complexities that have frozen GM in the past. Other leaders lead more overtly, through stirring presentations that motivate others to follow. In either case, the proof is in actions, more than in words. This becomes particularly critical in periods of accelerated change and crises. Sharing a vision can go a long way toward helping people endure the struggles.

Leaders don't wait for others to do something. They take responsibility for making things happen. Fred Smith has proven himself a master at verbally communicating FedEx's shared mission of 100 percent customer satisfaction, but he has also demonstrated proactive leadership through his own actions. Bob Brown, Personnel Manager at FedEx, recalls his first experience with Fred Smith.

> I remember the first day on the job when I met him, as we were walking across hangar 6, the hangar where we did all the airplane maintenance, and across the hangar, there was a rag on the floor. I remember Fred saying, "Whose job is it to pick up that rag?" And then he said, "It's mine, because I saw it . . . that's what I want to get across to all our employees, that it's their job to do the things that need to be done." That made

such an impression on me, and I think that's the sort of the philosophy that's permeated the company ever since. Back then, of course, we were a small company, and a lot of people had a lot of interaction with Fred Smith. He still tries to have that interaction, but with one hundred thousand employees, it's tough. His philosophy, though, is still the same.

Since becoming GM's President and CEO in November 1993, Jack Smith has led a remarkable transformation. He has accelerated plant closings and taken big swings at GM's bloated white-collar bureaucracy. He has established simple goals and streamlined the decision-making process. Despite that, he has managed to create a healthy one-on-one relationship with Steve Yokich, who heads the GM Department of the United Auto Workers.

Smith favors participation. He runs an open organization, and he relies on the people around him and defers to them. He doesn't try to micromanage.

He has demonstrated his commitment to destroying GM's bloated bureaucracy by his actions. During 1992 GM reduced its North American payrolls by twenty-six thousand, and by the end of 1995 planned to shed another forty-eight thousand white-collar and blue-collar workers. The number of central corporate staff has been reduced from 13,500 to 2,300.

Those who clearly expect high quality standards and who support the priorities that go along with that earn respect from their colleagues. And they do it all the time. They make clear what's really important.

Good leaders constantly communicate and find opportunities to focus employees on quality. They make their rounds and know what's going on. They take the guesswork out of what constitutes "exceptional performance" by giving employees clear examples in their frame of reference. Realizing that being "the best" comes from focusing people on details as well as on the overall picture, they model the way for continuous improvement in their own work. They share their optimism and get those they're leading to respond with belief in what can be accomplished. And they create the systems and structures to move other people.

## Valuing Customers—External and Internal

You can't legislate or coerce people into a commitment to customers and high quality. But you can show so much commitment to customers yourself that employees "catch" it or feel too self-conscious to omit it. Strong leaders sensitively and continuously determine and assess the wants, needs, and possibilities of their existing and potential customers. They continually send messages to their associates that the customer is the priority. They know that their business plan must include customers and quality in the strategies and action plans that surround them.

They listen to employees, customers, and suppliers alike on what will have value for customers. In turn, they ensure that all parts of the organization listen and respond consistently to information from customers. They reward employees who have gone the extra mile for customers. They demonstrate the courage to tackle anything—structures, systems, even beliefs and values—that is preventing increased value for users.

Successful business leaders provide the resources their people need to serve customers well. In its continuing attempt to link up customer expectations with delivery, Promus Hotels empowers its employees to enact the company's unconditional guarantee. It celebrates progress toward removing barriers to quality through its "best-idea forum" and its President's Award, given to an employee nominated by other employees for his or her ideas on how to improve customer satisfaction.

Customer-focused leaders make it easy for customers to complain and then use the complaints to address the causes behind customers' dissatisfaction.

Customer-focused leaders also recognize the significance of their internal customers to the creation of a high-quality product, as well as the relationship between how employees are treated and how external customers are treated. Earnie Deavenport, Eastman Chemical's Chairman of the Board, insists that the quality of management is more important than the management of quality—that the essence of quality is the sum of the "talents, intellect, creativity, and skills of the people making those products."

Fred Smith, FedEx's CEO, believes that "customer satisfaction begins with employee [internal customer] satisfaction." He has become the epitome of a leadership style that creates a people-first environment by tying company interests to individual concerns. Putting it simply, Smith says, "If you want people to be interested in customer service, you have to answer their fundamental questions, like "What do you expect of me?" and "What's in it for me?" You answer these through visible, understandable policies, procedures, and programs."

Robert Galvin served as CEO of Motorola for thirty-one years, from 1959 until 1990. In the early 1960s, fearing stagnation, Galvin decided that Motorola's future lay in an all-out commitment to microelectronics and semiconductors. Having to start from the bottom, Galvin laid out a ten-

year plan to make Motorola the industry leader by using an intense customer focus as the centerpiece and backing it up with total employee
involvement. He realized the equity of employee commitment to building
a world-class company.

Galvin began a massive effort to decentralize Motorola, changing the
entire management system. Realizing that it would help him surpass the
competition, he fostered empowerment and ownership throughout the
organization. The rest, as they say, is history. Even now, as it leverages its
high quality in Asian markets, Motorola is not content with the quality of
its international pager and cellular phone markets. It spends over $750
million annually on research and development.

Galvin understood that reducing process variability is critical to cap-
turing the market, but he also knew that there was more to the recipe;
employees had to be enthusiastic about it. He recognized the importance
of passion, along with measurement tools.

The systems and structures Galvin set in place still serve to motivate
employees. Motorola's unique bonus system, which reaches all employees, allows employees to increase their salaries by as much as 40 percent,
depending on team and individual accomplishments.

## Straight Communication—Especially During the Tough Times

There is a tendency during periods of downsizings and restructurings for
top management to take the Hussein approach of "hiding in the bunker,"
but this is the very time when employees need most to hear from leaders.
When an organization is under unusual stress, rumors abound and tem-
pers run short. Clear communication is particularly critical. Some managers who are struggling with problems of downsizings and mergers keep
everything to themselves. Because of their reticence, nobody realizes the
depth and complexity of what they have to deal with. Not only do they
keep their concerns to themselves when the numbers are down; they
often don't get all the credit they deserve when things get better.

Lee Iacocca, former president of Chrysler, was not at all silent about
discussing the deep hole Chrysler was in, beset as it was by serious financial and production problems. Nor was he quiet about discussing the
steps he was taking to turn things around. As a result, many people em-
pathized with him.

Most corporate leaders cannot appear on television as General
Schwarzkopf did when he told Americans how things were going during

the Gulf War, or as Lee Iacocca did when he touted Chrysler's progress. But they can keep people up-to-date on how they are doing and on how things are really going.

When leaders have tough assignments to carry out, they remind their staff that everyone is under similar pressure and that they all have to do unpleasant things. The best way to communicate this kind of news is in face-to-face interaction, rather than in impersonal memos. Not only is it critical that senior leaders communicate with each other during the hard times; they must send messages to their employees that they too want to hear the bad as well as the good news from them. During the 1970s managers often shielded senior leadership from reality, thinking that those at the helm didn't want to know about the problems. Consequently, the corporate office learned of problems only after they had escalated into major quality and productivity slippages that were tough to turn around.

Successful leaders don't just tell employees that they want to hear the bad, as well as the good, news. They make it easy for employees to see them at any time—to report not just successes but also failures. They also ask the right questions—not "How are things going?" but "How is the new assistant working out?" or "Is the process action team working on the procurement process making headway?" These questions tell the employee that leaders are vitally connected with the daily operations and that they know enough to comprehend the answers. And when messengers do bring bad news, leaders give them positive feedback, as in "Thanks for alerting me before this problem escalated."

## The Value of Humanitarianism

Bob Boruff, Vice President for Manufacturing at Saturn, always makes those around him feel that they're the most important thing to him at that moment. He never makes them feel they're taking up his valuable time. He is a willing and patient listener. He is enthusiastic. He is forgiving. And he moves others forward as a result.

The very first time I met Boruff, I was struck by how vibrant he is. Unlike many stuffy VP's offices where everything is very orderly and neat, Boruff's office is filled with symbols that represent his own dynamism, and it rings of activity. From his conference table to his flip chart, you realize that he is a man who never passes up the opportunity to teach and to learn.

Usually dressed in a casual short-sleeved sport shirt, Boruff often speaks with conviction about what he sees as the primary task of a leader:

to define the value system. Preferring to talk about values rather than cam shafts or engine transmissions, he speaks about the role of leadership. He believes in enabling systems that clarify the corporate value system and consequently has worked to create facilities and systems which facilitate high performance teamwork.

Boruff is an exceptional communicator. The language used in a company is one signal of its policies and practices. Boruff's lack of pomposity supports Saturn's overall democracy. With Boruff there are no overblown words—but there are profound ideas. Whether in a one-on-one conversation or in a business address, Boruff knows the value of speaking to his audience and uses frames of reference familiar to his audience to make his points.

Boruff is patient and forgiving. On my way to a recent appointment with him, I went tooling down the wrong interstate, traveling some forty miles out of the way, and ran out of gas. Arriving almost an hour late, I half expected him to have scheduled another meeting or, at the very least, to hurry me along with my presentation (although my previous encounters with him should have suggested otherwise). While I had telephoned him about my wanderings, I still expected him to feel annoyed and rushed. Here's a guy positionally next to the Saturn president, and I'm holding him up for an hour. As I stumbled through an apology about running out of gas, though, Boruff replied, with a twinkle in his eye, "That's because you drove three hundred miles out of your way—what do you expect?" I knew, with that, I could relax and proceed with my presentation.

## Empowering Others

In a fast-moving environment, orders won't work; the leader's job is to establish a process by which people learn together. If the relationship between leader and followers includes trust and shared values, the leader's vulnerability encourages followers to join in the task of transforming the culture.

It's up to executive leadership to give employees the opportunity to earn success. Leaders must find specific problems or issues that people can address and then let them devise solutions. That way, employees both add value and see how they add value.

Leaders also need to develop the capacity of their employees to put shared values into practice. Employees can't do what they don't know how to do. Training is at the top of successful organizations' agendas—

not just any training, but training that develops employees' skills related to quality and service. Leaders realize that if they are to build commitment to teamwork, for example, they must develop employees' capacity to work in teams. If they believe in continuous improvement, they must teach employees how to benchmark and how to formulate quality indicators. If they want employees to feel ownership in a 100 percent customer satisfaction mission, employees must be given the authority to act independently.

Promus Hotels' senior leadership realized that merely offering a 100 percent customer satisfaction guarantee wasn't enough. They had to make it easy for employees to enact that guarantee for guests. The hotels made certain that employees do not have to fill out cumbersome forms nor seek management's approval to pick up a guest's tab for lunch, or even for the entire stay, if the guest is not totally satisfied.

Square D's philosophy of empowerment is clearly embodied in Rick Agee's leadership. Agee, Manager of Metal-Clad operations at the Smyrna, Tennessee, Square D plant, backs up his words with actions. Metal-clad team members talk about Agee's willingness to get out of their way and let them solve their own problems. According to Jim Jackson, "Rick lets us do our work; he gives us guidelines and support, but he doesn't get in our way." Catherine Bradford smiles rather sheepishly as she remembers a time when the team couldn't get to consensus, and they went to Agee asking him to intercede. He did facilitate the discussion, but he refused to "fix" the problem. "Rick tells us we are the experts, and he will not baby us. He gives us the big picture, but he also gives us the independence to resolve our own conflicts and problems," says Catherine.

Square D team members talk about the impact of empowering leadership at Square D. Eugene Martin says, "When you're trusted to order copper, or any other material, it makes a difference in the way you feel about your job. Once employees were clock watchers. They just came to work, did whatever they had to do, and went home. Now they're enthusiastic and want to make our product better. We really feel that it's our plant."

## Staying Connected to Product and Process

In the 1970s many senior executives became remote and insulated. Real leaders, however, have always been vitally connected with product and process. Earning credibility is a factory-floor activity, a person-to-person process. Credibility is gained in large and small ways, but mainly through physical presence. By sharing personal experiences with their employees and joining in dialogue, leaders come to be trusted.

At Jimmy Dean Foods, individual contributors and plant managers alike respect Bill Hardison, former President of Rudy's Farm Company and later Corporate Vice President of the Sara Lee Meat Group, and Judy Baines, Director of Customer Service at Jimmy Dean Foods, for their willingness to stay connected to people and process.

Bill Hardison is one person I deeply regret not having had the chance to work with early on in my professional career. Had I been given this opportunity, I believe I would have been better able to reconcile some of the dilemmas that faced me in corporate America. He is the embodiment of balancing "high-tech" and "high touch"—high-tech in his intimate knowledge of product and high-touch in his close connectedness to people. According to those who worked alongside him, Hardison had that in-depth understanding of what creates worker frustration and fulfillment that can come only from close involvement with those he supervised. At the same time, he has an overriding sense of organizational mission.

Bill began his long career with the meat business at Rudy's Farm Company as a college student trying to earn his tuition. He eventually became the president of that company, a company that came to be acquired by Sara Lee. Later, as Corporate Vice President of the Sara Lee Meat Group, he was responsible for managing various meat companies within the corporation. As people talk about his contribution, inevitably they mention his knowledge of product and his willingness to share that knowledge. "Nobody knew the meat business like Bill Hardison. . . . His credibility results from that knowledge and his willingness to share that knowledge with others and meet them where they are," says one operations manager.

Managers at Jimmy Dean also mention Hardison's connection with people. Hardison stayed in touch with both his internal and his external customers. One person recalls Hardison's philosophy: "Bill always kept his door open to everybody—kill-floor worker to plant manager. . . . He cared about all his employees and wanted everyone to feel free to come to him at any time with a problem, or just to talk. . . . Remember, this was twenty-five years ago, before anyone had written about the benefits of the 'open-door policy.' "

People are not willing to follow people they can't believe, people who do not walk their talk on quality and customer satisfaction. Although now in a management role, Judy Baines shares all the responsibilities with those she supervises. I have watched her roll up her sleeves and do whatever needs to be done, including working on an assembly line production to get the product out. And that willingness pays remarkable dividends with those in the plant.

Federal Express's CEO Fred Smith is an example of a leader who's willing to stay connected to people and process. Obviously, in a company with more than one hundred thousand employees, that is quite a challenge, but FedEx has invested resources in systems and processes to keep him in touch. Smith is continually figuring out ways to interact with the internal and external customers.

Debby Johnson, Materials Analyst for the metal-clad work unit at one of the Square D plants, stays connected with those she supports. She affirms that what helps her the most in her support role to the teams is going to the factory floor, talking to the employees, and finding out what they need in their work and when. She is then able to support them better. Debby is also helped by the fact that she worked on the floor herself and has the trust of team members, which comes only from direct, personal involvement. One of the plant managers says of Debby, "She has been willing to take personal accountability in a big way."

## Valuing Diversity

In the late 1970s and even into the 1980s, people were considered "boat rockers" if they didn't buy into existing or past cultural rituals. I worked with managers who expressed sadness that they had not felt independent enough to say what they thought, believing that they had to parrot the company's power brokers. Today, in contrast, when we think of leaders, we think of people who make waves and who don't shy away from the uncomfortable. Credible leaders honor the diversity of their many constituencies. General Norman Schwarzkopf advises that leaders can't shoot the messenger, that they must have a standard within the organization that allows people to speak up when something is wrong. Contrast this to those organizations in which "birthday meetings" or any other interface between manager and employees take on an orchestrated look where employees ask the "right" questions and make the right comments.

Those who are able to influence others today (and the ability to attract followers is the ultimate test of leadership) encourage dissent and independence of thought from their associates—a far cry from the unanimity required by corporate managers in the 1970s and 1980s. Leaders recognize that surrounding themselves with only "yes" men and women may lead them in the wrong direction. These men and women have enough inner security to ask questions—and to hear the responses.

At the Smyrna, Tennessee, Square D Plant, the trait team leaders most appreciate about Metal Clad Manager Rick Agee is his willingness to back them, even when they may be surfacing "bad news," and even when bringing the issue to senior management's attention may not be politically expedient. "We feel we have his support, and that gives us courage," says Jim Jackson, a member of his team.

## Risk Taking and Entrepreneurism

When a key value is at stake, or when someone's behavior is inconsistent with the company's stated values, leaders must be willing to take risks and to make decisions based on principle—even if the decisions are not politically expedient.

Not only do leaders themselves take risks; they encourage others to do the same. Leaders allow people to be innovative without fear of failure. When it comes to new product development, they recognize that they need people who are willing to break the rules, to be mavericks. Even in government, there is increasing recognition of the need to be entrepreneurial. Until a few years ago it was rare to hear about entrepreneurism in government agencies, but that is changing with today's emphasis on a leaner and less layered government. Richard Guimond, Principal Deputy Assistant Secretary for Environmental Restoration and Waste Management at the U.S. Department of Energy, encourages entrepreneurism and encourages his staff to be creative and take risks. Guidmond observes that entrepreneurial leaders "don't try to change people's minds, since this takes too much time. Instead, they look for partners who already agree and can sponsor the change, or those who are neutral and can be won over." He stresses that these leaders avoid building elaborate layered organizations and keep staff procedures and policies to a minimum.

RC&D coordinators at the U.S. Department of Agriculture illustrate this entrepreneurism. Recently I delivered a program for these coordinators, who came from all over the United States. As I listened to their stories of how they got this or that community leader to jump on the bandwagon, I was struck by how renegade these governmental employees were—and how willing they were to move around regulations and policies to make things happen. Not one time did I hear any of them say, "We can't do that because of the regulations." And these were employees out of a system that has historically rewarded them for never making waves and never taking risks.

## Leading a Business Turnaround through Effective Leadership—A Case Study

Jim Clark embodies many of the characteristics of a successful leader. As Vice President of Engineering Products at Square D-Groupe Schneider, North America, Clark is still improving the bottom line of businesses through his keen business acumen coupled with a large dose of humanism. He has a long history of plant and division turnarounds at corporations such as Asea Brown Boveri, McGraw Edison, and General Electric, primarily because he is able to see more to the quality equation than measuring scrap at the end of the line. He realizes that quality means more than control charts and that the cultural infrastructure must be in place for high quality to result.

Jim explains that in the 1970s he experienced a general resistance to changing the status quo to effect higher quality. But things had gotten so bad in one of the GE plants that Jim was given a breakthrough opportunity to try to turn a failing business around. He did so through taking some creative approaches to personnel selection and building trust with the front-line employees in a day when many managers could not see the relevance of such issues to quality.

Jim Clark was only thirty-one years old at that time, with a background in manufacturing and finance. Though fairly inexperienced in plant management, he asked for and received the opportunity to become plant manager.

### High Tech, Low Morale

On arriving at the plant, Jim assessed the overall state of affairs. The plant's products were new and technically sound, so marketing them was not a problem. There were, however, other dilemmas. The main problem was in manufacturing, where Clark found that the hostile relations between management and the hourly union workforce were contributing to quality problems. He decided to deal with the poor labor relations first, because it seemed unlikely that he could overcome the manufacturing problems without the cooperation of the workers.

Clark needed to change the attitude of both the plant's management team and the union workforce. He realized he had to tackle management first and correct the problem if he were ever to improve relations with the union. That meant he had to work with three key positions.

## Non-Traditional Choices

The position of unit manager of shaft machinery was open because that manager—who, Clark says, was a good manager—had been frustrated with the startup of the new operation and left. Taking a bit of a gamble, Clark selected a young graduate of GE's manufacturing management program who had strong interactive skills and was eager to tackle a unit manager's position. Clark decided that this coachable young manager was worth a chance, figuring that what he lacked in experience, he made up for in enthusiasm.

The unit manager of heavy casting for the motorized wheel was very experienced but was a Theory-X-style manager, who had contributed to the plant's personnel problems. He also wanted out and Clark was able to find him another position in another plant. Clark hired in his place a veteran foreman from the propulsion section who had an excellent job performance record as a foreman but who had never been allowed to assume a manager's role because he lacked a college degree and was perceived as unsophisticated. This man had originally worked as a machine operator prior to becoming a foreman, a job which he had held for more than ten years. His people loved him, as they felt he understood their problems. Clark chose this man's credibility and experience over the more "slick" competition. Jim also replaced the materials manager, whose personality had alienated salaried and nonsalaried personnel alike, with a younger person who had demonstrated concern and care for employees.

With his new staff in place, Clark turned his attention to the labor relations problems in the hourly workforce.

## Gaining Trust From Both Sides

Since Jim realized building trust with the employees was essential to getting the plant operating properly, he spent a lot of time out on the plant floor talking to the employees. It became apparent that the company's union negotiator and the union's president were the main agitators at the plant. Clark told the plant's union stewards that if they could keep the union officers out of the plant, he would keep the company's union negotiator out of the plant. Since many of the employees feared and mistrusted the human resources group, the union stewards agreed. Even though they were a little skeptical, they saw this as a giant step in building the trust with the new management team.

When Clark notified the company's union negotiator that he would want him in the plant only if the union's officers came in the plant, the negotiator agreed, at least temporarily, because he felt that the union officials would never stay out of the plant. The union stewards got a similar agreement with their officers, who also felt that the company union negotiator would never stay out of the plant.

With the two main agitators out of the way, Clark formed work groups of both hourly and salaried employees to solve the problems in their areas. These were cross-functional teams in which everyone had a say regardless of positions. Clark and his team members—the manufacturing engineers, the foreman, and the hourly workers—knew they would have to eliminate the inconsistency and inequity in the old system. They decided to focus on three main problems—piece prices, quality, and work flow.

The team agreed upon a specific method and time allotment to manufacture each part.

Clark stopped all supplemental payments immediately and had the cross functional work groups agree upon the best method for manufacturing each part to achieve an overall quality product. He reviewed each one to ensure that it was fair and proper.

### Involving the Workers

At first Clark was intrigued by the results. The hourly workers identified operations that were not needed as well as operations that needed to be added. They also offered ideas on ways to modify current operations. The improved work flow reduced rework and resulted in lower piece prices. The net result was a reduction of more than 20 percent in the piece prices compared to the prices paid in Propulsion!

Clark later realized, however, that the hourly workers accepted the lower piece price because they had played an active part in setting the methods. There was a marked improvement in quality as rework began to decline at a rapid rate. Involvement had made the difference.

### Walking the Floor and Sharing Information

When Clark became Plant Manager, he initiated an open-door policy so that anyone could come to his office at any time, regardless of rank. Initially, the union stewards were the only ones to take advantage of this policy, but gradually others began to come around, although Clark spent so much time with them on the shop floor that they usually could discuss work problems there.

During his walks out in the plant, Clark talked to workers about things outside their work—hunting, fishing, their families—things that both union stewards and individual workers had in common and enjoyed. This enabled them to get to know each other on a more personal basis and established a basis for trust. It was important that they saw each other as individuals, not as adversaries. Some of these people, Clark came to discover, had never talked to "high-level managers," as they called them.

Clark affirms that trust must be two-sided. Employees will not develop trust with management if they think management is lying to them. He explains:

> During those years, the company embraced a philosophy that only senior-level leaders should have certain information [one of the reasons that in their attitude surveys employees typically gave low scores to questions related to whether they felt managers were giving them correct information]. During those days, certain components within the company felt that "lower level" employees did not have enough intelligence and maturity to grasp information about certain matters and that only the senior leaders should know the "big picture."

Clark says he could never agree with the company's philosophy that financial information was not to be shared with the lower-level employees. "If you want people to help you," he says, "you must never lie to them about anything, and you must be willing to explain to them why you need to do something and the economic reason behind it."

Consequently, Clark took a chance and explained to the plant employees that he would share financial information with them, but if it reached ears outside the plant, he would be forced to stop. This approach worked. They did not betray him. Clark says that this information sharing helped a lot when difficult decisions had to be made. People were more willing to accept them, because they understood the logic behind them.

### The Importance of Feedback

After establishing trust, the second most crucial thing, according to Clark, was giving people feedback when they began to suggest improvements.

"If the suggestion was a good one, and implementable," says Clark, "we made sure to adopt it and give the person the recognition for suggesting it . . . not a cash payment, but a more personal recognition, perhaps being spotlighted in the plant paper. If the idea was not adopted, we explained why, but they were still recognized for suggesting it."

### The Outcomes

In less than eight months, the rework and manufacturing losses at the plant dropped from 1,200 percent of direct labor to 200 percent of direct labor. As improvements were made in the machining process, the plant was able to trace the cause of one costly type of problem to quality problems of the vendor. When Purchasing was notified and given solid facts to back up the complaint, it began to work more closely with the vendor to solve the quality problem.

Output increased from fewer than five units per week to more than forty-five per week during this eight-month period, and union grievances virtually dried up. Of course, this caused concern with both the top union officials and the company's union relations group. Clark explains, "They wanted our work groups stopped, and felt that the management and hourly workforce had grown 'too cozy' by working together. Fortunately, the financial and shipment improvements were so dramatically improved that the general manager prevented either of these two groups from interfering."

At the end of the eight-month period, Clark was promoted to take over a larger plant. But the new management team remained in this plant and continued with the policies that had been initiated while Clark was there. And the positive performance of that plant continued. The basic ingredients of the cultural infrastructure—creativity in selecting people, trust gained from walking the floor and sharing information, listening to employees' suggestions, and giving feedback—all contributed to the plant's quality and productivity turnaround.

### So Who Are the Heroes of the 1990s?

Certainly the likes of Fred Smith, Jack Welch, Bob Boruff, Jim Clark, and Bill Hardison come to mind as business heroes of the 1990s. But there are many other heroes who work on the front line—like Mickey Williams of DuPont, Judy Baines of Jimmy Dean Foods, Debby Johnson of Square D, Mike Warner of Eastman Chemical, and Mike Park of the U.S. Army

Corps of Engineers. They, and others like them, have turned organizations around by their dedication and commitment to quality. They have put together teams that capitalize on their members' strengths and produce more than those members ever could working independently.

These men and women have generated passion about a high quality product; they have pulled—not forced—people around them to do more than they ever thought they could; they have encouraged the exploration of new ideas as a corporate philosophy; they have directed their efforts toward doing those things that are critical to customer satisfaction; and they have considered building interpersonal bonds more important than policies and protocol. These are the ones others are following, and these are the ones who are keeping their organizations on track.

# 16

# Switching the Tracks

## *Transitioning to a Quality Culture*

The American people are going through major culture shock. Their jobs are vanishing in mergers, takeovers, and downsizings. They are being asked to learn new ways of thinking about themselves and their jobs. Many skills that were valued during the derailment are now maligned. And people are scared. They are being forced to do something they hate to do: change. Many Americans can't understand how or why they are being forced to play a desperate game of catch-up in industries they invented. They ask, "How could this have happened?"

During the "derailment" U.S. business practices were still governed by Frederick Taylor's theory of scientific management, which many consider the single most significant management philosophy ever. At the turn of the century this theory offered a way to make management centralization work in the industrial age. The theory provided the means and methods to perpetuate a management style that included functionality and close supervision. In this philosophy, planning and working were distinct functions. The style worked well for years, most successfully in corporations like the highly centralized and functionalized General Motors. Although it is no longer appropriate to our times, its staying power is evident in some corporate cultures that are struggling for survival.

The major problem with this management style in terms of moving to a quality culture is its omission of a vital ingredient in achieving and maintaining a high-quality product—the human spirit. The theory assumed that the human being is a machine tool. American business paid a high price for that way of thinking during the derailment.

To respond to the quality challenge, all organizations are being challenged to shift from Taylor's scientific management. Implicit in that movement are monumental changes—from changes in markets to changes in the way people operate. "Global" is replacing "domestic"; "lean" is re-placing "layered"; "continuous improvement" is replacing "status quo"; "horizontal" structures are replacing "vertical" ones; "coach" is replac-ing "boss"; "team" emphasis is replacing "individual" emphasis; and "personal" power is replacing "positional" power. The transition is not easy, because, for some employees, the formulas and structure of scien-tific management have acted as a security blanket. As workplace democ-racy sweeps through corporations like GM, it can be real scary for "bosses" and employees who may be unsure of how to act. Roles have changed; along with that, so have the rituals.

## The Challenge of Transition

Transitioning from a culture as deeply rooted as Taylor's to a flatter, con-tinuous improvement culture takes time and persistence. Technical, polit-ical, and cultural elements must be aligned. And sometimes it's easier for management to change structures and systems to match the new para-digm than it is to change employees' values and beliefs. It is tough to let go of the philosophy that a company is successful primarily because of its manufacturing equipment, rather than because of its partnership with customers. When the new paradigm is introduced, people cling tightly to the company's old ways and often feel a great loss as the old ways disappear.

One thing is clear: Managers have to involve the whole organization in order to reengineer it. They have learned the hard way that however great the design of a new system is, its ability to change the culture is limited to people's responses to it. Ultimately, cultures emerge when in-dividuals interact around common missions and use straightforward principles of interaction.

A couple of years ago I was conducting a training session for a Sara Lee company when the president of the company—who sat right along-side his marketing manager in the training—remarked to me that he was "having a tough time with this team business." I appreciated the honesty of the statement. This man was sixty-two years old and had been pro-grammed in the days of "tough-minded management," when the man-ager alone was the problem solver and senior leadership alone possessed the vision statement and long-range strategies and didn't share either with those on the assembly line. The empowerment idea can be threaten-ing if people feel that it takes away whatever created their value in the first place. Sometimes all their skills and abilities appear obsolete, and they feel they don't have enough in reserve to transition to the new culture.

There is nothing more difficult to take in hand, or more perilous to conduct, than a cultural change. It makes terrible demands on leaders. When you're trailblazing, you have different values from your management—the people you work for and those who work with you. The risk of failure is great. Snipers and cynics are everywhere. But you can take heart from companies like Motorola, which has changed to a quality culture fairly readily. This company grabbed continuous improvement in the early 1980s and has been relentless in hanging on to it. Eastman Chemical enjoyed a steady cultural evolution after 1984, when it began inviting customers to visit its plants and become part of its improvement efforts.

The cultural changes at these companies, as well as others which have moved to continuous improvement, were driven by an understanding of where the organizations wanted to go, by skills and talents that would serve them in the future, rather than by where they had been. These companies recognize that people and culture—the human systems of an organization—are what make or break any change initiative. They understand that change initiatives require the right mix of psychological, communication, and management skills.

In the late 1970s and early 1980s, companies did not take these required components into account. During the derailment organizations ignored the need to dig up the old cultural infrastructure and instead tried to impose quality initiatives on top of it. There was no plan to liberate organizations from their past.

Today, however, successful organizations have learned that changing to a quality culture requires a plan, one that factors in both innovation and the cultural infrastructure of that innovation. They realize that they must start with the cultural infrastructure. For example, you just can't tell people all of a sudden that individual effort doesn't count, when for years you have recognized them for that. You have to begin by transforming your "boxed" organizations into faster, smarter team structures where individual strengths will still be valued but where the value will show up in a cross-functional marketing plan that benefits the organization, or in a new product, put together by representatives from various functions, that benefits everyone.

## How Fast Can or Should We Change?

Modifying a structure from vertical to horizontal or moving from being a domestic to a global company cannot happen suddenly. When moving from a vertical to a horizontal structure, managers are looking at eliminating a social order that's been around since medieval feudalism. The durability of this monumental structure as a concept for social organizations is amazing. Obviously, we are not going to do away with it overnight.

Nor can we expect people who came into manufacturing plants twenty-five or thirty years ago, when the vision of companies was domestic, to relish the idea of going global. They are charged now with developing product capabilities to serve markets around the world. This requires them to look beyond traditional product definitions to future customers' needs, which may very well mean grappling with vast cultural differences.

Further, global management requirements can be quite different. Managers who acquired all of their knowledge and experience in these North American organizations have been expected to make adjustments—like relocating within the United States—but not to move to another country. And people have to be trained in new skills and capabilities, which takes time.

Some business leaders, including Jack Welch of General Electric, advocate radical change that is out of sync with the old culture, change that generates enough shock effect to immobilize the old culture. They advocate hitting the organization with enough force to shatter the status quo and to wake people up. These companies have concluded that the competitive rigors of the new economy—the demand for speed and global reach, the struggle to respond to the increasing demands of customers, the need to exploit information technology—are too big and too urgent to be addressed by anything less than change on a grand scale. Many leaders feel if they promote incremental change, they'll never achieve anything meaningful. They recognize that crises can lead to creativity as people step out of their normal behavior, do only what's important, and are forced to resist riding on their past successes to sustain their future.

Others suggest incremental change more in keeping with the Japanese culture, where, as Pascale and Athos note in *The Art of Japanese Management*, "corporate direction evolves from an incremental adjustment to unfolding events" in order not to put everything at risk. They recognize that monumental change can make people panicky and impulsive. Esprit de corps unravels, so tighter controls become necessary.

The major problem with grand strategic leaps is the temptation for some with positional power to grab the ax and start chopping. They grab quick solutions—much as they did in the late 1970s—and do things they wouldn't do if things were more stable, including purging themselves of anything related to the old culture. This can be dangerous and expensive.

Neither seismic nor incremental change, in and of itself, results in sustained creative energy. While heavy-duty intervention on the part of senior management may be desirable, the organization also contains many people who have not been programmed or rewarded for being risk takers or entrepreneurs but who have made legitimate contributions, nevertheless. They can still. These men and women are steady, "follower" types, who know and understand system and structure and are valuable because of it. While many today call them "deadwood," they can be the very ones who can work on structure and system to produce real cultural change. Sometimes, however, they may not be able to survive an emotionally wrenching and terrifying sudden revolution.

Having worked with organizational cultures embodying both these philosophies, I have found that too much subtlety can breed lethargy, but too much force can breed panic. Every business must design its own system and go at its own pace. If the organization is now centralized, with high control, a measured and steady change is probably best.

Consider, for example, that in just a few years, government employees have had to move from considering themselves civil servants, entitled to their jobs, to justifying themselves and defining quality from the customer's view. While private industry gets impatient with what it thinks is the government's sluggishness in changing its structures and systems, in many ways federal agencies have made more progress than some private companies. Today, they are being trained in the same total quality precepts as private industry. They are mandated to downsize and restructure; yet, because federal regulations dictate most of their policies, federal agencies don't have nearly the authority that private industry does to change its classification, compensation, measurement, and selection systems quickly.

Bill Hardison, Corporate Vice President of the Meat Group at Sara Lee during the merger of two of its companies, Jimmy Dean Sausage and Rudy's Farm Company, believes that in a major change, such as a restructuring or merger, you must change one thing at a time. "If you have too many changes introduced to people at once, then if something goes wrong, you can't always pinpoint it," says Hardison. Is what went wrong something that would have gone wrong anyway, or is it the result of inattention?

Saturn Corporation's self-managed team structure has received much publicity. But it has taken years for the people working in these teams to become high-performing team members. Employees were hired from GM, a top-down hierarchical structure with vastly different rituals, and the required change in attitudes, skills, and systems did not come as fast as some might think. Saturn officials point out that, although they have made great progress, they are still evolving in that structure.

When we speak of high-velocity change, therefore, we have to consider whether the necessary infrastructure is in place. For example, if an organization is going to implement a self-directed team structure, it must first consider whether senior leadership really trusts employees to make their own decisions, whether the employees really value team effort, and whether the employees know how to work synergistically. If they don't, the organization must be willing to do one of two things—bring in new people who do value team contributions and have team skills or train and develop existing employees. If the organization really values a team culture, is it willing to alter its selection and rewards systems to bring them into alignment with this new culture? That means no longer evaluating employees merely on their technical competence, but also considering how well they perform as team members.

## Requirements for Changing a Culture

Whether piecemeal or radical, change begins with an awareness that some change is necessary. Usually a forced change is short-lived. Only when people internalize the need to change will they be committed to it.

But it takes more than knowledge and awareness to change a culture. Intellect may guide and direct, but it does not carry the force that leads to action. The force must come from passion—and passion that drives organizational consequences is not as easy to evoke as passions, such as hate and fear, that drive personal actions. Managers must tell people over and over that the new organization isn't going to disappear, and they must continually work to rid the organization of the old rituals that are out of sync with continuous improvement. You must instill change by selling continuity and you have to convince people that world-class quality is the price of just being on board. At the same time you must help people realize the overall opportunities for the organization and its employees.

No matter how measured the approach, you must have a clear vision of what you want the organization to become. And that vision has to be shared with everyone. Then you must get the mandate from everyone else to go forward with that vision. A couple of years after the merger of Jimmy Dean Sausage with Rudy's Farm Company, some managers from both companies were still operating using rituals and philosophies from the old cultures. Consequently, they were having difficulty working as a team. What helped them meld together as much as anything was bringing together members who had come from both companies and crafting a new vision statement, which embodied the ideals and values of the new culture.

Almost as important as a clear vision of a customer-focused, continuous improvement culture is an alignment of the political and cultural elements of the organization with the desired cultural change. That means putting into place structures that will reduce the effects of the "chain of command" structure and enable employees to have decision-making authority about their jobs—in other words, diffusing power, rather than consolidating it. Employees should be given the opportunity to develop their own customer-focused goals in concert with their managers and team leaders. Alignment also means rewarding managers who give employees a broad sense of direction but at the same time know and care about what's going on throughout the organization and develop opportunities for creating customer value. It means changing selection systems and reward systems to focus on continuous improvement and customer value.

Leaders and followers both need something to grab onto before they will let go of their old behavior. When change means laying people off, managers must do it fast so that they can fill in the void and give the people still at work survival skills. No one can be very productive in an environment where you say you're going to restructure over the next three years. The major source of frustration I have heard about from U.S. Army Corps of Engineers members during the past several years has been the sluggishness with which restructuring and reorganization have taken place. They have expressed the difficulty of becoming proactive when the political overtones of restructuring cause continuous stalling. The irony is that when senior leadership doesn't take the bull by the horns and push on through, change is ultimately mandated, which takes all sense of control away from the organization and greatly increases the stress on its members.

Often people seek safety in work. Use that instinct: Give them ownership of their work and a clear definition of the results they are accountable for. Then the new way becomes the safe way.

Another major requirement of changing to a quality culture is convincing people to accept personal accountability for the success of their organization by creating value for their products and services. Many people expect senior leadership to provide them their direction and to come up with the new product or service that will save them. Today, however, everyone has that responsibility. Instilling that belief in itself requires changing the thinking of many employees—especially those in government—who had always seen goal setting and leadership as the special province of senior managers.

Leaders must drive change by focusing not on programs or policies but on work and customer needs. Most workers would have a hard time recalling any "program" that in and of itself evoked passion. But when concepts of value-added properties for customers (internal as well as external) are translated to everyone's work—from the data-entry person to the project manager—and come to life for the employees themselves, that is a different story. If employees don't understand what customer needs are, they don't know what to put first.

A transforming leader must look for those factors that motivate followers and seek to satisfy workers' higher needs. Everyone in the organization must have a voice, but cynics must not be encouraged. The most ardent foes of change are those with the most to lose, which means they have power. To avoid letting them create obstacles to change, decisions must be made by those close to the action.

A final but very important requirement of change is the responsibility of senior leadership to make the employees feel that they are the organization's most important asset. Virtually no mission statement exists today that doesn't include this thought, but proving it to employees is another matter in periods of cutbacks and downsizings.

One of the ways some organizations do this is by giving people survival tactics to both those who stay and those who go. This may mean offering training in "recareering" skills, which teaches employees how to "rechannel" their knowledge and skills to reinvent value for themselves and to become more proactive by examining trends and forces and anticipating how their own skills fit into those trends and forces. Other training might include learning new skills, such as computer technology skills, to facilitate career cross-over. Business leaders must continually examine world trends that are likely to impact their employees, consider what talents and skills exist in organization and which ones need development. Organizations must get employees ready for the future so that if their "present" jobs disappear they can still be salvageable. The difficult part is convincing employees to look beyond their current job descriptions to what their mission will look like five years from now and who their customers will be.

We must help people rethink their jobs and assess their transferable skills so that they can reposition themselves either in new slots in their current organization if it downsizes or in other companies. Flexibility has wide application; so does innovation. These skills transfer.

Employees' sense of self-worth is affected when their jobs are threatened. Even though productivity and quality sometimes increase in a plant that's in trouble, driven by a sense of urgency, that surge of energy comes more from the hope that if employees remind the organization of their skills, top management will decide to keep the plant open. But this is usually an artificial high, a nervous response, that cannot sustain high quality.

On the other hand, with a daily focus on mission and a daily demonstration of care, people can come through restructuring with their self-worth intact. Even if their job disappears, they will have the strength to transition themselves—either within the organization or outside it.

## Unifying Elements in the New Culture

When any organization is changing to a quality culture, the one thing that will motivate employees to give their all is the message leaders send them on the organizational mission. If the mission is continuously evolving, as many are, this can be pretty tough to do. Even cultures like Sara Lee, which have been able to keep people excited by brand leveraging, will have to do more to unleash excitement. Employees have to be given something that they feel is worth working toward, a mission employees can "get their hands around" and can feel daily. If organizational values are part of that mission, they have to be demonstrated continuously, and they have to be lived outside the organization's formal communication channels.

The goal of the transition has to be repeated over and over, in lots of different ways. If the goal is a global market, employees need to be reminded that the old organization, which supported a domestic market, isn't going to support the new goal. You have to be willing to admit that you may not have the skills in place to address a global market. You must realize that many of your managers came up through the ranks and that their knowledge and experience are limited to the United States. Their past success in fact can trap them if it leads them away from the future. You must bring together marketing, manufacturing, and engineering leaders to examine their product designs and assess how expanding and diverse consumer needs affect them. And you have to do it regularly.

Another unifying element in the new culture is the focus on valuing contributions from all members. The author Warren Bennis says that you can't lead what you can't value. During downsizings, corporate leaders tend to pontificate on how the organization can't afford deadwood employees and mediocre performance. Well, the organization somehow has afforded them up until now and has encouraged their mediocrity by doing very little about it. Chances are that workers are performing in a way consistent with the way they've always performed. Rather than focus on those statements, it seems more logical to focus on processes that have value added for customers. If those employees are performing actions that don't add that value, then there is an opportunity to either eliminate the process (which may in some cases lead to eliminating the employee) or improve the process by showing the employee what will add value to it.

Stories and rituals can help unify a culture. For example, to illustrate the importance of risk taking and development, the story is often told about IBM's first president, Tom Watson, and an employee who botched an assignment to the tune of several million dollars. When Mr. Watson called the young man in and began asking him how this happened, the young man finally wearied of the questions and responded, "Mr. Watson, why don't you just go ahead and fire me?" Mr. Watson responded, "Young man, I can't afford to fire you; I've just invested $10 million in your training."

In some retail organizations employees are called "associates" instead of "subordinates," signaling the passing of the old chain-of-command structure and the ushering in of a culture that treats everyone with respect and equity. And some managers have literally taken their office doors off their hinges, signaling an open-door policy. Some manufacturing organizations have done away with reserved parking spaces and dining rooms for executives to signal the flattening of the organization.

In some hospitals the cleaning staff offices of a hospital have been moved from the basement to the first floor to validate the impact of clean rooms on patient compliance and recovery. And federal agencies give employees—not managers—awards to give to their associates who have been the most helpful to them, signaling that often employees more than managers know who is contributing the most.

Many organizations allot time in every staff meeting to discuss ways to increase customer value, others have brown-bag lunches where employees discuss solutions to customer problems, others take office employees on field trips to see the earth-moving project, and still others have periodic meetings to celebrate successes of individuals in enhancing customer satisfaction. All signal an external, rather than an internal, focus.

Many writers, including Tom Peters, Tom Watson, Stephen Covey, and, before them, Eric Hoffer, have written about the importance of principles and values in keeping people stabilized and unified in a climate of instability and flux. As Covey so aptly explains, principles are not capricious, like jobs and people; they enable people to realize that their worth is not dependent on other people or organizations. They enable people to survive struggles, including layoffs and downsizings.

Observers may question whether personal values or organizational values are more important in changing an organizational culture. One thing is certain: If your personal values and the organizational values of your employer are out of sync, you will go through your worklife under tremendous stress. At best, values of equity, integrity, compassion, and caring show up in both repertoires.

Perhaps the least an organization can do is help give people the courage to face their futures by giving them the tools to become proactive. That may mean formal training, or it may be one-on-one counseling. Either way, leaders need to help those who leave—and those who stay—to feel that they have the internal control and strength that comes from clearly knowing what they value and the knowledge to make decisions congruent with those values.

## Balancing the New With the Old

Turnover has its virtues. Used correctly, it gives the organization the chance to change its chemistry more quickly than it would otherwise. It's harder to convert employees who have been part of the old culture than to bring in eager, new outsiders, without investment in the old culture and the old political power structure, who will embrace the new culture. Many times I have preferred to hire people who are relatively new to the training field and who have not had the chance to stagnate or to establish bad work habits.

As a matter of fact, one year I had become so disgusted with the sluggishness of our senior instructors and their unwillingness to continually reach up that I was determined to hire an all new training staff. I was angry with myself for carrying these inept employees so long! Since I was not able to pay them what they demanded that year, that made the decision for me and them less painful than it otherwise might have been.

I found, however, that, even though loyalty to the old ways could be a liability, bringing in an entirely new breed also had a downside. Because these new workers didn't know our company's history, our core competencies, our processes, or our clients' preferences, their actions were sterile and mechanical. They may have read or been told about our quality product and service standards, but they hadn't lived them. That made it harder for them to feel ownership. I came to learn that I really did value the historical perspective employees acquire only by being around a while.

Bill Fightmaster, now Director of Quality, Worldwide Operations at Allen Bradley and the former Vice President for Corporate Quality at Square D-Groupe Schneider, explains that after the launch of its quality initiative, for three years Square D hired primarily people from the outside in order to "reshape" its new culture. According to Fightmaster, "Prior to that time Square D had hired virtually no one from the outside, and really most of its products and processes had been outpaced technologically as a result." Fightmaster explains that while in some ways bringing in outsiders was good because the company had developed a case of tunnel vision, it was also demotivating for those who had been "grown in the company." Those who remained felt they needed to maintain a low profile.

Unlike the situation in the 1970s, when only insiders were considered to have correct answers, Square D leaders came to believe that those who had been conditioned by the old culture were less than bright. And it came to be accepted that you had to have come from the outside to be able to shape the new culture. There was some pull and tug, though, because some of those who came from other cultures were able to recognize skills and talents within the old culture. Fightmaster explains that, as a result, the company ended up having a more balanced culture than one might expect.

## The Reengineering of DuPont

DuPont, a diversified chemical, energy, and specialty products company headquartered in Wilmington, Delaware, recognizes the importance of reengineering values, attitudes, and organizational structures to take care of internal customers. DuPont officials explain that historically, DuPont's information technology (IT) department had a "push environment where we [DuPont] knew what was best for users, and would give it to them." Now, however, DuPont is moving toward a "pull environment," where, in the words of Craig Binetti, general manager of the DuPont plant at Old Hickory, Tennessee, "our internal partners tell us what they want and we provide it."

DuPont's central IT department has shifted from having a line organization with a tight chain of command to a structure that combines line and network and is moving from functionality to a horizontal organization. DuPont managers explain that a networked organization works best when determining strategies and setting direction, while priorities are best served by a line organization.

DuPont achieved this culture shift by consulting with outside management experts, studying other corporations, and encouraging IT staff members to focus on the needs of the corporation and the individual business units. In the new DuPont environment, leadership is more important than management. Employees are judged on how well they lead efforts to improve quality, cost competitiveness, and responsiveness.

DuPont has worked hard to change the narrow mind-sets of corporate specialists who have spent their careers climbing a vertical hierarchy to the top of their function. Craig Binetti explains that the company is trying to do away with the disconnects that come with function and departments in favor of multidisciplinary teams that support core processes. It's challenging, explains Binetti, to those who have been honored for decades for supporting function. But DuPont's efforts have paid off in terms of decreased cycle time and increased customer satisfaction.

## The Evolution of the Jimmy Dean Quality Culture

Even if the managers from both companies in a merger have taken the time to understand thoroughly what they are getting into and feel the need to meld as a quality culture, the process of coming together is still usually tougher than either side anticipates. This was true for the merger of Jimmy Dean Sausage and Rudy's Farm Company in 1989. The crafters of both companies were willing to build a new culture, but, as with most mergers, it took time for individual managers and employees to adopt that willingness. The senior leaders knew there were commonalities between the two cultures, but it took more than two years for the other employees to see them as well.

### The Background

Technically, the Jimmy Dean Sausage Company, based in Dallas, merged with Rudy's Farm Company, based in Nashville, to form the Sara Lee Sausage Division (since renamed Jimmy Dean Foods) in 1989. But as with any merger, merging didn't imply melding. It took years for a third culture to actually develop.

Several factors contributed to the decision to merge. First, some of the Rudy's sausage plants were facing environmental pressures from various business concerns, particularly the tourism industry in Nashville. The Nashville plant was located next to the Opryland Complex, and some people were concerned that waste might get into the water surrounding the complex, causing environmental hazards. Environmental concerns, then, were one factor behind the relocation.

Second, the Sara Lee Meat Group (of which Jimmy Dean and Rudy's Farm were members), the original crafters of the merger, believed that Jimmy Dean's marketing advantage, coupled with Rudy's reputation for high intrinsic quality, was a potentially powerful combination. Jimmy Dean had already been successful in leveraging the Jimmy Dean brand of sausage nationally, making it the number one sausage in retail sales. Rudy's Farm Company was known for using the whole hog in its sausage production, which set it apart from the competition in having a relatively low fat content. So the combination of the two companies looked like a "dream team."

## Cultural Differences

The cultures were remarkably different, although commitment to quality was high in both. The historical practice of Sara Lee had been to buy good companies with name brands, work with existing management, and then let the companies run fairly autonomously. Even though the companies had common systems and processes that reflected corporate policies, each retained an individual culture that stemmed from the men who had started the companies and who had maintained close involvement with the product and process.

Rudy's culture reflected, deliberately, a down-home style that matched its product ads. To an outsider the company may have appeared "laid back," but in reality it was participative. When I first visited the company in the mid-1980s to present a training proposal, I was struck by how friendly everybody was and how nobody seemed to emphasize titles or position. The employees were proud of their sausage and wanted me to know why. I had the opportunity, on that first visit, to tour the plant, including the kill floor, observe the pride workers took in their product, and see their commitment to the company.

Rudy's was founded by the family of Dan and Frank Rudy, and the two brothers had direct involvement in the daily operation of the business. Bill Hardison, past President of the company and later Corporate Vice President of the Sara Lee Meat Group, explains that Frank was the entrepreneurial visionary and Dan was a "tough, pragmatic" manager. He says that the company would have never been started if it were not for Frank Rudy, the visionary, but that it would have gone out of business in six months, if it weren't for Dan, the "tough-minded" one of the two.

Hardison explains that the Jimmy Dean culture was more autocratic and top-down than Rudy's, mostly because of Jimmy Dean's continued involvement (although Rudy's could have been characterized that way in the beginning, because most family businesses start out that way). "As for Jimmy Dean himself, it is quite natural for one in the entertainment business to have a persona that demands attention and control, and Dean was no exception," says Hardison. Hardison explains that the Jimmy Dean culture was one in which there was a lot of control, vested in one person, the owner of the company. "There was good and bad in that," he says. The good part was that Dean was integrally connected with the people and the product, and all employees knew where they stood with him and what his vision was. According to Hardison, "There was no ambiguity. . . . But the negative part was that a culture like that may have a tendency to produce only 'yes men' and demolish those who are not." Hardison recalls the first management meeting he attended at Jimmy Dean; six or seven managers were present, but none of them said anything. Hardison remembers watching them wait for cues from Dean before they expressed their opinions.

I did some work for the company before the merger, and although I did notice evidence of intimidation, I also sensed that the employees really adored Dean. Hardison agrees.

The survivors of that culture, those who came to know Jimmy Dean's preferences and responded to them, regarded him as something of a protector. They speak highly of his attention to detail and his involvement with both them and the product. In explaining how the Jimmy Dean culture worked as well as it did, Bill Hardison says that it worked because Dean's "hardness" was consistent. "If you're not going to let a person use his initiative, you've got to force that initiative all the time. If you step back and quit doing their work for them or stop going the extra mile and depend on them, then you've got trouble. You can't be soft on one thing and hard on another," says Hardison.

The challenge of developing a new, merged culture was difficult for both companies. Both had to change from a family-run, personally managed company to a corporate culture. Hardison explains that that transition was tough on everybody. Employees from both companies had to give up something and to make significant adjustments. The Jimmy Dean people lost the close connection to Dean himself. Even though the new culture from the beginning acknowledged the need for his involvement, as it recognized the marketing advantage of his name, Jimmy Dean's role was diminished in terms of involvement with the staff. The new company recognized that it had to establish its own identity.

Rudy's people, on the other hand, felt that they had been swallowed up. Since the first president of the merged company came from Jimmy Dean, many of the initial rituals of the emerging third culture derived from that company. Many of these rituals, including the dress code, the way secretaries addressed their bosses, and what was allowed on the office walls, were drastically different from the old Rudy's culture. Dress at Jimmy Dean was much more formal, and the offices were much more homogenous than those at Rudy's. In fact, so clashing were some of their rituals, and so different in management styles were their senior leaders, that, according to Bill Hardison, "this merger could have ended up as a marriage made in hell."

In other ways, the crafters of the new company tried to demonstrate impartiality. They chose a neutral geographic location for the new company's corporate office and selected managers and vice presidents from both companies.

### The First Phases of the Merger

The first stage of the merger was filled with the usual loss and grief associated with the dying away of any "old order" and was emotionally wrenching. There were so many changes—social change, change in working relationships, change in work habits. In the beginning, Jimmy Dean folks felt they had lost Jimmy Dean, and many of the Rudy's folks felt that they had lost their entire company. According to Bill Hardison, "Actually, that's reality now." Fortunately, most of those from Rudy's had anticipated the merger and resigned themselves to it.

According to Hardison, "For the Jimmy Dean folks, the primary loss was the lessening activity of Jimmy Dean. Because he had had the control he had, this was a major adjustment." Some employees missed Jimmy's protective and paternalistic approach, explains Hardison: "I'm sure that they were a little uneasy with his decreased involvement." Furthermore, Hardison explains, some of the Jimmy Dean employees felt that the president of the merged company (who had been Jimmy Dean's president) made excessive concessions to the "other side"—to Rudy's management. As for the Rudy's people, they felt they had to keep a low profile since at the beginning the culture of the new company and its power brokers came from Jimmy Dean. Both sides felt the loss of having to move to another geographic area.

Certainly the crafters of the new culture considered all the components: people (choosing employees from both cultures to fill job slots);

time (deciding on the appropriate cycle times for strategic business reviews); space (deciding where people and activities would be physically located); and social concerns (considering what people would best fit which activities). The designers began developing leaders for the new culture.

This first phase lasted about two years. Says Hardison, "We got over the hump of deciding who we wanted to be part of the combined company; we got over the next hump of getting the people we wanted and losing the people who could not buy into the new culture."

Frustrations and fears subsided as energy was channeled in new directions, and people began to accept the change. But this acceptance was not consistent. This was a chaotic phase; at times people expressed acceptance, and at other times they reminisced about the "good old days" before the change.

During this second phase, three aspects of the culture began to change: the technical system (organization of people, capital, information, and technology to produce the product); the political system (the allocation of power, rewards, and career opportunities, which did not change significantly); and the cultural system (the set of shared norms and beliefs).

### The Third Phase and the Emerging Third Culture

The emerging new culture has taken on characteristics of both companies, as well as some entirely new ones. It is more open than the old Jimmy Dean culture and probably more structured than the old Rudy's culture. Bill Hardison explains that the key to unifying the new culture is to focus on what the customer really expects, rather than what management thinks the customer wants. He says that while this philosophy has not been easy to swallow, everybody has begun to embrace it.

A significant sign that the third culture was indeed emerging was the formulation of a new vision statement that connected people as well as product with profit. This statement was not directed by Sara Lee, nor was it the work of any single person or culture. The vision blended the ideas of individual contributors, middle managers, and senior managers at the local level and reflected a people, product, and customer promise that the contributors felt reflected what they were becoming. I had the opportunity of a lifetime to facilitate the formulation of this new statement, in which senior and middle managers, including the company president, and individual contributors came together and agreed on what they really valued.

The degree to which the new culture has responded to emerging customer tastes and preferences is seen in its 80 percent fat-free sausage. Fat-free sausage—sounds like an oxymoron, doesn't it!

There are still problems to be resolved, among them the relationship between the new company and Jimmy Dean himself. Since Jimmy Dean's name appears on the product, he naturally wants to know about product development and about marketing strategies. But there is a new president, one who came from neither company, and he also has his own vision of where the company should go. He came from neither of the old cultures and is determined to develop the new culture into one where the customer is the centerpiece.

A new vision, a new president, a new culture. It took five years to create, and it is still evolving.

## A Quality Revolution at Square D

In 1987 Square D intensified its quality focus. While the company had been known since 1903 for a high-quality product, that product wasn't always what the customer wanted, explains Jim Clark, Vice President of Engineering Products: "In many cases Square D overdesigned the product and gave the customer more than what he wanted." Now the customer's voice is the key.

Bill Fightmaster, former Vice President for Corporate Quality, adds that the quality "revolution" had to do with more than just product—it was an entire cultural transformation. "Quality became a way of life. Whereas previously Square D's top management had reflected a top-down style where decisions had been made mostly by management, with the change to a quality culture, anyone could make suggestions of improvement. This was a radical departure." Furthermore, according to Fightmaster, "employees could make suggestions without fear of reprisal." Square D called the initiative its "3 P's"—the power to make changes, the permission to do it, and the protection to do it.

Fightmaster explains that although there was similarity in cultural philosophy among Square D's various components, the quality movement lacked a unified direction for a while: "Because of the diverse offerings of Square D at the different plant locations, different regions were doing their own brand of the quality process." Each plant was a separate business and had its own profit and loss statement.

> So although there had been a quality thrust, we didn't have people moving in the same general direction. We might have

people at Middletown, Ohio, doing Deming, others at the Smyrna plant attending the Juran Institute. And there was not a position which would integrate quality across the organization. Consequently, our quality initiative had not achieved the results we had hoped for.

Senior leadership put together a task force, including employees from marketing, manufacturing, engineering, and human resources, that formulated an overall quality plan for the entire organization, "The Quality Leadership Network." One of the first things the task force decided was that it would have to ask people to do things differently. According to Fightmaster, "Not only was the leadership paradigm changed, but so were the rituals." He explains that things that had established people's sense of identity, like exclusive signature authorization, were dropped. This meant that things that once only a manager could sign for can now be signed for by anyone. Says Fightmaster, "All of a sudden you are giving your secretary authority to purchase office supplies, while the manager is saying, 'I don't want to see office requisitions for supplies; you can sign up to $1,500.00.' " (Fightmaster explains that senior management had told managers that they could do things differently back in their "Vision-Mission College" in 1987 [see Chapter 11] but unfortunately neglected to tell them how. When roles and rules change, people have to given guidelines.)

Even good changes carry with them great stress. Skills that brought rewards in the past become obsolete. Consequently, Square D began to train its employees by bringing team members together to troubleshoot and solve problems.

In 1991, the company introduced the C2Q process, which represents its commitment to quality. This process included developing criteria and quality indicators, some similar to those required for the Baldrige Award, and customizing them for Square D's business. Fightmaster elaborates: "A team went to other companies that had similar manufacturing processes to ours and looked at what they have done and put together a program that was molded strictly for our company. We put it together in twelve months. Once we rolled out this C2Q process, we determined we were going to do it across the whole company."

Square D's quality effort has paid off. At its Middletown, Ohio, plant (which only a few years ago was slated to be closed because of low productivity), 99 percent of the employees have participated in the certified work group program for ISO 9002 standard, and all of the thirty-two individual line and staff departments at this facility are now certified. Four of the work groups are now self-directed. Bob Sheffield, former Middletown plant manager, describes the benefits that have accrued from this endeavor: "Employee involvement and awareness are its highest point ever. Employee pride, once a serious problem here, is now our strong point, as evidenced by eagerness to participate in Square D problem-solving and quality-improvement teams." Further proof that this initiative is paying off is the fact that there have been no employee grievances filed since June 1991.

## Shifting the Culture One Behavior at a Time

This book's overall theme is that the cultural infrastructure must be in place for any quality focus to be sustained. One of the biggest challenges for people is understanding what organizational "culture" really means and seeing the relationship between their actions and that "culture."

People on the front line have a tendency to think they will be handed the new culture. They have a tough time understanding that real culture change is usually grass-roots driven and comes from their own actions. People seem to exaggerate the difference between behaviors and systems and "culture." One clearly produces the other. When I do training, I have to deal with changing systems and structures and behavior, since these are concrete and are all that can really be measured. Actually, many times these must precede belief and attitude, which make up an organizational culture.

Leaders can take specific steps to drive cultural change. Leaders have a responsibility to create conditions that enable the organization to grow and thrive. Even though no one can mandate cultural change, senior leaders can mandate a performance plan that includes continuous improvement. They can reward teamwork and measure quality improvements. Employers like General Electric and Motorola have discovered that a key ingredient in getting employees to acknowledge and embrace organizational change is compensation. Instead of handing out automatic annual pay increases based on title and seniority, which was the common practice in the old paradigm, these companies reward teamwork, measurable quality improvements, and employees' acquisition of new skills.

Senior managers and team leaders can factor creativity and innovativeness into selection criteria and formulate probes that can uncover these. They can begin every staff meeting with success stories about the quality initiative. They can share financial data with all employees—even if they don't think the employees will understand them. And they can make empowerment a two-way street by expecting better goal achievement and competitiveness in return for sharing responsibility and ownership. These are the actions that make up an organization's culture.

## A Checklist for Change

Following are some questions organizations need to answer to facilitate change to a quality culture.

1. Does the company place higher value on past rituals and behavior than on innovation? If so, why?
2. What specifically do people value about the past culture?
3. How often are employees' conversations infused with references to what customers value, rather than what is good for the organization?
4. Do employees talk about the future on a regular basis, or is it reserved for R & D labs?
5. Has the company attempted to define what its products and services will be in the future?
6. To what extent are current systems (performance appraisal system, compensation system, selection system) aligned with where the company is trying to go? Does the performance appraisal system reward people for both team and individual effort? Do selection standards include creativity and the ability to manage change?
7. How often do people in the organization cross over functions and develop products and services together?
8. How often do multidisciplinary teams include major customers and suppliers?
9. Are managers and team leaders given clear guidance regarding their roles in creating and executing strategy? Are they empowered to change processes and systems at the local level to serve the customer better?
10. Are champions of the quality culture positioned throughout the organization, from clerks to project managers?

# 17

# Proceed With Caution (in Chopping Limbs)

## The Danger of Arbitrary Downsizing

Xerox Corporation was the first U.S. company to recapture from the Japanese a market leadership position that it had lost. Xerox's revenues increased 50 percent between 1984 and 1994, producing good profits and providing steady employment. Despite this, the company announced a decision to cut ten thousand jobs, or 10 percent of its workforce, over three years, most of them white-collar jobs. This represents just one example of an economic paradox evident in American industry.

There is a good side to this economic picture. The United States is no longer losing ground to Japan; service exports to Eastern Europe have increased at a 25 percent rate in recent years; thousands of American companies have taken a new, aggressive approach to selling in the international arena—and they are succeeding. U.S. businesses are venturing into new markets, exporting goods and services that had never gone abroad before, thinking up new ways to apply their technological know-how. This new spark is coming from the energy and vision of American managers and entrepreneurs who are overcoming obstacles to stake overseas claims. American manufacturers are accommodating foreign preferences and are customizing products for these markets.

Now for the bad side of the picture. Increased market share has not led to additional jobs at home. In order to compete effectively, corporations must have a lean and flexible organization that can deliver the most cost-effective products and services. For large corporations that often translates into trimming the workforce.

Mergers and acquisitions and competitive pressures have driven many U.S. companies to the belief that arbitrary layoffs are necessary for continued profitability or, in some cases, corporate survival. Those layoffs, however, are not producing the benefits companies had hoped for. Only 34 percent of downsized companies have reported increases in productivity since 1988, and fewer than half have seen their operating profits improve, according to an article in *Fortune* magazine in January 1994. Employee morale among the survivors has plummeted.

## Downsizing—Not a Panacea

Downsizing is now pervasive, and cost-control, head-count, and staff-related costs are major priorities in U.S. industry. But there is no magic in cutting employees. If a company thinks about what it's doing only in terms of downsizing, it will be unsuccessful.

Many organizations view downsizing as a panacea for quality without reflecting on what caused them to be so labor-intensive in the first place. They have not realized that downsizing done in a vacuum can cause more problems than it solves. Unless they are part of a broader corporate strategy, layoffs are a short-term fix. Arbitrary downsizing is expensive.

Downsizing actions are generally accompanied by lots of golden parachutes, such as attractive early retirement terms offered to workers as young as age 50. While these actions are humanitarian, paying people not to work increases production costs and certainly doesn't help your competitiveness.

Downsizing is expensive in other ways. Companies are left with scared, dispirited, downsized people who are then expected to revitalize and reengineer the organization. Corporate performance expectations are not realistic in this scenario.

In the late 1970s and early 1980s many corporations used a depressed order rate and a general downturn of the national economy to rationalize laying off personnel. In the 1990s, the reason given is the need to build and maintain global competitiveness. While the reasons are different, the result in many cases is the same—slashing, especially middle-management jobs. This cutting is often done without examining what caused the labor intensiveness in the first place and without considering the consequences of that slashing on those who are left.

It seems ironic that at a time when American industries are eagerly embracing total quality principles, which are in large measure responsible for their again becoming competitive, many are actually undermining their own efforts through improperly planned and chaotic reductions.

### Purging of the "Undesirables"

During the 1970s and 1980s, the phrase for "downsized" was "laid off," but in reality these people were rarely called back. These employees involved were usually the "undesirables"—either older employees who were considered to be no longer productive, boat rockers who were perceived to cause discontent among employees, or merely those who were perceived to be disloyal to the cause.

I saw personal values wither as unit managers or section managers were pressured to go along with the layoffs, regardless of their personal convictions.

Performance appraisals were often used as a way to rid the organization of older employees and trim back payroll costs. One particular employee, who had a degree in engineering and in law, worked for twenty-four years doing substantially the same thing within GE: filing patent agreements, writing license agreements, and litigating patent agreements. At the end of that time he was told he wasn't qualified. The attorney claimed that his supervisor gave him an unfair performance appraisal which led him to resign. He retorted, "If I was qualified for twenty-four years, why wasn't I qualified for twenty-five? I hadn't had brain damage."

Likewise, I worked with a master's degreed engineer who had been with the company for twenty-five years and was known by managers and individual contributors alike to be a dedicated hard worker. He was terminated because of recent low performance appraisal scores, which he never really understood. Subsequently, he applied for more than ten jobs within the company, none of which he was successful in getting.

## Downsizing Today: Valid but Still Tough to Swallow

Today, there are certainly valid reasons to reduce labor intensity. First, low inflation rates make it difficult for companies to raise prices, thus putting continued pressure on profit margins. To stay competitive, companies must keep a tight rein on expenditures and make sure budget requests are flat. Corporations recognize that they simply can't afford labor intensiveness if they are going to respond to the global challenge. But many employees find the need to compete globally an even harder pill to swallow than the need to compete domestically, which was the major driving force in the 1970s.

Those companies that have a strong quality consciousness and the *entire* quality formula are now handling the layoffs more openly and fairly. Employees are generally told the truth about the need to reduce staff. There appears to be less manipulation, like lowering performance appraisal scores to justify layoffs, than in previous years. Many organizations offer recareer options and outplacement services. For example, when GM eliminated its in-house security force in 1993, seventy former guards were sent to school to become automotive engineers. Companies now pay more attention to the survivors. Still, it's tough on everybody—for those laid off, for those doing the layoffs, and for those left behind.

Some executives, in an attempt to avert layoffs, try running their departments slightly understaffed. But this can lead to overworked and dispirited people.

## Breaking the Contract

While I was conducting training for the Soil Conservation Service of the U.S. Department of Agriculture, the participants were read a faxed communication from Washington informing them that a certain number of slots were available to those eligible for early retirement. Anyone interested had twenty-four hours to sign up. I reflected on the irony of this—normally government moves at a sluggish pace on even the most insignificant decisions; now, people had one day to make a decision that would affect the rest of their lives.

This offer of early retirement was part of the downsizing of government that is being driven by both the taxpayer and Congress. Those who signed up were to receive $25,000, in addition to their regular pensions, as an incentive. Some saw the offer as a poker game and speculated that another offer later might mean more money. The problem was that there appeared to be no criterion for determining the reduction other than the need to chop so many slots. While listening to the news, I wondered how taxpayers would react if they knew of these "golden parachutes" being offered as a way to make government look leaner. Leaner, yes, but at what price to the taxpayer and the survivors?

Still, many of these federal employees believe that this is the least government should do for them. Like many corporate men and women in the 1970s who gave their entire lives to their companies, many government employees feel betrayed. They accepted work as civil service employees, sometimes at lower wages than those in private industry, in exchange for job security. Now that contract has been broken.

We would like to believe that those who dictated the cuts considered the costs of increased stress, lower morale, and even higher operating costs from the creation of new alliances, to say nothing of quality short-cuts. Ironically, although downsizing is supposed to give employees greater control of their work, workers have an increased need for some-one "in charge" during these difficult times. With broken alliances, they may not find this sense of security.

## Rightsizing, Not Downsizing

If companies are going to continue to increase quality, they must have an efficient, content, and productive workforce. Those companies that are "back on track" have higher morale and higher productivity than those who aren't. They are squeezing the cost out of manufacturing while at the same time improving quality. What are they doing differently from the rest in terms of downsizing and layoffs? The answer is that they are rightsizing, not downsizing.

They treat downsizing not as an end in itself but as a means to be-come more productive. They see it as a part of a long-term program to renew corporate health. They take a good, long, hard look at what led to the downsizing in the first place. They don't begin with the question, "Which people should we cut?" They ask the more important question—which is more difficult to address—"How do we change the way we oper-ate? How, indeed, do we change our culture?"

World-class organizations have been willing to depart from the tradi-tional American tendency to solve problems in a linear fashion, step by step, without looking at the reasoning processes beyond the problem at hand. They have adopted the Japanese approach of looking beyond what's on the table and factoring in broader issues having to do with the corporation's place in society. In Japan, the contextual rationale, personal values, and individual workers' skills are weighed in corporate decision making, along with the cost and efficiency considerations that have tradi-tionally guided American reasoning.

Restructuring means cutting out overcapacity and getting rid of bloated bureaucracies. It is taking the unnecessary, nonvalue-added cus-tomer work out and getting back to essentials. It's almost creating that mom-and-pop operation of many years ago. Flattening should mean fewer reports and meetings. It should mean more risk taking and greater speed.

Those companies whose quality remains high after downsizing do not downsize capriciously. They continue to apply total quality principles during the process of reduction. They analyze what tasks are most significant to an efficient and effective organization. They don't spend time worrying about how much work has to be done but consider instead *what* the work is that has to be done. They keep evaluating the work and asking themselves, "Does that work add anything to the bottom line of the company?"

They ask the right questions: Which tasks can be performed well by temporary staff or contract employees? What business status reports are really necessary? Where is the bulk of customer concerns coming from? (Pareto's law is useful here, as 80 percent of complaints usually come from 20 percent of customers.) What is the source of most of our rework? Which of our activities really contribute to our bottom line? Which ones have the most customer impact? What would happen if we quit doing them? They ask people at all levels to look for ways to eliminate reports, approvals, meetings, policies that don't add customer value. In particular, work areas that have chronic overtime and high turnover profit greatly from this scrutiny.

Successful organizations determine what their core business is going to be, stick with it, and keep striving to make it better. They realize that fat is likely to reappear unless cost cutting is done strategically. People in these organizations are moving away from the idea of the company as protector. They're starting to consider how they add value to the group. They are becoming more entrepreneurial. They are looking beyond just cost cutting to see how they can increase sales and ensure value for the company.

Simplifying operations saves costs. That's often the motivation for drafting SOPs. However, if left unchecked, these procedures tend to last long after their usefulness has worn out and can end up being very expensive. A few years ago, I was struggling with writing a course manual as part of a Department of Defense contract. Frustrated with trying to reconcile the contract requirements about the writing style and format with the principles of good writing (which was one of the focus areas in the training), I eventually telephoned my course proponent. She seemed confused about my question and responded that these requirements were no longer applicable to this type of training contract and that I should ignore them.

Organizations should regularly take a look at their systems and procedures to determine which ones need to be eliminated. Particularly in periods of downsizing, they should encourage staff to scrutinize which procedures are valuable and which ones have outlived their usefulness.

### Why We Prune in the First Place

If downsizing is done in a vacuum, without examining the processes that most impact the customer, it is an expensive proposition, and the benefits are usually short-lived. What companies must do is examine why they have to downsize in the first place. Labor intensiveness, you say. But what led to that?

Bill Hardison, former Corporate Vice President of the Sara Lee Meat Group, explains the hazards of becoming too labor-intensive and then having to downsize to stay competitive and fast.

> One of our biggest problems today in industry is that we haven't had to make do. Perhaps we've not had enough crises we've had to rise up to. . . . It has become too easy to borrow money. . . . We build up the orchard, and then we say that we have to chop down some of the limbs. But if we don't remember why we're chopping, to produce trees that are more fruitful, then our chopping is in vain.

He says that one of the toughest parts of the president's job is cutting staff. He concedes, however, that the downsizings and restructuring of companies and core industries will continue as the U.S. battles to remain competitive.

Dr. Armand Feigenbaum, a quality guru who worked at GE early in his career, affirms a similar belief in an interview that was reported in *Industry Week* magazine for July 4, 1994. He maintains that the problem with downsizing is that "you will cut off the good heads with the bad heads . . . that you'll simply move costs from one part of the organization to another without ever getting at them."

### Chopping Is Easier Than Analyzing

Of course, it is a lot easier to just eliminate boxes on the organizational chart than to consider those processes that have the most impact on the customer and eliminate jobs on that basis. The first step, defining the processes, can be time-consuming. Initially, AT&T's Network Services Division, which has more than sixteen thousand employees, tallied up some

130 processes before it narrowed them down to 13 core ones. The second ordeal is trying to get people whose whole security has been based on what they have done for marketing, or sales, or manufacturing, to agree to move beyond territorial function. They have to come to grips with the fact that the function cannot be a basis for their future.

## "Sizing It Up"

Downsizing alone can occasionally produce a positive impact on the bottom line. A downsized Hewlett Packard not only cut costs but bolstered sales and earnings and launched new products. At a minimum, downsizing forces organizations to address questions about the nature of employment in the future, questions such as, "If you can't offer workers job security, how can you expect them to be committed to the future of the organization?"

If downsizing is done in a vacuum, it is generally very costly. Companies can't lay off people without examining what led to the layoffs in the first place and determining which processes have value and which do not. This is a time-consuming process, but it will pay dividends in the long run. If the company just restructures or downsizes without fundamentally changing its way of working in terms of quality, the downsizing will only be a bandaid, and it will not stick. And it will have such a devastating effect on the survivors that it will not raise the quality level in the long run. Rightsizing, on the other hand, provides a framework that organizations can use to question long-held assumptions. It can then use the answers as a basis for organizational redesign.

When automation replaces people, the company needs to reassure nervous employees by focusing on the total costs of production, not just the labor costs. Those people replaced need to get the first shot at new openings around the company. It is critical that positions, rather than people, be eliminated.

# 18

# Troop Trains—
# Defending Defense

## Quality—Not the Special Province of Industry

If it is true that culture can be changed only one action and one process at a time, it may seem virtually impossible to really change our federal government, which employs 2.9 million civilians and maintains a military force of more than 1.5 million. It has become trendy to beat up on the government for its sluggishness, its labor intensiveness, and what appears to be its lack of operational improvement goals. We shake our heads at scandals, from $600 toilet seats to Congress's inability to balance a checkbook.

Before I became a Department of Defense (DOD) contractor, I, too, believed that all civil workers were lazy bureaucrats who had become too comfortable with their jobs. I had a disdain for the inefficiency of government agencies and believed that all government employees were trying to steal from taxpayers. Having worked with the DOD for more than ten years, now I have changed my mind, at least in some respects. I still become frustrated with the arrogant, often godlike, attitude displayed by some functions. And I stay amazed at how the simplest task can be stretched over such a long time, causing tremendous schedule pressures for contractors in the field. I have learned, however, that many government employees are hard-working and dedicated to a high-quality product. I have learned that many of them believe, as I do, that government is too bureaucratic and too wasteful, and they are as eager as I am to see a reduction in government regulations.

The condition of federal agencies is not so different from that of U.S. companies during the "derailment," when businesses were also incredibly bureaucratic and labor intensive. Lest we in industry become too smug about our "superiority" to government, we might remember that until the late 1970s, and in some cases the 1980s, employees in most private corporations were rewarded for following "the GE way" or "the GM way." Creativity was endorsed only if it was seen as compatible with the existing culture. Many of those same companies have now been recrafted and are on the road to recovery.

I may be naive, but I believe that the government can also be fixed. In fact, things are already changing as a deficit-laden United States and the resulting fiscal austerity are driving federal agencies to adopt total quality management practices. Agencies recognize that they must be customer-driven, and partnering efforts are decreasing the costs of doing business. The Department of Defense is benchmarking some of its functions against world-class performers, such as FedEx. Like many corporations, the U.S. Army finds itself going through a massive overhaul. It has suffered cuts that are deeper and in some ways more painful than those at General Motors and IBM.

## An Overview of the Government's Quality Journey

The quality effort has been under way throughout most government agencies for several years. Public service visionaries have been embracing TQM ideas since the late 1980s, and most have incorporated techniques into a variety of governmental programs. In 1990 the Office of Management and Budget cited quality and productivity-improvement efforts under way in 265 government programs. The seriousness of the government initiative is reflected in the *National Performance Review*, a 1993 study of federal agencies that contains recommendations for cutting red tape, focusing employees on customers, and eliminating programs that are valueless and rules that are senseless. The study, the result of work begun under former President George Bush and accelerated by Vice President Al Gore, recommends reducing regulations and empowering employees to make decisions that will benefit both internal and external customers; its findings have been described as "reinventing government."

Reinventing Government (REGO) is an effort to improve efficiency and effectiveness of government. It projects a savings of $108 billion, and the elimination of 252,000 civilian jobs by the year 2000. Most of the members of the council responsible for these recommendations are federal employees who, because they have suffered the consequences of strangling regulations, should know more about the waste and mismanagement of government than anybody else. They have sought ideas and advice from all across the United States, from management experts, business leaders, and private citizens.

The report has been hailed by the private sector as a policy statement that spells out a clear vision and gives government executives the responsibility for their agencies' missions. The Council for Excellence in Government claims, "The last ten years in the private sector have taught us that lower costs and leaner structures are not in themselves ends or goals; they are the consequences of well managed, mission-driven organizations. They are tools used to deliver quality, value and customer satisfaction."

Some of the quality effort in the federal government has been sporadic and piecemeal. In the words of a report by Colonel Michael Diffley and Lt. Colonel Robert Slockbower of the New Orleans District of the U.S. Army Corps of Engineers, "it may be several years before the paradigms and business skills characteristic of a mature TQM program will be common." Nonetheless, government agencies have come a long way from thinking of themselves as "entitled" to work to realizing that they must be held accountable for results produced. In the Army, middle management has been reduced by 25 percent, and there will be more reductions. The Army is facing the challenge of recruiting young people when a lifetime "career ladder," once a primary lure, is becoming less of a possibility. In my twelve years as a government contractor, I have never seen government and private industry share so many common challenges and initiatives as I have seen in the quality initiative. The government initiative is serious, and the results are dramatic.

## Restraining Forces

When plumbers at the Sacramento Army Depot found leaking traps, their manager followed standard operating procedure. He called the procurement office where an officer, knowing nothing about steam traps, followed common practice. He waited for enough orders to buy in bulk, saving the government about $10 per trap. No regulation required him to wait, just a powerful tradition. So the Sacramento Depot didn't get new steam traps for a year. In the meantime, each of their leaking traps spewed $2,500 worth of steam. To save $10, the central procurement system wasted $2,500.

Presently, government faces even greater restraints than industry in moving to a quality culture. From voluminous regulations regarding travel authorization to the budget process, the federal government is handicapped by outmoded laws and practices. Government employees believe they can do little about these moribund systems and structures. Or if they can, the process is painfully slow.

## Regulations

First, regulations, practices, and systems can't be changed as easily as those in private industry. Even if they envision what those systems should look like, managers are inundated with obsolete regulations that prevent them from recreating relevant ones.

### Procurement

In a recent training seminar activity for the U.S. Army Corps of Engineers, teams were asked to determine value-added steps and nonvalue-added steps in a process that affected internal and external customers. One team delineated a seventeen-step process for purchasing a $40 calculator!

Until the recent passage of the Simplified Purchasing Act, which is intended for small purchases (at the time of this writing it had yet to become operational at all field levels), this $40 calculator ended up costing thousands of dollars. An employee working in private industry would run down to Walmart and purchase it for $40. A government employee must follow processes with redundancies. These employees see better than anyone the waste here, but they have been powerless to change things, since regulations drive each step.

### Environmental Protection Laws

Likewise, the implementation of environmental regulations to clean up toxic hazardous waste in remediation (restoring the environment to its original state) is extremely costly to the federal agency involved and ultimately to the taxpayer. For example, because of mandates to clean up former defense sites, the DOD must spend tons of money burning dirt— literally. In the case of underground storage tanks, the laws mandate a convoluted process of dealing with them that is often costly and unnecessary, according to engineers. If in fact these tanks are leaking enough toxic gas to create harmful effects, there are other ways of preventing it, including capping the tanks in some instances. In any event, installations should be given authority to develop cheaper and more efficient ways to resolve these toxic hazardous waste issues, since they understand the problem better than congressional members—sometimes even better than DOD headquarters staff.

Other environmental regulations are equally costly to implement, such as those required to reduce trauma to migratory fishes. In some local agencies, employees on the front line have been given the opportunity to develop less costly ways of progressing migratory fishes to reduce this trauma.

## Military Construction

Another costly example of too many regulations is the Construction Appropriations Program. If a military installation wants to build a new building or add to an existing one, and it has funds for it already, it cannot use its own funds over a certain dollar figure without getting congressional military construction appropriation. This is one reason we see so many "patchwork quilt" barracks and military buildings at installations.

## Personnel Practices—Punishment and Reward

Virtually all federal managers express frustration about their powerlessness to reward good performance or get rid of the deadwood, because of the voluminous amount of documentation required by regulations. The current system makes termination so difficult and time-consuming that few managers are willing to try. Instead, they are compelled to isolate these poor performers, give them virtually nothing to do to reduce their negative impact, and wait until they retire.

Conversely, strictly defined merit systems, when they exist at all, make it hard to provide incentives for high performers. Managers and individual contributors alike are often evaluated on "form filling" rather than on mission accomplishment. Government employees have traditionally been rewarded for *following* systems, not creating them. They have been rewarded for administering the status quo, not moving beyond it and creating their future by defining ways to streamline their operations. Like managers in private industry during the derailment, these employees have been conditioned to be keepers of the system. Although in recent years they may have worked on "solving problems," this focus is still different from improving those processes where gaps aren't apparent. The philosophy of "if it ain't broke, don't fix it" pervaded government, as it did industry, until the 1990s. The Government Performance and Results Act of 1993 should help force clarity of goals and objectives and a focus on outcomes.

### Budget Process

Another barrier is the budget process. One of the most contradictory practices to operating our federal government agencies in an innovative and entrepreneurial way is the manner in which money is appropriated. Unlike those in the private sector, federal managers and other employees have little incentive to save money in a single year, since if they don't use it, they lose it. They cannot use the leftover money for training, improved technology, or program innovations. This process is a major impediment to encouraging quality improvement and scrutinizing processes for value-added components. Federal employees often feel as if they were actually being penalized for saving money, so they feel they must learn to manipulate the system in order to "balance the scales."

## Emphasizing Product Over Process

Second is the challenge of emphasizing product over process. Just as the concentration of product over process got U.S. industry into serious trouble in the 1970s, so the government's emphasis of process over product has been a problem. Government managers admit that they've gotten so caught up in "coordinating" that at times they have forgotten what the coordinating was supposed to accomplish. They have been compensated for inputs, not outcomes. For example, managers are recognized for the number of reports generated, or the RFPs written, not for the results of either. Of 103 federal agencies studied by the National Performance Review task force, two thirds were found to have strategic plans, but in only nine were they linked to outcomes (*National Performance Review*). Employees are still rewarded for spending (inputs), not saving (outputs). For the most part, their performance objectives have been written in terms of process, not outcomes. This challenge stems, in part, from the difficulty of thinking of government as a business with customers and stakeholders.

## The Challenge of Becoming Entrepreneurial

For government employees, the changing paradigm is not just about learning to operate "outside the chain of command," but learning to become creative and entrepreneurial. In industry, at least before the derailment, we were expected to be creative and entrepreneurial. And today we either vaguely remember that expectation, or still see the results of it in

American innovations. Governmental agencies, however, have never really expected their employees to act in this way, and employees themselves don't have such a reference point. Therefore, these employees must actually change more than those in industry.

Some government employees possessed an entrepreneurial spirit when they began working in the government but have since lost that spirit, becoming strangled by convoluted procedures and reward systems that do not endorse risk taking or creativity. Consequently, they have either catered to the system or sought jobs elsewhere.

## The Entrenched Chain of Command

For me, as an Army Corps of Engineers contractor, the layered bureaucracy has been one of the most frustrating barriers. In our training classes, many of the middle and first-line managers have indicated that they have never seen or heard their own vision and mission statements around which we build their training. A consultant should not be the first person to show them the direction in which their agency is going! This gap illustrates one harmful consequence of bureaucracies: By the time information and direction make their way down through all the layers to first-line and middle managers (who are the ones who must translate the information into *action*), they are often obsolete or meaningless. So while much money and energy have been spent on words of total quality in federal agencies, those agencies have not yet been able to fully capitalize on that effort.

## The "Cushion" of Bureaucracy

Another major barrier is that some employees and managers really do not want the government to change. They are comfortable with entitlement. The bureaucracy enables them to hide mediocre performance. Jerry Liebes, Corps of Engineers Deputy Chief, Human Resources Planning, Development and Evaluation in Washington, D.C., has insisted for years that the internal customers should often go ahead and take action, instead of blaming everything on the regulations. According to Liebes, "Regulations are sometimes used as an excuse for inaction." Federal agencies themselves are responsible for many of the regulations; if employees challenge the utility of these and demonstrate that they are inhibiting their efficiency, there's a good chance they can be eliminated.

## A Lack of Belief

A final barrier to change is the lack of belief that government really *can* change the way it operates. It's tough for many to believe that a Congress that has in many ways justified value for itself by legislating and regulating is really going to work to decrease government. Nowhere has bureaucracy grown more than on Capitol Hill, where some 37,000 aides and functionaries serve the House and the Senate—an average of sixty-nine per legislator! The number of staff members has nearly tripled since 1960, and the proliferation of committees and subcommittees has spawned fiefdoms that ensnare serious legislation efforts.

## Additional Challenges for the Military

The military faces still another barrier. It's hard to find any organization with a longer history of honoring the chain of command than the military, but the structure poses more challenges than it does in private industry.

And the reluctance to benchmark is also cultural. According to Captain James Fritz, Air Force Quality Control (AFQC) Quality Advisor, the military system of awarding promotion and high performance ratings fosters competition but discourages teamwork. This competitive spirit certainly serves the military well during wartime, but during peacetime, it may discourage units from working together so that everyone can improve. Fritz explains that if an Air Force unit discovers through benchmarking that another group or squadron is more efficient than it is, it is unlikely to publicize the fact that a group of peers has built a better mousetrap. He emphasizes the need for the military to face its own culture and change to systems and structures that will enable a quality culture to evolve.

### Recognizing the Need for Empowerment

It's widely recognized that the DOD's existing command and control management style is outmoded. Even though people still talk about the command and control components of leadership, a great deal more is said about communications and empowerment. The word "intelligence" has taken on new meaning—making decisions consistent with the overall mission.

This is not all talk. The quality initiative in the Army and the Air Force is in some ways as serious as that in private industry, if not more so. The Gulf War victory in 1991 is attributed to speed, surprise [contingencies driven by initiatives at the lowest levels], and stellar technology, rather than the sheer muscle strength of the Allied forces.

In many ways the Army is ahead of other organizations in understanding that it can no longer micromanage its troops, given the rapidly changing and expanding mission of the Army. It has grappled with the question of how officers can lead in situations that are highly unpredictable and at which they cannot even be present. (Remember the many times during the Gulf War when General Schwarzkopf was in Washington and the troops, because of a shared mission, did not even realize it and were able to act anyway?)

The Army has recently recognized that most major battles have been won not by a general's orders but by low-ranking officers' action based on a "commander's intent." Furthermore, some of the humanitarian missions undertaken by the military have required as much tact, intelligence, and discretion as the command of platoons in combat. Army officers have had to move beyond SOPs and think on their feet.

Today Army training emphasizes leadership, not just decision making, especially leadership that motivates the troops and works to build a cohesive work unit.

### Ensuring Predictable Results Without Hands-On Management

The U.S. Army and Air Force are struggling with the same issues surrounding empowerment as private industry. The overall challenge often cited by military leaders is to determine how a leader can help to create excellent and predictable results without hands-on management. The military, not unlike Sara Lee or Federal Express, is focused on how to move information everywhere in the organization without knowing ahead of time who will need what. The DOD has helped units enjoy greater access to one another by keeping them small.

The Army, for example, is determining in detail how to move information that formerly was held only by commanders all the way to lower-level soldiers, such as the crew members of a tank. As General Norman Schwarzkopf said, "You can stand in front of a tank and yell, 'right face,' but it's only when you have people lined up to the rear that the tank is going to move." The Army and the Air Force recognize that they will need to support more decision making within local units because it is that level of local autonomy that gives the troops their highest effectiveness. The Army has had proof of the effectiveness of rapid information exchanges at local levels in initiatives such as Desert Storm and the disaster relief effort that helped victims of Hurricane Andrew.

These departments also recognize, however, that if they're going to liberate people from policy and procedural manuals, they have to provide something for them to use instead. And that means promoting a clear sense of mission, shared organizational values (what is important and what is not), and the skills to make decisions.

## Creating a Quality Air Force

Realizing that rules and regulations strangle empowerment, the Air Force has eliminated more than one-third of its regulations. A lot of people may sneer when they hear the words "quality" and "headquarters" used together—in any organization. But in the U.S. Air Force, these two words are no longer mutually exclusive.

The quality vision began at the Pentagon, the headquarters of the DOD, with senior leadership's commitment to a quality Air Force. The Air Force Quality Institute at Maxwell AFB has been empowered since 1991 to provide commanders and their organizations with advice, concepts, methods, educational resources, and a common frame of reference for attaining a quality Air Force culture. The center advocates customer-driven service based on the concept of continuous improvements. It offers education, training, resources, support, and consulting services in continuous quality improvement.

A group of Air Force trainers work together as an informal network, sharing information and developing training for anyone in the Air Force to use. They operate on the belief that every little bit helps to implement a quality culture.

In addressing the quality challenge, Colonel Hank Firumara, Commander of the Air Force Quality Institute, sounds remarkably similar to CEOs in private industry when he says that:

> Quality is the unleashing of human potential within the organization. Quality has a truly human dimension . . . it's not something we can put in the context of a cookbook or menu of options. People want to do well . . . give them opportunities . . . focus on mission . . . give people the training they need, mentor teams, and watch your organization excel.

The criteria for judging the quality of the Air Force are based on the Malcolm Baldrige National Quality Award and span seven broad categories: leadership, information and analysis, strategic quality planning, human resources development and management, management of process quality, quality and operational results, and customer focus and satisfaction.

In the category of customer focus, the Air Force addresses the interface between each organization and the outside organizations it supports. For example, in an operational environment, it might include those customers who need support through weapon systems, or perhaps through combat, mobility, or space resources. In a support environment, customers might include a system program office's weapon system acquisition; another customer might be a logistics center's repair of an operational command's aircraft.

### Only One Secret Formula

MSgt Susan Holmes, AFQC resource team (now retired), summarizes the cultural change in the Air Force. She says, "Maybe we're finally realizing our professional well-being is directly linked to our ability to meet the customer's needs."

She explains the Air Force journey, saying that when it first started, officials spent a lot of time searching for some basic answers to the question, "How do we get there?" She clarifies, "Like lemmings to the sea, we followed the crowd and went to Deming . . . to Juran . . . to Crosby. . . . We flew around the world visiting major commands, talking to teams, and read every case study ever written on the subject of quality implementation." She explains that, as they returned with their heads full of theories, they realized that nobody had cornered the market on the "how-to-TQ" business. There were no instant, prepackaged formulas. Holmes advises, "Read books, watch videos, talk to people—then just roll up your sleeves and get to work!"

According to Holmes, team processes are difficult to benchmark, because individual and group personalities are rarely identical. She emphasizes that common sense is the key tool for applying other organizations' solutions to your own company or unit. "If you like another team's actions, try it on for size," she says. "It's basically simple to collect information, ideas and techniques of managing through quality; the hard part comes when you take the plunge from the abstract world of theory and charge headlong into your everyday work world."

### The Quality Effort at Robbins Air Force Base

One of the biggest quality efforts is taking place at the Air Force Logistics Command at Robbins Air Force Base in Georgia. This major command has various functions, including procurement of products for the Air Force and the repair and maintenance of aircraft—fighter planes and cargo planes—and black boxes from submarines and tanks. About 99 percent of aircraft used during the 1991 Persian Gulf War were dissembled and repaired by this command. In 1990 the quality strategy at the base, called QP4—people, process, performance, and product—was stepped up and included (1) transforming functional managers into process managers and quality leaders; (2) using statistical process control and other analytical techniques to improve processes; and (3) transforming the workforce into an empowered team performing at its full potential.

According to Colonel Scott Wangen, some of the major commands were having difficulty trying to follow the Federal Quality Institute's guidelines for total quality. The commands wanted to go further and switch to following the Baldrige criteria. The four-star major council, which included General McPeak, then Chief of Staff, and General Ron Yates, gave them the go-ahead to proceed "to do what was right." Explains Colonel Wangen, "We [Warner Robbins Air Logistics Center] were the baby of the Air Force Logistics Command, and we had in the past primarily focused on how good we were doing, and patting ourselves on the back. For the first time, we had to examine how we were really doing." The colonel explains that the command had help from an IBM partner in avionics, whom they asked to be the senior examiner and to use the same evaluation criteria as would be used in private industry.

Wangen recounts this "most sobering exercise": "These product directorates are like individual companies, each run fairly autonomously. That great strength [the strength of autonomy] was in some ways our weakness, because each 'head' is a champion of their product center, called category champions." Wangen explains that it was challenging to move these product heads from thinking of their own entities to considering common processes and problems. According to Wangen, process definition and assessment were especially challenging because of the amount of time and effort involved; it took more than six months and required a total of about six thousand hours of labor (some installations have spent as much as fifty thousand hours).

Wangen continues, "We found that even though these centers have responsibilities for vastly different things, there are common problems." Some bottlenecks in procurement, for example, occurred across product centers. Other problems, he explains, were identified as corporate processes that the centers didn't have the authority to fix and which they had to refer to headquarters. When they did so, they discovered that the corporate council in some cases had not thought through how the quality initiative would compel changing systems and processes—even though it had endorsed the quality vision.

Wangen explains that the process of referring these "corporate processes" to senior leaders was definitely a wake-up call for the corporate office. Partly as a result, the corporate council began deploying the quality initiative through strategic planning. This required formulating action plans to translate the vision into the daily operation for those that are closest to the customer.

### Changing a Culture One Action at a Time

Continuous improvement usually doesn't happen in a once-a-year dramatic event. Accomplishments from the quality initiative show up on an ongoing basis—on the front line, usually one step and one action at a time. At Kessler Air Force Base, for example, Captain Tom Powell, who led a team from the Seventh Air Force Command and Control Squadron in identifying problems with the existing communications setup, ultimately discovered and eliminated a critical radio "dead spot," fostering reliable communications at the base.

Sergeant Gregory Voss, also at Kessler, demonstrated how simple scrutiny of what people are doing in terms of need and value added can pay off. While packing office supplies in support of a lengthy TDY (temporary duty) Voss noticed that most of the space was taken up by Mission Accomplishment Report forms, used by crew members to log flying events. Each crew position had separate forms, and each crew member had to use a separate form to log each day of flying. That amounted to roughly 480 forms over a two-week period! Sergeant Voss designed a new form, allowing a crew member to use a single form during the entire TDY to log all flying events. The number of forms dropped from 480 to 48! Besides saving space, this dramatically reduced administrative processing time.

Still another team member at Kessler put his quality knowledge to work and improved the squadron's procedures for overhauling brakes. TSgt Richard Nichols worked with others in the pneudraulic section to produce a continuous improvement process to reduce overall cost and improve the brake overhaul procedure. Their quality effort has saved over $50,000.

## Continuous Improvement at the U.S. Army Corps of Engineers

Since the late 1980s the U.S. Army Corps of Engineers has been promoting a "customer-focused, values-based, people-powered" vision. A great deal of energy has been put into this focus, including the development of nineteen specific leadership competencies needed to promote the vision. As Jerry Liebes, Deputy Chief of Human Resources, Planning, and Development, explains, "This development of leadership competencies, as well as corporate literature, has stressed the idea that all managers are human resources managers who must align their actions with their words." The Corps's material on its vision, long-term strategy, and values could easily be in any industrial vision.

The extent to which the quality improvement in the Corps is recognized by those outside government is illustrated by the partnership between the Corps and the National Society of Professional Engineers (NSPE) to improve the quality of services and design. The Corps and the NSPE are benchmarking against each other, with the intent of improving the design and construction process. The NSPE recognizes that the Corps has highly qualified professional personnel but is limited by regulations. The NSPE wants to understand better the limits imposed on Corps personnel and then develop procedures to eliminate or reduce those limits, thereby reducing design construction costs and time. The New Orleans District's excellent safety record is acknowledged within the petrochemical industry and is being used as a benchmark by others in the industry.

Over the years the quality of work in the various districts has improved as a result of the normal problem-solving process. Unfortunately, the improvements were often too late to keep the customer satisfied. In the words of Joe Theobald of the Louisville District, "When something went wrong, we performed damage control to get through the crisis and tried to fix the problem so it wouldn't happen again. . . . This reactionary method of achieving quality made us a repair shop, and customers who had paid a high price [for our mistakes] didn't want to spend time in a repair shop. . . . They want quality built in at the plant." Many of the district's initiatives are focused on doing just that, preventing problems up front to keep customers out of the repair shop—in other words, building in quality from the beginning.

Various districts within the Army Corps of Engineers have achieved some dramatic results from implementing TQM. In the Portland District, for example, since the introduction of TQM more than fifty error cause removal actions (ECRs) have been submitted, saving $500,000. At the same time forty-six ECRs requiring Corrective Action Team involvement have saved close to $18,000, and the Army Ideas for Excellence Program has prompted 269 suggestions that have saved the District nearly $300,000.

## TQM *in the New Orleans District*

While recognizing that the New Orleans District (NOD) had enjoyed good reputations with customers and the people of New Orleans, its executive team saw much room for improvement, including the need for a corporate commitment to continuous improvement, a way to measure improvements, a rigorous review of business processes, and mechanisms for identifying and communicating with customers. Among other initiatives, NOD discovered a cheaper, faster way to work on a navigation lock—one that applied TQM to the dewatering and repair of Algiers Lock and saved $2 million and twenty-two days of out-of-service time. For details on this initiative, see Chapter 10.

The district learned some valuable lessons from this quality initiative. The first lesson was that operating budgets may be good financial management tools, but they are poor quality management tools. NOD discovered that the operating budget told them only who spent how much on what; it didn't tell them if employees were spending the right amounts in the right way on the right things. To learn that, the district had to examine its decision-making processes, which weren't captured in operating budgets or organizational charts. It identified fifteen major, relatively independent activities where business decisions were made, the people who were primarily responsible for decisions in those activities, and the major customers and suppliers.

According to Colonel Michael Diffley and Major James Duttweiler, "The easy part was filling up the blank sheet; the hard part was realizing that existing tools didn't work." They explain that the new framework emphasized what they believed to be the right things: daily business decisions and the critical relationships that drive them. As an engineering, design, and construction organization, the district believes that the quality of its products directly reflects the quality of its planning, engineering, design, and construction decisions. "The quality of these decisions, in turn, depends on the quality of relationships and extent of communication among internal and external suppliers and customers," say Colonel Diffley and Major Duttweiler.

The new framework was also designed to reflect how the district runs its business. It's built around major processes that are used daily. As a result, quality improvement initiatives are developed by the same teams responsible for daily business decisions. NOD avoids cumbersome quality architecture and ad hoc quality committees. And it does not restrict itself to its organizational structure since its business services and activities cut across departmental lines.

Another discovery—which seems surprising at first blush—was that the best opportunities for early quality improvements were found in some of NOD's best-run business units. The district found ways to save millions of dollars in areas that weren't broken. These units were staffed with talented people who had been practicing many of the tenets of TQM for years; empowerment, customer focus, continuous improvement. But some parts were missing, like senior management's commitment to explore innovations and a disciplined approach to measuring business decisions. NOD discovered that those business teams that operated closest to a TQM model without knowing it were best positioned to initiate early quality improvements. Those furthest from the model needed to devote more time to building their teams and evaluating their business processes before beginning the process of continuous improvement.

Another discovery was that good quality measures are critical to sustaining the focus, but some are tough to identify. One measure that is relatively easy to identify is periodic maintenance operations at navigation locks. The per day costs of closing a lock is extremely high to the district's navigation customers. Thus, the single measure "days of closure" fits the definition of a good quality measure for lock dewatering operations.

In their report the executive team at NOD clarifies what it would mean if TQM were firmly embedded in the district's culture.

> Each of NOD's fifteen major business activities consists of about a dozen processes in which decisions are made and initiatives are developed for improvement. For example, the bidability, constructibility, and operability processes of their construction business aim at improving construction quality through better designer-constructor-owner communications. They involve teams from the engineering, construction, operations, contracting, and project management divisions at NOD, as well as outside customers. In total NOD has over 200 such sub-processes.

The executive team presents the fruitlessness of trying to centralize management of the task.

> Clearly a fully functioning quality program will behave more like two hundred independent motors than a single big machine. One key to its success is that process leaders are empowered to improve their processes, and that they have the

opportunity to go from opportunity recognition to improvement implementation with near-zero upper management involvement. The other key is that customers be well-defined and that process teams communicate effectively with them and management empowers teams to make changes that improve customer satisfaction.

## Partnering Within the Corps of Engineers

The U.S. Army Corps of Engineers' Louisville District has boiled the concept of partnering down to a few basic elements. It uses a teamwork approach between government and the contractor to achieve customer success that embodies total quality management principles and seeks to change from a traditional project relationship to a shared culture. It focuses on building cooperative relationships, avoiding or minimizing disputes, and actively pursuing common goals by the contracting parties. The result is cost savings and a more satisfied customer.

Why is this beneficial? The life cycle of a project can be shown as a downward sloping curve when the impact one has on the project is compared to specific points of time during the project's construction. For one thing, the dollar benefits of changes made prior to actual construction of a project compared to costs are much greater than the benefits of changes made after construction is under way. As the project proceeds, changes become more costly. Partnering with contractors is one way to deal with questions and crises closer to the beginning of the project. Trust and communication commitments can be achieved early in projects by partnering and can save the cost of changes made later on—as well as litigation expenses.

Partnering has enabled districts to move from adversarial relations to cooperative teamwork and away from a litigation focus to solutions and accomplishments. It has promoted risk taking and helped dissolve bureaucracies. It has moved from a finger-pointing to a hand-shaking mind-set.

## The Process of Partnering

The Corps has learned that partnering can be successful only if it is part of a total quality paradigm. And it recognizes that before the TQM process can begin, there has to be a corporate vision to which all employees are committed.

Partnering in the Corps begins early, before the initiation of studies or real estate actions. It begins at the acquisition strategy meeting, and project managers include tentative workshop dates as milestones in their project schedules. The project manager, engineering manager, area or resident engineer, and customer form the project team leadership and the spirit of partnering requires consensus in decision making. To set the tone for working relationships, the workshop should be scheduled as soon as possible after the contract is awarded.

The workshop's purpose is to establish commitment, trust, mutual goals, and objectives among all the members of the partnership. The result is an agreement or charter to commit to the goals. This charter is signed by all who participated in its development.

### Partnering Initiatives and Results

The Corps's Louisville District is participating in fifty-five formal relationships—all started within a span of twenty-four months. These partnerships range in value to as much as $53 million. They include district and civic commitments, as well as design and construction projects. Two partnerships are concerned with design facilities with programmed costs of approximately $80 million, and twenty-eight partnerships deal with construction projects with a combined value of almost $250 million. To date, Louisville's partnering efforts have saved more than $900,000 and more than a month of workdays.

Partnerships include the construction of a $13 million Sewage Treatment Plant; a $1.6 million rehabilitation of the Fort Knox Commissary; an $18 million project involving construction of dormitories and dining hall and levee at Scott Air Force Base; and a $10.2 million project at Wright-Patterson Air Force Base. On this last project, the contractor has made exceptional efforts to schedule work to minimize impact to airfield operations, and what could have been a serious problem was resolved to the mutual satisfaction of the partnerships. Twenty-seven thousand hours of work have gone into this project without a lost-time accident.

## The Government's New Customer Focus

Federal agencies have made progress in streamlining processes and considering quality from the customer's view. In the training arena, for example, there is a genuine attempt on the part of training headquarters to find out what internal customers really desire in training and then to offer training to meet those needs. The Corps of Engineers sends out questionnaires every year to districts throughout the United States to discover which of the topics they have been trained on have proven to be most helpful in their operations. This tracking keeps them continuously responsive to the needs of their internal customers.

This sensitivity to fulfilling customers' needs and expectations also shows up in the evaluations required for all training courses. These evaluations are quite involved, covering everything from course manual design and content, to instructor presentation skills, to practical value of case studies and application exercises. The Corps' Training Division headquarters tracks all these evaluations, graphs them out, and forwards them to the contractors. This continuous tracking ensures that contractors know at all times how they are doing and enables them to continuously revise and improve the programs during the contract. The challenge, like the challenge facing private industry, is to anticipate customer needs by examining trends that are likely to affect those customers and to offer training in those areas before the need becomes a crisis.

## The Government's Continuing Challenges

Not unlike many private sector companies, government agencies are still struggling to understand what the quality revolution means. Some federal agencies have made major investments in TQM training, some with good results, some with not-so-good results. One district within the Army Corps of Engineers spent $500,000 on what was termed "TQM training." All employees in the district were trained, and the consultant tossed a lot into the program, from values to scattergrams. The employees appreciated the district's willingness to invest money to bring them "up to snuff" in this initiative. All employees received the training, and they have since improved on old processes.

A major challenge facing the federal government is to continue the effort to reduce regulations so that its quality improvement initiatives will not become thwarted. It must speed up its "reinvention" of systems and structures to sustain its pockets of energy and enthusiasm, which are needed to translate total quality ideas into actions. Federal employees now recognize the need to recreate value for themselves, but they also need to feel a sense of urgency to accomplish the change. Reducing the regulations that have protected them will help create that sense of urgency. Not only must government agencies continue reducing regulations that they themselves have generated (and at least 50 percent of the regulations are agency-generated); they must pressure Congress to reduce those that lie within its purview.

Government managers must recognize that not all inefficiency can be blamed on regulations. Some government employees—managers as well as individual contributors—maintain that managers often use regulations as an excuse for inaction. They claim that sometimes the obstacle lies in the interpretation of the regulations, rather than in the regulations themselves. It is often these interpretations that actually determine policy and practice. Jerry Liebes, Army Corps of Engineers, insists that the internal customers have the opportunity to do more than they may think. He urges employees to question the utility of regulations that were written many years ago, when conditions were very different from the way they are now. He also urges government agencies to reduce the amount of "explanations"—briefings, assessments, commentaries—and replace them with action that produces valuable results.

Finally, as is often the case in private industry, the government faces the challenge of integrating quality into the strategic goals of local operations.

Even with the challenges, this movement within government for accountability and product focus is real. Few federal employees disagree with the move to "reinvent government."

The federal government is moving on its quality journey. Agencies are considering outcomes, examining processes in terms of intent and value-added properties, and designing continuous improvement training around the mission and values of the organization, using the input of those on the front line.

There is a strong quality consciousness. Leaders, like those in private industry, are urging action and entrepreneurism and restructuring to enable employees to act. They need patience and understanding, though, as they struggle to rid themselves of strangling, obsolete regulations and policies that many of them had no part in creating.

# Part IV
# Staying on Track

# 19

# More Powerful
# Than a Locomotive

## Leveraging Your Quality Around the World

On my first trip to Japan, what struck me immediately—more than the neon Panasonic or Sony signs—was the sight of McDonald's golden arches. Here they were, symbolizing the payoff of quality assurance—international customer value.

Ray Kroc, the founder of McDonald's, has revolutionized restaurant quality assurance, from the way farmers grow potatoes to the way packers process beef. Turning hamburgers rather than flipping them, discarding french fries seven minutes after they're cooked if they haven't been purchased, checking the sweetness of ketchup, and smiling at the customers—all have resulted in a consistency of product and service that people around the world have seen as high quality.

### Differentiating Market Leaders From Market Followers

Quality products and processes are key factors in differentiating market leaders from market followers. Some U.S. industries have proved the effect of superior quality on efforts to acquire international market share. Just as a focus on quality turned Japan from a maker of trinkets into an economic powerhouse, a similar quality focus has enabled many U.S. businesses to regain considerable market share. In 1990 the U.S. share of the $168 billion global hardware market was 60 percent, compared to 17 percent for Japan and 16 percent for Europe. In the more profitable global software and services market, the U.S. share was even greater—70 percent to 80 percent of the $144 billion pie. American companies continue to dominate in the manufacture of such computer components as microprocessors and hard disks. And American software manufacturers, including Microsoft, IBM, and Apple, still set the standard for the rest of the world.

Superior-quality products have enabled Motorola to hold its own in the fiercely competitive semiconductor market. That company's commitment to build in "robust design" in order to attain six sigma quality enabled it to win the largest share of the cellular subscriber market worldwide. Its MicroTAC portable cellular telephone is the hottest-selling portable in Japan and the rest of Asia. Superior quality has also enabled Motorola to enter the international market for low-priced two-way radios. These products were once imported from Pacific Rim countries to the United States. In 1986 Motorola had virtually no share of this market; in the mid-1990s, its Radius line of two-way radios was the largest selling brand in the world.

Globalization of U.S. companies has resulted from more than just zero defects. Jack Welch's use of decentralizing principles to restructure GE and his holistic approach to quality improvement paid off internationally. By the end of the 1980s, GE was earning 40 percent of its profits in international markets. In the mid-1990s it was seeking opportunities for its lighting business in Mexico and India.

Some federal government agencies also have demonstrated the impact that high quality can have on their future. While they don't have bottom-line profits to worry about, these agencies must respond to the increased pressure from taxpayers for accountability and recreate value for themselves. High quality is enabling them to support international initiatives.

The solid reputation of the U.S. Army Corps of Engineers for high-quality construction and environmental cleanup expertise has prompted other governments to seek the agency's help in construction and environmental projects around the globe, including dam construction in South America, environmental cleanup in Kuwait, and military construction in Japan. To sustain that quality advantage in exporting its services, the Corps, like the private sector, must seek to understand preferences, environmental regulations, and cultural practices that differ from those in the United States.

Global forces have spurred rapid changes in the marketplace, making it more difficult to establish systems that can be depended on for years on end. Leveraging quality components can enable organizations to remain competitive in the international market.

## Losing Competitive Position and Retrieving It

The United States has made a remarkable comeback in only a few years. It was only during the mid- and late 1980s that most U.S. industries recognized the United States's diminished global economic competitive position. Particularly troubling was the loss of significant market share in the automobile industry. Since the causes of this loss have already been alluded to in earlier chapters, only a recap will be given here.

Primary among the causes was the growth of modern, large corporations that stressed mass production for mass markets. As they grew, companies lost sight of customers and ceased to create and deliver value competitively to them. They also became overly functional and harder to integrate. The country that had invented mass production found itself no longer able to compete for routine manufacturing jobs against low-wage countries like Taiwan and Mexico.

Another major cause was the smugness and self-assurance that often accompany a lack of competition. The United States and its allies had destroyed major industrial and infrastructural components of the principal economies of Europe and Asia during World War II and had reigned as the world's foremost productive power until the late 1970s.

In the meantime, countries like Japan made great strides in regaining economic power, primarily by offering higher quality and keeping their eye on the customer. Despite the Japanese recession of 1994, that country's economic power has steadily increased, and Japanese companies are establishing manufacturing facilities in the United States to build a variety of consumer products.

Many observers argue that it was easier for Japanese industry to focus on improved products since it had little choice, that it had to rise "from the ashes." Certainly, poverty can be a terrific motivator, and in the wake of World War II Japanese companies were devastated. They knew that if they were to survive, they would have to export, and the goal of economic planners in war-torn Japan became creating industries that could bring in foreign currency.

As European and Asian economies began to rebuild, however, they didn't just restore what they had lost; they began focusing on using new technologies to make what they had lost better. After focusing on replenishing domestic needs, both Japanese and European companies turned their eyes toward global markets and began making headway in industries such as steel. The United States simply could not fathom that the backbone of its war effort, the steel industry, could ever take second place to anyone, especially to Japan and Germany. When some overseas steel companies began making inroads in foreign markets, most U.S. industries dismissed the shift as the result of low wages. It had only seemed like yesterday that "Made in Japan" was synonymous with low price and shoddy quality. Americans couldn't believe there could be this much turnaround.

For the past few years, however, the leading U.S. steel companies have been recovering. They are operating in the black and turning back much of the foreign competition. Through downsizing and investments to modernize, a ton of steel that required 9.3 hours to produce in 1980 now takes only 5. And management is more willing today to work with labor. Steel workers have gained representation on the boards of America's biggest steel companies, and their situation is more stable. But still the threat of competition looms, as recessions in Europe and Japan have led to oversupply and lower prices there. Even with the shipping costs, foreign steelmakers find it profitable to sell to U.S. companies.

## No Such Thing as an American Industry

The term "American industry" is increasingly irrelevant, because it assumes the existence of a separate American economy in which all jobs associated with a particular industry are bound together. The reality is that factories and equipment move everywhere. This mobility makes it harder for individual industries to control their economic destinies.

Jim Clark, Vice President for Engineering Products at Square D-Groupe Schneider, North America, cites the example of the electrical distribution manufacturers in the 1950s and 1960s.

> The major manufacturers were Allis Chalmers, I.T.E., General Electric, Westinghouse, and Square D. By the 1990s, Siemens [a German company] had bought Allis Chalmers. Gould had bought I.T.E. and split it, selling part of the business to Siemens and part to Brown Boveri [a German and Swiss company]. Brown Boveri merged with Asea [Swedish] in the late 1980s to become ABB. Westinghouse sold a major part of its plants to ABB in 1990, while Groupe Schneider [French] acquired Square D in 1991. In the 1980s, Schneider had also acquired Federal Pioneer in Canada, Federal Pacific in Mexico, and Tele-mechanique in France. It already held the majority of shares in Merlin Gerin in France. In the early part of 1994, Westing-

house, in bad financial shape, was forced to sell the remainder of its transmission and distribution plants to Cutler-Hammer. Only General Electric's electrical business has remained virtually the same during the last thirty years.

## Defining a Global Corporation

It is important to understand just exactly what it means to be a global business, how it operates, and why it is critical to reaping the benefits of quality efforts. A global corporation is one whose marketplace is the entire world, not just a section, such as the United States. Until a company considers the entire potential market for its products without restrictions of geography, it is only a niche player. Just because a regional manufacturer ships some of its products to a foreign country doesn't mean it's a global company. International manufacturers aren't truly global if, even though they have acquired or established businesses all over the world, their regional or national divisions still operate as autonomous entities.

Only when a company has a plan to get into markets worldwide can it be considered a global business. A comprehensive analysis of the entire global market and an assessment of how to participate in it set global companies apart. A 40 percent market share in the United States may be only 2 percent or less of the global market. Jim Clark points out that at one time ABB shipments of $4 billion in the United States constituted only 10 percent of its total global business.

About 500 of ABB's 25,000 managers are global managers, people whose daily work is focused on gaining and maintaining global advantage. They are expected to have global vision, understanding, leadership, and integrity.

## Qualities That Enable a Company to Compete Globally

Ultimately, companies and federal agencies must see the potential power their capabilities can give them in the global market. That implies more people in the organization than just the CEO. CEOs and company presidents must focus people in the right direction and create processes and structures to keep that focus, but for the effort to be sustained, employees must also think and behave globally. This cannot be accomplished through mandates alone.

## A Unified Vision

To successfully compete in the global market, a zero defects product is only the ticket for boarding the train. You must create an organization whose people are adept at exchanging ideas, processes, and systems across borders—people who are constantly working together to identify the best global opportunities and the biggest global problems facing the organization. People pursuing global ends across organizational and geographic boundaries must have a unified vision to guide their efforts.

A lot of managers assume that since consumers differ from location to location, their businesses can't operate effectively as a unified entity. They see their industry as a bunch of specialized businesses. Their thinking is understandable. The primary reason hurried efforts fail to establish a global presence in a country like Japan, for instance, is people and the often provincial *values* they carry with them. These values, which once held the company together, cannot become part of another culture overnight. The importance of making shared values explicit grows as distance and diversity increase. Assumptions that made sense in a local market with a definite set of customers may not apply that well to your colleagues operating in different regions.

But still there is the need for a unified mission statement—which reflects no one nationality—in which values can take root. Leaders must communicate that unified vision, and then follow through and design processes that force interaction of all their people across borders.

Just formulating such a statement is not easy. We have all seen how difficult it is for even a small organization to come up with a vision statement that all employees can really buy into. Clearly, when companies become global, the challenge of formulating shared values is greater, as the very values that once kept people together may now drive them apart if they are not rid of their provincialism.

## Knowledge, Flexibility, and Adaptability

When Jim Clark begins a business turnaround, he assesses several basic factors, including assessment of the competition, product comparisons, future technological needs, and market requirements. He explains that the amount and quality of this information determine the strategic direction of the business and the tactical planning needed to achieve its long-range goals. But Clark insists that you have to go beyond this view and consider what it will take for the business to compete internationally. He explains that even with the theoretical recognition, some U.S. industries have been slow to understand its full implication, especially in terms of tailoring their products for foreign preferences—unlike Japanese and German economies, which have accommodated American tastes. How many Americans would have purchased a Honda Accord if the steering wheel had been on the right side? Historical cultural prejudices and nationalistic pride, egotism, and ignorance have to be overcome if a company is to become a global player, according to Clark. Sensitivity to local desires in foreign markets is required. Failure to recognize these preferences will cause the corporation to fall short of its goals. "For example," says Clark, "ABB had a common practice of spending R&D money to develop a product or technology that the Swiss already had developed within ABB, but because of nationalistic pride, it was not shared throughout the company. Groupe Schneider had similar problems with Telemechanique and Merlin Gerin competing against each other for various products and technologies, even though they were owned by Groupe Schneider."

Expanding your business beyond national borders requires flexibility and adaptability. It takes the right attitude. And the right attitude is shedding the "our way is the only way" kind of thinking. It means listening and making modifications to accommodate foreign preferences. It also means developing additional competencies.

In Japan, the product development process is driven by engineers, not marketing people. Unlike the Americans, Japanese engineers personally research market needs and competitive products themselves. Before the Lexus went into production, Japanese engineers lived in the homes of potential U.S. buyers to learn about and understand their lifestyles and the features these customers preferred in their automobiles.

For those designing and manufacturing office chairs, responding to local preferences might mean designing for people who may be physically smaller than Americans. For financial departments, it might mean having the knowledge to deal with foreign currency, international tax laws, and tariffs.

Companies trying to expand into foreign markets without understanding local customs, laws, and cultures have made some major blunders and learned hard lessons. General Motors, for example, has learned that a regional product may not be a global product. In the electrical business, there are different electrical standards that must be taken into account. In some countries, such as Japan, an appealing home appliance may be sold directly to customers through each manufacturer's company shops. But in the United States and Europe it is not so simple, as unions and EPA and OSHA regulations, as well as EEO laws, have to be accommodated. Or consider the antitrust environment. If U.S. and European competitors and bidders communicated with each other as they do in Japan, they would be in prison. While the Japanese can concentrate mainly on meeting customer needs without a host of other organizations to worry about, the same is not true in the United States. Thus, only part of the skills and know-how that make Japanese producers successful at home can be transferred to these other environments. In order to succeed there, other competencies are needed, such as knowledge of environmental laws. It means realizing that it takes time for a country such as Russia to become a democratic culture.

## Eastman Chemical's Response to Worldwide Customers

In the past, if chemical companies met U.S. health, safety, and environmental regulations, they were almost assured of being in compliance with foreign requirements. But things have changed. Eastman Chemical has learned that keeping up with a wide variety of developing international regulations is a big challenge.

"Now if we sell a product in six different countries, there may be six different laws governing the sale of that product," explains Ed Miller, a member of the global MEPS (Make Eastman the Preferred Supplier) team to provide the Eastman Health, Safety, and Environmental Services Division (EHSES) with support for the sale of products on a worldwide basis. "By being able to give prompt responses to questions about health, safety, and the environment, we're able to meet our customers' requests for product more readily."

As a result of the MEPS team's efforts, all process teams within EHSES recognize that their jobs affect a worldwide operation, rather than only domestic sales and production. This means, for instance, that Eastman employees must possess a knowledge of regulations in Europe and other parts of the world for industrial, food, drug, and cosmetic chemicals. They must be able to communicate hazards through material safety data sheets in a variety of languages. And they must be able to assess how Eastman products can be used safely worldwide.

EHSES stays close to marketing, the business organizations, and manufacturing for information about the Far East and Latin America. Although Eastman sells about one third of its products overseas, most of the manufacturing is done in the United States, Miller explains, so there's a major effort to understand what goes on in other countries. He goes on to say that EHSES also uses international trade associations and Eastman personnel stationed abroad as sources of information about health, safety, and environmental topics.

## The DOD and Cultural Differences

As the U.S. military becomes more global, it is faced with challenges of working with "customers" who have difference cultures and different sets of expectations and value systems.

One project laden with these challenges is the role of the Japan Engineering District (JED) of the U.S. Army Corps of Engineers as the DOD's design and construction agent for U.S. military funded construction in Japan.

The Government of Japan (GOJ) began the Facilities Improvement Program in 1979 to ease the cost of stationing American troops in Japan. What began as a modest program for constructing housing and community support facilities has grown to a $1 billion program that includes numerous, one-of-a-kind, complex operational facilities. While the design and construction of these projects are funded by the GOJ, JED plays a significant role in their completion. The Department of the Army supports the Japanese Host Nation Funded Construction Program (HNFCP), with central funding from Military Construction, Army (MCA) Planning and Design (P&D) funds. JED has the responsibility for design and engineering surveillance and for preparing criteria for the Japanese contractors. Support operations within the district include logistics and supply management, budgeting and resource management, and contracting and information management. JED also provides a full range of environmental services, including training, testing, and assessments.

The GOJ host nation construction program is replete with codes, regulations, and design and construction methods different from those found in the United States. This difference became clear to me while I was doing some work for the JED. While in Japan I talked with several construction engineers who spoke of the "political" nature of construction bidding in that country and the differences between the Japanese values system and its American counterpart. Engineers report invisible profits earned by Japanese builders and the distribution of hidden profits around the system, including considerable sums given to politicians. It seems to be a common view that the root cause of this corruption in public works is not the bidding system but the willfully negligent pricing policy of some of the bureaucrats who commission the work.

The point is that JED must understand and work with that system and understand these differences between Japan's bidding process and expectations and those used in the United States. Other differences are found in environmental regulations and engineering specifications. To meet this challenge, JED has recruited Japanese and American engineers and support professionals who have multiservice and bilingual skills.

JED's product niche is not to compete with its partners for work they already do well, but to fill in the voids. JED provides quality products and services where, through economy of scale, it can coordinate all services to consolidate all requirements to get one big economical contract everyone can benefit from. Because of JED's expertise in the field, it can provide technical support more cheaply than a partner can develop his own in-house capability. Corps engineers are able to leverage their quality beyond the United States.

In order for the U.S. military to realize the maximum benefit from HNFCP and for JED to execute its mission properly, JED must receive sufficient P&D funding. JED must ensure this funding on a continual basis by performing efficiently and effectively.

## Understanding Where the Gaps Are and Filling Them In

Many companies may never get their employees to think globally because their leaders don't understand what they must do. For one thing, leaders must understand where gaps are—gaps in understanding of cultures, currency exchanges, and different needs and standards—in order to become global. Part of the human resources challenge critical to global business success is recognizing the limits of one's own experiences and doing something about them. Building an understanding of an international business requires hiring new people who do have these skills and understanding and training the existing managers who do not. Companies like Square D have developed courses in conjunction with major universities to train their managers to think at the global level.

Because of these demands, one of the biggest constraints on the success of western companies in Asia has been the human resources constraint. Many western companies don't have managers on staff who can go to Asia and be successful. Leaders must be willing to take risks in environments that are not within their own understanding, which means they must hire competent people who know the areas the leaders are weak in. It may mean getting an Asian manager to the point where you trust him to manage your investment in a manner consistent with corporate expectations.

### Leveraging Your Core Competencies

You must do more than produce defect-free products. The only way to gain lasting competitive advantage is to take the best capabilities you have and leverage them around the world. That means looking at your "core competencies," those technologies or processes that make you competitive. As Clark explains, even though the features and dimensions of the switch gear, the washing machine, or the automobile may vary from locale to locale, much of the technology and many of the manufacturing processes are similar. The application is what differs, and that requires an understanding of local markets. Just as it was important in the 1980s to understand the particular company's internal infrastructure before beginning quality initiatives, so today companies must consider the cultural infrastructure of markets other than those in the United States and understand their developing preferences.

Managers will be required to borrow management techniques from one culture and apply them elsewhere. Just-in-time techniques are proving to be comparatively easy to adopt for some U.S. companies. Letting teams get on with it is easier in the West than in Japan. You can learn these techniques that come from around the world and adapt them for your own individual culture, changing them slightly quite often.

Although a few American companies that have strayed "from the knitting" (as Tom Peters puts in his book *In Search of Excellence*) and diversified beyond their major competencies have been successful, most have failed.

Japanese industries historically have "stuck to the knitting" and concentrated on what they do best—their core competencies. In developing new products, Japanese companies have emphasized what they know and have built new products that extend the utility of these products. The Japanese believe that continuously improving the existing product line enables them to extend market share, as well as build on the core competencies of a company.

That is not to imply that there has been no diversification. But the diversification takes a different form in Japan than in the United States, where companies often think in terms of moving in radically new directions, as when GE moved into the retail credit arena. In Japan, diversification means transplanting core competencies applications into a range of other products. For example, in the 1970s, Seiko Instruments, one of the world's largest manufacturers of quality watches, decided to diversify beyond its relatively mature category. But instead of inventing totally new products, the company looked at its own production processes—the proprietary technologies and applications it knew best. In commercializing these processes, it developed more than fifteen product lines ranging from precision assembly robots to computer peripherals.

Determining exactly what a company's core skills, techniques, and processes are is the most critical step in the ongoing product development process.

### Flatter Structure

To successfully compete in the international market, and to quicken reaction times and speed up the flow of ideas, organizations will have to be flatter and eliminate the bureaucrats. At ABB, there is only one layer between the top ranks and the business units. Only 171 people work in ABB's modest and functional suburban-Zurich headquarters. But an equally telling sign of its flat organization is the self-directed work groups at ABB's relay and railway-signal equipment plant in Katowice, Poland. The groups handle suppliers, production, inventories, quality control, and customer complaints.

Organizations with more layers require e-mail and financial reporting systems that can bring everyone into the information loop quickly.

## No Single Recipe for How a Global Company Must Operate

There are no discernible patterns or common trends in how manufacturers are approaching the production and distribution of their goods in Europe, no broadly used logistics strategies that transcend all industries or even parts of one industry.

For example, regulatory impediments bar the sale of common medical and pharmaceutical products across the entire European marketplace. Also many products carry large pricing differentials from country to country.

Consumer electronics is one field where pricing differentials exist. In a country like Germany, VCRs often sell for twice as much as they do in a country like Spain where the standard of living is lower. Because the German market prefers a VCR that carries unique features and German-language packaging and instructions, manufacturers believe they can't realistically sell a standard VCR in both Germany and Spain.

Pricing differentials are so significant that firms still want to sell unique products in each country-market rather than standardize on one product that could be sold across the community.

Consequently, there can be no hard and fast rules on how a company should be structured for global success. Although the matrix system has taken a lot of heat lately, companies such as ABB—the pioneer and champion of the global electrical business—have fine-tuned the matrix system to suit their particular goals and corporate cultures. ABB's system, like most successful matrix systems today, is product-driven.

Jim Clark of Square D-Groupe Schneider, explains: "Headquartered in Switzerland, ABB's matrix system of organization is on a regional basis which has its own profit and loss and a second system made up of strategic business units. These SBUs are formulated by product type, an example being the medium-voltage SBU."

Clark adds, "Groupe Schneider established a matrix similar to ABB's upon acquiring Square D." Schneider's CEO, Didier Pineau-Valencienne, explains that traditionally, standards and regulations forced electrical products to be produced in the countries in which they were to be sold. But new products were designed in such a way that "we could manufacture 95 percent of them for world use and change the last 5 percent at the end of the process for use in a specific country." According to Pineau-Valencienne, this new concept was a huge breakthrough in cost structure and helps explain why his definition of "global business" is built around product strategies and capabilities rather than marketing plans or management teams.

Square D-Groupe Schneider's strategic business units are referred to as DAS, an acronym for the French word for Division of Strategic Activities. The main responsibilities of the SBU or DAS are product-focused. Here, global R&D is coordinated for the entire company. Clark explains that some other aspects of the business, like the quality system, are also coordinated.

There are advantages to this matrix system. Clark explains that it ensures consistent strategy of product and process for those aspects of the business that *should* be consistent:

> The SBU reigns as the overall coordinator of the products and technology. For instance, if the corporation determines that the market in Asia requires a particular product—a certain type of circuit breaker, for example—then SBU managers review all existing products made throughout the company to determine if this product already exists. If it does, then the SBU managers will coordinate the logistics of bringing that product to the Asian market. When the market requires local manufacturing,

the SBU will have the technology transferred and help set up the manufacturing plant.

Not only does the matrix system then reduce replication of effort, it enables the entire company to leverage the lessons it has learned and its "best practices"—its core competencies—to all areas of the business.

The DAS also coordinates other company practices. For example, Square D-Groupe Schneider, North America, has adopted the CQ quality system, which is used throughout the company. There is a DAS that ensures that all business operations within Square D use it. Local plants, though, can modify the program to accommodate their particular customers and products.

The matrix system is somewhat like a baseball game, where the DAS leader establishes the boundaries, saying, in effect, "Here is the diamond, and you must play within those boundaries. Outside those boundaries is foul ball territory. But within these boundaries there are variations on how the game is played."

Clark explains that "the DAS or SBU goes beyond just coordinating existing technologies or products. Its main charter is to plan for the future of its products and technology. Market research and analysis are done by working with the regional managers to formulate the strategic direction of the SBU. Regional inputs are critical as standards and usage requirements vary by country. Based on these inputs R&D plans can be formulated to project needs well into the future."

The Ford Motor Company also uses a product-driven matrix system. Its CEO, Alexander J. Trotman, wants to transform Ford from an old-style multinational to a streamlined global company. The first step will be to merge the once very separate North American and European car operations into one big organization that can capture world economies of scale.

Trotman's most controversial move has been the integration of Ford's car development groups across boundaries. Until recently, regional fiefdoms designed vehicles for their own markets. That pleased local tastes, but resulted in duplication. Trotman is eliminating self-contained country units and the separate vehicles, engines, and components they produce. In the Mondeo, Ford's try at a "world car," an elaborate system using teleconferencing and shared computer-aided design allowed staffers in Germany, Britain, and the United States to work on the project together.

## Benefits of Becoming Global

The benefits of being a global company are many, as are the benefits of a federal agency that exports its services internationally. The more global markets an organization participates in, the more recession-proof it becomes. For example, in 1993 the U.S. economy recovered from a recession, the Canadian and Western European markets stayed depressed, the Pacific Rim countries grew strong, and China started to grow. The Eastern European countries have huge growth potential but are strapped for cash, as are other Third World countries in Africa and South America. With such fluctuations in the global economies, a corporation participating in only one or two regions will become vulnerable to the fluctuations of the local economy and will be limited in its future growth only to those regions. Obviously, this can eliminate the advantage of growth opportunities in China, Eastern Europe, and the emerging Third World nations.

Besides the benefit of providing a buffer against recessions, operating globally offers the opportunity to share technology and to leverage manufacturing operations. While a company may need plants in Europe, the United States, Latin America, and Asia to make products that meet the special needs of local markets, it's possible and desirable for those plants to share the best available product technologies and manufacturing processes. This allows increased productivity and nurtures future technological growth. Clark explains that "the DAS is able to measure the cost of manufacturing throughout the world to evaluate where each product should be made for the benefit of the total group. Without a strategic overseer like the SBU or DAS, it is very easy for a company to get locked into regional practices without a strategic direction." At Square D prior to its acquisition by Schneider, for example, when a product was to be replaced in the United States with a new product or technology, the old product was sent to Canada to become the Canadian offering; therefore, the product that Canada was producing was generally a generation behind the United States offering. The product offering in Canada that was being replaced was then sent to Mexico. This left the Mexicans with a product offering two generations behind that in the United States and one generation behind the one in Canada. As Square D took on a global focus, it began offering the same product in the United States, Canada, and Mexico, with slight modifications possible to meet local needs. Hence, one plant could produce the requirements for the entire North American market instead of having multiple plants to make multiple models. Square D realized tremendous savings through the rationalization of its manufacturing plants in the United States, Canada, and Mexico.

The consolidation of resources, the market data input by region, and the multiplicity of product offering a global corporation can accumulate give it a formidable advantage over regional players. In addition, global recognition of the corporate name helps give the customer base confidence in the supplying corporation. Having a quality product remains an important required foundation for a move into the global marketplace by any manufacturer. Quality suppliers nearly always receive preference over the competition if all other factors are equal. Similarly, federal agencies that have demonstrated the capacity to respond to emerging trends and fractures around the globe are given preference over agencies that have not.

## The Challenge of the Twenty-First Century Marketplace

Senior managers are struggling to adapt themselves and their organizations to the twenty-first century global business world that is rapidly taking shape. The rate of technological progress will accelerate; breakthroughs in digital electronics and biotechnology are already coming from such unexpected places as Israel, China, and Malaysia. Business opportunities are predicted to explode, but so will competition as technology and management know-how spread beyond brand-name companies to new players in Asia and Latin America. With more countries viewing protectionism as economically incorrect, it will become cheaper and easier for expansion-minded CEOs to steal their rivals' market.

There is much more involved in being able to capitalize on these opportunities, however, and economists and strategists vary on what should be done. Most agree that businesses must discover new ways of managing and competing. Many economists insist that there is a need to boost investment and get economic growth on the fast track again. They argue that sizable investments in machinery, infrastructure, and R&D would shift annual output from consumption to productive investment and that an investment-oriented program would enable U.S. businesses once again to compete in world markets on the basis of technology and productivity rather than price, for price is too capricious to count on.

U.S. business leaders' response to competing in a global economy must be, in part, to change the way it manages business to promote flexibility and adaptability. Some observers predict that thriving in this environment will require a combination of Western-style accounting and Japanese-style teamwork. As global competition has increased, some of these changes are already taking place, as American businesses adopt team structures, just-in-time production, and lean production, all borrowed from the Japanese. As a result, they have dramatically reduced cycle time and manpower requirements and adopted a customer focus.

One thing is for certain. Thriving in this fast-paced global environment requires a new kind of company, one that includes all the usual ingredients of a quality culture—zero defects, customer satisfaction, fast response time, continuous improvement—but also another dimension—universal values and an understanding of the variation in national environments in each of its businesses. No longer must the organization merely concern itself with how to combine these disparate business units into divisions or sectors based solely on assumed similarities among customers or markets. Now it must consider how to combine them into coherent cultural units that provide a common framework in which each of its businesses can flourish. Success ultimately depends heavily on how well you are able to balance local needs with shared global values.

# 20

# Riding the Silver Bullet

## *On Track and Moving Forward*

During the derailment, corporate America was not able to capitalize on its innovation and entrepreneurship because it lacked the needed cultural infrastructure. Ironically, the very qualities that had once accounted for America's high-quality products engendered a hubris and a self-assuredness that made American industry vulnerable. Anytime we get so smug and inward-looking that we stop focusing on whom we're trying to serve with our innovations, the end is in sight. As organizational structures became more complex, empires were built, and functions began to compete internally, our competitive spirit became directed inward. If that same spirit of innovation had been used to stay focused on the customer instead of on ourselves, we probably would have improved the quality for the customer and therefore retained our industrial lead. Because we had the technology and we had the technical talent.

Organizations that are being revitalized are recapturing that spirit of creativity and innovation, but they are now directing it outward to the customer. Today's consumer expects continuous improvement in product and service, and continuous improvement focuses on bettering existing products and services as well as creating new ones. Creativity and innovation mean not "glimpses of the divine" but a sustained focus coupled with the ability to apply new and old information in new ways to add value for the customer.

Peter Drucker observes that innovation has become particularly important because the accumulated competence, skills, knowledge, product, services, and structure of the present will not be adequate for very long. Organizations that have retrieved market share and that are continuing to succeed globally are reexamining both past and present practices and procedures and determining whether they are recreating value for customers. They are considering which of their product lines adds more value than others. They are considering which steps in their processes are completely unnecessary and result only in higher costs for the customer.

Government agencies also are encouraging their risk takers and entrepreneurs to "come out of the closet" so that their energies can be used to make government more useful for its customers. In the past, the federal employees who were innovative had to be quiet about their creativity, because their innovations implied a departure from standard policies and rules. That's all changing.

Organizations today know that since customers' preferences and expectations are quickly changing, they have to restructure to decrease their cycle time. They are therefore transforming their cultures and operating more like small companies by decentralizing authority and organizing into teams to bring people closer together. Teams can outperform individuals and restore that sense of community within corporations that have been crippled by a decade of downsizings and restructurings.

Leaders like GE's Jack Welch have made sweeping changes to reduce layers and to recraft organizations to enable employees to move from administration to execution. Judging from GE's bottom line, Welch has been successful.

Organizations that are back on track have a strong quality consciousness—however differently it may be translated and however varied the approaches toward continuous improvement. Some companies stress internal performance measurement, conformance indices, and technical specifications; others stress more external factors, such as shifting customer preferences and technological advances on the horizon. When people focus more on internal process than on what that process is for, they may end up with a better process, but one that no one wants. Organizations that have been the most successful in recapturing market share are those that are both inwardly and outwardly focused.

The self-sufficient corporation is gone forever. The command and control structure that remained a model for decades made managers responsible to each other, rather than to customers. In its place is a new paradigm that values teamwork over individualism, seeks global markets over domestic ones, and focuses on customers, not on short-term profits. Quality is no longer viewed in terms of what managers can afford; it is seen as an area in which they can't afford to make compromises. Quality is not so much a competitive tool as a ticket just to board the train.

We must be mindful that if our quality focus—be it TQM or something else—results in number crunching or paper chasing, and the *appearance* of quality rather than a real improvement, then we're still off track.

If quality directors are viewed as having a special claim on achieving quality, rather than coordinating the quality efforts of all employees, then business is still on the wrong train. If the quality focus commands the organizational quality guru to spend vast sums of money on pet strategies and quality consultants, then we've purchased the wrong ticket.

The bottom line is that authentic quality improvement is not the special province of the corporate quality director. Quality directors who are sincere about integrating quality across the culture are the first to say this and the first to insist that quality must be everybody's job. Authentic quality improvements, while not demanding organizational additions (councils, subcouncils, sub-subcouncils), do demand some flattening, the liberation of line management from corporate control, and the release of front-line people from line management. They also demand that the organization become more horizontal and less functional. Cross-functional efforts that include not only representatives from various functions but also suppliers and customers mark those organizations that are doing well in market share and in employee pride and morale.

In the early 1980s U.S. business tried to catch up by focusing primarily on the competition that had beaten it. That focus promoted reaction, rather than proaction. While it is important to benchmark and to consider the "best in the class" in establishing standards, companies should not ignore their own strengths. Nor should they benchmark just to say they've beaten the competition. All measurement should be done in response to customers. Anyway, the best in the class may not be good enough to really delight the customer. Anticipating the customer's needs and striving to exceed them gives greater assurance of staying on track than just beating the competition.

We are getting back on track primarily because we recognize that the entrepreneurial spirit and pride of craftsmanship is not the special province of the executive office. We are back because we now recognize the relationship between cultural infrastructure and sustaining a quality product and service. And we are redesigning our industries in light of that recognition. Those driving the train today recognize the relationship between culture, character, and quality and have had the courage to recraft organizations so that they can regain some of that character and culture we had before the derailment. Those that are back on track realize that they must have more than financial capital. They must have human capital, which translates to quality and customer commitment.

Although industries are coming back, they must be vigilant. They must be disciplined. They must keep close to the customer. They must resist success by remaining austere.

Reducing defects and rework can be stimulating, but we need to remember that customers really expect more than this. To customers, minimum defects is the minimum expectation. They expect new things that add ease and value and even fun to their lives—things that enable them to have more flexibility. Sometimes, those customers are not as concerned about a shrinking sausage patty as in the time saving that a microwaveable sausage and biscuit can give them. While we may protest that we sacrifice intrinsic quality with that microwaveable sausage, the time saved may be worth more to the customer than the lost quality. However painful this compromise may be, it is the customer's voice—not the company's—that will determine the future of the business.

## Just Do It

Kahlil Gibran wrote that "believing is a fine thing, but placing those beliefs into execution is the test of strength. . . . Many are those who talk like the roar of the sea, but their lives are shallow and stagnant."

Talking about cross-functional teams isn't enough. People can easily get so stuck in the talking mode, with lengthy discussions about the barriers to change, that they never get on with it. While it may be legitimate to spend time designing the future, at some point people have to begin living that vision.

Some readers may be weary of hearing the words "walk the talk," but when all is said and done, it's the "done" part that people remember. If the top people don't become the role models for the new values and vision, chances are that vision will not be used to make daily decisions. Change can happen from the inside out, but it's a lot tougher and it takes a lot longer. For every step forward, you may have to take two steps backwards.

To those in the Department of Defense who sometimes protest, "You don't understand; we get a new CEO every three or four years, and each seems to have a different style of managing the organization," I suggest that if a movement does become cultural, if the train is moving at a high enough speed, then whoever comes into that organization will probably have to move in the direction of that train. It doesn't make too much difference what that individual's behavioral preference is, or even what his or her priorities are, if the needed cultural elements are in place. Even if the new leader simply refuses to go along on the trip, workers can still continue their journey by focusing on actions they can take within their own world and, if need be, suspending thought about the CEO.

How do you start your journey? You can do it in one of two ways: You can look underneath actions and structures that contradict where you're trying to go to the beliefs and value systems that have produced those actions and systems, or you can change the structures and systems and hope that belief will follow. It is often easier to start by requiring a change in behavior. When that change yields improved performance, excitement and belief follow. Some leaders have had success by just plunging in and changing systems and structures, whether developing some team objectives in performance development process or examining letters and reports to see if they reflect a customer, rather than an organizational, focus. Other managers prefer to begin with the values and beliefs found in the infrastructure, but this takes longer and they risk losing employees' enthusiasm for action.

No matter which way they choose, leaders must eventually change the organization's culture and character: how people relate together to accomplish a result, and how decisions are made. Leaders must ask themselves: If we were managing and leading the way we say we want to do—the way our mission statement and our values statement read—how would we act? How would we recognize behavior? What behavior would we recognize? How would this behavior be rewarded?

## A Challenge Still

Even though it has become part of the private industrial culture, and is fast becoming part of the public-sector culture, adopting continuous improvement is still challenging. Because it implies a loss of the "old order," it continues to be threatening for many employees and consequently painful for the quality champions who are trying to stay on track in this journey. Even though America's efforts toward high quality have become a boon overall, rather than a threat, and virtually nobody quibbles any longer with the basic philosophy, the daily reality is that leaders still have to push and push and not relent. I have found that the only way to do this is to believe in the correctness of the journey, continually visualize the ultimate impact on the customer, and avert the critics who try to derail you.

# Recommended Reading

Bennis, Warren. *Why Leaders Can't Lead*. San Francisco: Jossey Bass, 1990.

Bennis, Warren, and Burt Nannus. *Leaders: The Strategies for Taking Charge*. New York: HarperCollins, 1986.

Bridges, William. *Surviving Corporate Transition*. New York: Doubleday, 1988.

Covey, Stephen. *The 7 Habits of Highly Effective People*. New York: Simon & Schuster, 1989.

———. *Principle-Centered Leadership*. New York: Simon & Schuster, 1992.

Creech, William. *The Five Pillars of Total Quality*, 1994.

Crosby, Philip B. *Quality Is Free*. New York: McGraw-Hill, 1979.

———. *Quality Without Tears*. New York: NAL/Dutton, 1985.

Deming, W. Edwards. *Out of the Crisis*. Cambridge, Mass.: MIT Center for Advanced Engineering Study, 1986.

Federal Quality Institute. *Federal Quality Handbook*, 1991.

Gibran, Kahlil. *The Wisdom of Gibran*, 1966.

Hammer, Michael, and James Champy. *Reengineering the Corporation*. New York: HarperCollins, 1993.

Hoffer, Eric. *The True Believer*. New York: Harper & Row, 1951.

Iacocca, Lee, and William Novak. *An Autobiography*. New York: Bantam, 1984.

Juran, Joseph. *Juran on Leadership for Quality*. New York: Free Press, 1989.

Kanter, Rosabeth. *The Change Masters*. New York: Simon & Schuster, 1983.

Kearns, David. *Competitive Benchmarking*, 1993.

Ludeman, Kate. *The Worth Ethic*. New York: Dutton, 1990.

Nakatani, Iwao. "Sun Setting at Alarming Clip," *The Daily Yomiuri*, November 16, 1993.

National Performance Review. *Creating a Government That Works Better and Costs Less*, 1993.

Osborne, David, and Ted Gaebler. *Reinventing Government*. Redding, Mass.: Addison-Wesley, 1992.

Pascale, Richard, and Anthony G. Athos. *The Art of Japanese Management*. New York: Simon & Schuster, 1981.

Peters, Thomas, and Nancy K. Austin. *A Passion for Excellence*. New York: Random House, 1982.

Peters, Thomas, and Robert Waterman, Jr. *In Search of Excellence*. New York: Warner Books, 1985.

Pritchett, Price, and Ron Pound. *High Velocity Culture Change*. Dallas: Pritchett Associates, 1993.

Russell, Bertrand. "The Taming of Power," in *The Basic Writings of Bertrand Russell*, Robert Egner and Lester Denonn, eds. New York: Simon & Schuster, 1961.

Schaaf, Dick, and Margaret Kaeter. *Pursuing Total Quality*. New York: Warner Books, 1992.

Schonberger, Richard. *World Class Manufacturing*. New York: Free Press, 1986.

Senge, Peter. *The Fifth Discipline*. New York: Doubleday, 1991.

Sloan, Alfred P. *Adventures of a White-Collar Man*. Salem, N.H.: Ayer Co., 1941.

Stayer, Ralph, and James Belasco. *The Flight of the Buffalo*. New York: Warner Books, 1993.

U.S. Air Force. *The Quality Approach*. U.S. Air Force, 1993.

U.S. Army Corps of Engineers, Louisville District. *Partnering Progress*. March 1993.

Watson, Tom. *A Business and Its Beliefs*. New York: McGraw-Hill, 1963.

Wheatley, Margaret. *Leadership and the New Science: Learning About Organizations From an Orderly Universe*. San Francisco: Berrett-Koehler, 1993.

Womack, James P. *The Machine That Changed the World*. New York: Macmillan, 1990.

Wright, J. Patrick. *On a Clear Day You Can See General Motors*. New York: Avon, 1979.

# Index